DO ALL INDIANS LIVE IN TIPIS?

DO ALL INDIANS LIVE IN TIPIS?

QUESTIONS AND ANSWERS
from the National Museum of the American Indian

STEVEN PAUL JUDD
2016 1/1

Smithsonian Books

IN ASSOCIATION WITH THE NATIONAL MUSEUM OF THE AMERICAN INDIAN
SMITHSONIAN INSTITUTION, WASHINGTON, DC

Copyright © 2019 Smithsonian Institution.

All rights reserved. No part of this book may be used or reproduced or utilized in any form or by any means, electronic or mechanical, including photocopying, recording, or by any information storage and retrieval system, except in the case of brief quotations embodied in critical articles and reviews, without permission in writing from the publisher.

This book may be purchased for educational, business, or sales promotional use. For information, please write: Special Markets Department, Smithsonian Books, P.O. Box 37012, MRC 513, Washington, DC 20013

The National Museum of the American Indian (NMAI) is committed to advancing knowledge and understanding of the Native cultures of the Western Hemisphere—past, present, and future—through partnership with Native people and others. The museum works to support the continuance of culture, traditional values, and transitions in contemporary Native life.

For information about the Smithsonian's National Museum of the American Indian, visit the NMAI website at www.AmericanIndian.si.edu. To support the museum by becoming a member, call 1-800-242-NMAI (6624) or click on "Support" on the website.

Director: Cynthia Chavez Lamar (San Felipe Pueblo/Hopi/Tewa/Navajo)
Associate Director for Museum Research and Scholarship: David W. Penney
Publications Manager: Tanya Thrasher (Cherokee Nation)
Assistant Publications Manager: Ann Kawasaki
Project Editor: Arwen Nuttall (Cherokee ancestry)
Editorial, Permissions, and Research Assistance: Sally Barrows, Christine G. Gordon, Alexandra Harris (Cherokee ancestry), Wendy Hurlock-Baker, Fernanda Luppani, Bethany Montagano
Design: Julie Allred/BW&A Books, Steve Bell
Index: Kate Mertes

Published by Smithsonian Books
Director: Carolyn Gleason
Senior Editor: Christina Wiginton
Editorial Assistant: Jaime Schwender

SECOND EDITION

Library of Congress Cataloging-in-Publication Data

Names: National Museum of the American Indian (U.S.), issuing body.
Title: Do all Indians live in tipis? : questions and answers from the National Museum of the American Indian / by Smithsonian National Museum of the American Indian ; foreword: Cynthia Chavez Lamar, Director of the National Museum of the American Indian, introduction to first edition: Wilma Mankiller, Former Principal Chief, Cherokee Nation of Oklahoma.
Description: Revised edition. | Washington, D.C. : Smithsonian National Museum of the American Indian, [2017] | Includes bibliographical references and index.
Identifiers: LCCN 2017045193 (print) | LCCN 2018002669 (ebook) | ISBN 9781588346209 (e-book) | ISBN 9781588346193 | ISBN 9781588346193 (pbk.)
Subjects: LCSH: Indians of North America—Study and teaching. | Indians of North America—Public opinion. | Indians of North America—Social life and customs. | Indians in popular culture—North America. | Public opinion—North America. | Questions and answers. | Stereotypes (Social psychology)—North America.
Classification: LCC E76.6 (ebook) | LCC E76.6 .D6 2017 (print) | DDC 970.004/97—dc23
LC record available at https://lccn.loc.gov/2017045193

Printed in the United States of America.
23 22   6 5 4 3

The questions in this book originated for the most part in letters, emails, phone calls, and in-person visits from the public to the learning center at the George Gustav Heye Center, the New York branch of the National Museum of the American Indian, and to our flagship museum in Washington, DC. Special recognition goes to the museum's esteemed Cultural Interpreter staff, whose expertise working with our audiences contributed directly to the revised set of questions in this edition.

CONTRIBUTORS FROM THE
NATIONAL MUSEUM OF THE AMERICAN INDIAN

Mary Ahenakew (Cherokee/Piscataway-Conoy)

Stephanie Betancourt (Seneca)

Jennifer Erdrich (Turtle Mountain Chippewa ancestry)

Alexandra Harris (Cherokee ancestry)

Liz Hill (Red Lake Band of Ojibwe)

Nema Magovern (Osage)

Bethany Montagano

Rico Newman (Piscataway/Conoy)

Arwen Nuttall (Cherokee ancestry)

Edwin Schupman (Muscogee)

Georgetta Stonefish Ryan (Delaware)

Tanya Thrasher (Cherokee Nation of Oklahoma)

Sincere appreciation also goes to the museum's photographers and staff for their contributions: Katherine Fogden (Mohawk), Cindy Frankenburg, Ernest Amoroso, Walter Larrimore, R. A. Whiteside, Doug McMains, and Hayes P. Lavis. All photos are by museum staff unless otherwise indicated.

Special thanks to Ellen Jamieson, whose long experience at the museum's learning center and extensive research into Native cultures has greatly contributed to our collective knowledge.

*To Dr. Helen Maynor Scheirbeck (Lumbee),
whose lifelong commitment to creating educational opportunities for Native people
was matched only by her dedication to educating all Americans about Native cultures.*

CONTENTS

Foreword *Cynthia Chavez Lamar, Director,*
National Museum of the American Indian   *xiii*

Introduction *Wilma Mankiller, Former Principal Chief,*
Cherokee Nation of Oklahoma   *xv*

American Indian Cultures

Do Indians celebrate Thanksgiving?	*2*
What is the importance of music to Native people?	*5*
What musical instruments do Native people play?	*7*
What did Indians use for paint and dye?	*10*
What are kachina dolls? What are they used for?	*12*
Did all tribes have totem poles? Does anyone still carve them?	*14*
Do Indians make art?	*17*
How do I know if something I purchase is really made by an American Indian artist or tribe?	*20*
Why are there different spellings for words—such as tipi and teepee—in Native American languages?	*23*
What is a powwow?	*26*
Did American Indians invent lacrosse?	*28*
What was the first game ever played with rubber balls?	*30*
Did early Mesoamericans practice human sacrifice during their ball games?	*32*
Did any Indians practice cannibalism?	*34*
What did Indians really smoke in those peace pipes?	*35*
What is "counting coup"?	*37*
Do Indians do rain dances?	*39*
Are dream catchers an authentic tradition?	*41*
Why are most Indian ceremonies and dances off-limits to non-Native audiences?	*43*
What is the Native American religion?	*45*
How can I find a shaman (or medicine man) who will teach me?	*48*

Do Indians have funerals?	50
Was Tonto a real Indian?	52
Why did carved wooden Indians stand outside cigar stores?	55
How authentic are contemporary movies that try to tell stories from a Native perspective?	58

Time, Continuity, and Change

Where did Indians come from? How did they get to the Americas?	62
How many Indians lived in the Western Hemisphere when Columbus arrived?	65
Is it true that Indian languages are now extinct?	67
Did Indians have alphabets and writing before contact with Europeans?	70
Did Indians really help the European settlers?	72
Is it true that Pocahontas saved John Smith from execution?	75
Is it true that Indians sold Manhattan for twenty-four dollars worth of beads and trinkets?	78
Did Europeans purposely use smallpox to kill Indians?	80
Was Sacagawea really all that important to the Lewis and Clark Expedition?	82
What happened to white people captured by Indians?	84
Is it true that white people invented scalping, or did the practice originate with Native Americans?	87

People, Places, and Environments

What is the relationship of Native Americans to the environment?	90
Were the Americas a vast, untouched wilderness when Europeans arrived?	93
Did Native peoples and European colonists have different perspectives about land?	96
Do Alaska Natives really have hundreds of words for *snow*?	98
Did Indians really use smoke signals? Do they today?	100
Did Native Americans use sign language?	102

What kinds of foods do Indians eat?	105
Before contact with Europeans, did Indians make all their clothing from animal skins?	108
Is it true that Native people used all parts of the animal?	110
Is it true that Native Americans hunted a great number of large animals to extinction?	113
Why do Indians wear feathers? Why are eagle feathers important to Indians?	115
How did Native Americans acquire horses?	117
Where did Native people get glass beads to decorate their clothing?	119
Do Native American parents still put their babies in cradleboards? Are the cradleboards comfortable?	122
Are Indians more prone to certain diseases than the general population? Why?	125
What are the rates of alcoholism, drug addiction, and suicide among American Indians?	127
Do all Indians live in tipis?	129

Individual Development and Identity

What is the correct terminology: *American Indian, Indian, Native American,* or *Native?*	132
Should I say *tribe* or *nation?*	134
Why do many tribes have more than one name?	136
How do I prove my Indian ancestry and enroll in my tribe?	138
Did Native American tribes have royalty?	140
Why is the word *squaw* offensive?	142
Why is the word *Eskimo* sometimes offensive?	144
What's wrong with naming sports teams *Indians, Braves,* etc.?	145
What is the origin of the term *redskin?* Why is it offensive?	148
Why do some people believe there are no "real" Indians left?	149
Why are coming-of-age ceremonies important?	152
How have Native Americans viewed sexuality and gender?	155
Why do some Native people not like having their photo taken?	158

Individuals, Groups, and Institutions

Before the arrival of formal schools, how were Indian children taught? — 162

Why did the US government force Indian children into boarding schools? — 165

What distinct roles did men and women play in Native communities? — 168

Why was the Navajo language chosen for military code in World War II? Were all Indian "code talkers" Navajo? — 172

How did some tribes get a reputation as warlike and others as peaceful? — 175

Did any Indian groups practice polygamy? — 177

Power, Authority, and Governance

What are the Indian populations of the United States, Canada, and Latin America? — 180

How many Indian tribes are oﬃcially recognized in the United States today? Why is recognition important? — 181

Why didn't Indian tribes band together to fight off Europeans? — 183

What was the Iroquois Confederacy and how did it contribute to democracy? — 186

Are Indians US citizens? — 188

Did Native Americans own slaves? — 190

Did women serve as chiefs and leaders of Native American tribes? — 193

Can Indians leave the reservations? Why do reservations still exist? — 196

Why do American Indians run casinos? — 198

What happens to the revenue from Indian casinos? — 200

Do the rich casino tribes help out the poor tribes? — 203

Why is there still poverty on some reservations? — 206

What benefits do Indians receive from the US government? — 209

Do Indians have to pay taxes? — 212

Do Indians have to follow state hunting and fishing regulations? — 214

Do museums have to give back everything in their collections that was taken from tribes without permission? — 216

Science, Technology, and Society

What were some of the accomplishments of Native Americans
at the time Europeans first arrived in the Western Hemisphere? *220*

Did Indians have mathematics before contact with Europeans? *223*

How did foods native to the Americas influence global cuisines? *226*

Who really built the mounds? *229*

Native Knowledge 360° *232*

Further Reading *233*

Index *241*

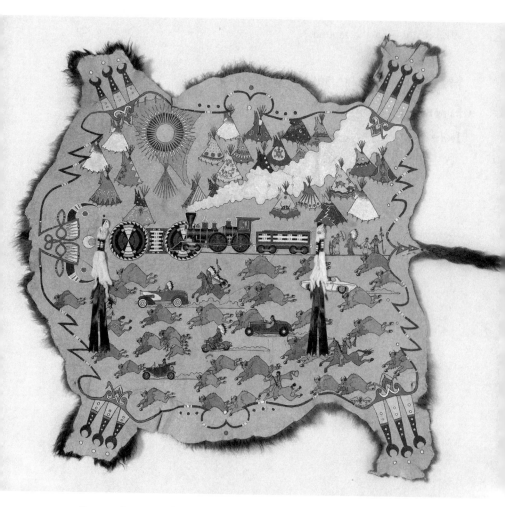

Dallin Maybee (Northern Arapaho/Seneca), *Conductors of Our Own Destiny*, 2013. Commercial-tanned bison hide, cut-glass beads, glass seed beads, gold beads, steel beads, copper beads, ermines, Swarovski crystals, acrylic paint, ink, and brass bells.

26/9328

FOREWORD

Often edgy and always surprising, the works of three Native artists featured on this book's front and back covers—all shown in NMAI programs, exhibitions, or publications—show how Indigenous people are always forging new paths for sharing their history. As you may not know, American Indian images, words, and stories infuse our lives today, and many students are unaware of how much Indigenous people have shaped the history, pop culture, and identity of the United States and well beyond.

The National Museum of the American Indian exists to challenge long-held stereotypes and showcase the contributions that Native cultures have made to American history and contemporary life. The museum's Native Knowledge 360° web-based educational initiative (known in classrooms as NK360°) stands out as an anchor project in this effort, and at the center of this long-term initiative are Indigenous peoples themselves. We discuss the NK360° project in more detail at the end of this book, and I encourage you to learn more.

This edition of *Do All Indians Live in Tipis?* is a natural extension of the museum's educational effort, with the table of contents reflecting the ten core concepts of the initiative, known as Essential Understandings. These concepts embrace a wide range of perspectives. This book highlights seven of those concepts, and the other three have been incorporated and explored throughout the essays. Native Knowledge 360° is a tool for the museum and Indigenous peoples to correct, broaden, and improve what is taught in our nation's schools and to provide materials for students and teachers. Moreover, it serves as a stimulus to the national conversation on education for and about American Indian communities. We have many partners in this endeavor, and by reading and sharing this book you become our partner as well.

Today there more than 570 federally recognized tribes in the United States alone and tens of millions of Indigenous peoples across the Americas—far too large and diverse a population to discuss in one book. Part of our mission here at the museum is to change how and what our audiences worldwide learn about Indigenous perspectives, and I think that you will agree that *Do All Indians Live in Tipis?* is one more way we are leading by example.

—Cynthia Chavez Lamar
(San Felipe Pueblo/Hopi/Tewa/Navajo)
Director, National Museum of the American Indian

Three Native artists featured in this book use today's media to tell their stories, equal parts unexpected, educational, and entertaining:

COVER: According to Northern Arapaho/Seneca artist Dallin Maybee, his 2013 work *Conductors of Our Own Destiny* ". . . reflects my personal perception of the evolution of Native traditional and contemporary art forms. I have always felt that one of the strengths of our culture has been our ability to adapt to and evolve in an ever-changing technological landscape. Our art has reflected that evolution."

BACK COVER: For Terrance Houle (Blood), his *Urban Indian Series* "serves to question ideas of tradition, identity, and culture that are often negated or replaced by Western cultural standards." *Urban Indian Series* (no. 3), 2007. Eight digital C-prints, 35.6 × 27.9 cm each. Collection of the artist. Photo by Jarusha Brown.

TITLE PAGE: Through his pop art satire, Steven Paul Judd (Kiowa) wanted to make art "geared toward Native peoples" but that anyone can also "learn from it, starting from a humorous point." *The Summer They Visited*, 2014.

INTRODUCTION

The opening of the National Museum of the American Indian in the fall of 2004 represented the most significant Native American cultural event of the early twenty-first century. The museum's exhibitions, publications, and educational programs allow Native people to tell their own stories about their histories, rich cultures, and contemporary lives. It is fitting, then, that *Do All Indians Live in Tipis?*, which is grounded in the diverse experiences and research of its Native authors, is being published by the museum.

Even after hundreds of years of living in formerly Native villages, towns, and communities, many Americans know very little about the original people of this land. Our names (my own last name is a mistranslation into English), histories, reservations, governments, ceremonies, identities, and even our clothing—all are subject to a great deal of confusion and oversimplification. I think this book is the kind of effort that recognizes the power of education to profoundly alter the public perception of Native people in the Americas. For several years the contributors to *Do All Indians Live in Tipis?* went about the daunting task of collecting and synthesizing information on diverse topics, propelled by a fundamental belief in the public's willingness to learn about cultures that may be geographically near but very different from their own.

In 1963 President John F. Kennedy said, "For a subject worked and reworked so often in novels, motion pictures, and television, American Indians are the least understood and the most misunderstood of us all." Regrettably, this statement is as true today as it was more than forty years ago. Many negative stereotypes persist.

A surprising number of non-Natives apparently believe tribal people still live and dress as they did some 300 years ago. During my tenure as principal chief of the Cherokee Nation, the onslaught of summer visitors often included crestfallen tourists who wanted to know, "Where are all the Indians?" With tongue in cheek, I would answer quite truthfully, "They are probably at Walmart!"

Presented in an easy-to-navigate, question-and-answer format, *Do All Indians Live in Tipis?* is an impressive effort to address some of the most common misperceptions about Native Americans. The book will help eliminate stereotypes and misinformation created and perpetuated by a lack of accurate information about Native Americans in the schools, the media, and popular books and films. Providing detailed, factual answers to many of the most commonly asked questions about Native people, the book is an important reference for anyone interested in Native American history, government, culture, life, and issues.

—WILMA MANKILLER (1945–2010)
Former Principal Chief,
Cherokee Nation of Oklahoma

AMERICAN INDIAN CULTURES

DO INDIANS CELEBRATE THANKSGIVING?

The Thanksgiving Day feast that is celebrated in the United States first took place over three days sometime between September 20 and November 9, 1621, among the settlers of Plymouth Colony (in Massachusetts) and approximately ninety Native people of the Wampanoag Nation. Contrary to popular myth, the Pilgrim/Wampanoag gathering was probably not the first public feast of thanksgiving held by the English in the "New World," but rather was one of approximately three that had likely occurred since 1610, most notably at the Jamestown Colony. It is the Pilgrim/Wampanoag story of the "first" Thanksgiving, however, that has been passed down to generations of schoolchildren as a time-honored part of American history.

Perhaps the most enduring part of the first Thanksgiving myth is that the Pilgrims hosted the feast for the Native people present. The reality is that after a cautious approach on the part of the Wampanoag, both groups contributed to the feast. Without Wampanoag agricultural expertise, however, the English would not have survived to celebrate their first Thanksgiving. Unaccustomed to the extreme weather conditions of New England and without enough food, warm clothing, or other provisions to see them through the particularly harsh winter of 1620–1621, the Pilgrims had quickly become destitute and were on the verge of starvation. On the other hand, the Wampanoag people—members of one of the most powerful confederacies of Native nations of the time—had plenty of food, some of which the English stole to survive. It is both ironic and tragic that the Wampanoag Nation in the coming years would suffer an almost complete decimation of their once-enormous numbers, power,

"We're here to escape religious persecution. What are you here for?"

Donald Reilly, The New Yorker Collection/
The Cartoon Bank; © Condé Nast

and influence—at the hands of the same people whose survival they had helped ensure.

In 1863, during the depths of the Civil War, Abraham Lincoln proclaimed that a day be set aside to give thanks publicly for life's bounty. Today, Thanksgiving is a national holiday in both the United States and Canada (in the United States on the fourth Thursday in November, and in Canada on the second Monday in October). Most Native people observe the holiday alongside everyone else, with the foods that have become traditional Thanksgiving staples, such as turkey (which was documented as one of the foods served at the feast in 1621) and stuffing. Indian people also use Thanksgiving as a time to get together with family and friends.

The idea of reserving just one day to give thanks for food, shelter, and the blessings of a healthy life is alien to many Native cultures, however. Most Indian people, even today, say that they give thanks each day for the bounty in their lives. It is customary for people in many Native cultures of the Western Hemisphere to greet each day with special prayers of thanksgiving and to give thanks at various times, including at harvest festivals and ceremonies, throughout the year.

On Thanksgiving Day, while most Native people are sitting down to turkey dinners, some prefer to observe the day as one of mourning—for what happened to the millions of Indians who lived on the North and South American continents before the arrival of the Europeans.

—LIZ HILL

WHAT IS THE IMPORTANCE OF MUSIC TO NATIVE PEOPLE?

According to Native American belief systems, music is intimately connected to everyday life and, especially, to the spiritual lives of Native peoples. Sacred music is an essential part of ceremonies and other important traditional activities. Social music is performed for personal enjoyment, at social events such as community or family celebrations, or as accompaniment to social dances. The idea of music for art's sake is not part of traditional Native thinking. Although singing is sometimes used as a form of artistic expression, there was no such thing historically as attending a concert of Native American music. Indeed, in most Native languages there is no word that means "music" in the sense that we know the word today. Instead, music and singing are linked to their many functions in Native cultures.

Song is the most common form of traditional Native American music. Frequently accompanied by various drums, rattles, and other percussive instruments, songs are sung at many different kinds of events for a wide variety of purposes. Sacred songs are considered to have a power of their own, and they help Native people communicate within the spiritual universe. Sacred songs are sung by people such as traditional healers and participants in many types of ceremonies. They are used, for example, when seeking help from the spirit world with a problem, for success in hunting or fishing, during times of mourning, when honoring someone, or when praying for the well-being of one's family or community. Sacred songs are often considered gifts from the Creator, and it is believed that many of them originated long ago in powerful dreams or visions. In the Native way of thinking, such songs must always be treated respectfully because of their

A drum group at the National Powwow, August 14, 2005. Washington, DC.

power. They can be harmful if misused, and they are only sung by people who have the appropriate cultural authority.

Native American singers use their voices in many expressive ways. Depending on the context, songs are sung solo or in groups, in unison, multipart, and even call-and-response textures. Some are peaceful and introspective, while others are forceful and dynamic. Some songs are sung only by men, some only by women, and some by both. Certain styles call for singing in a very high vocal range, while others are low. Occasionally singers express themselves and the cultural meaning of their music by quivering their voices, imitating animal noises, yelling, and making other special sounds. Sometimes the songs include words, either in the Native language or English, and other times they are just syllables, sometimes referred to as vocables.

The unique world of Native American vocal music is richly varied, steeped in traditions, and an essential element of Native identity and cultural continuity.

—EDWIN SCHUPMAN

WHAT MUSICAL INSTRUMENTS DO NATIVE PEOPLE PLAY?

Although the most familiar instruments played by Native Americans may be the flute and drum, peoples throughout the Americas have played diverse styles of music on many different kinds of instruments.

Drums are used at various social gatherings and in many ceremonies. Among Native Americans, drums are held in respect no matter where they come from or what events they are used for. Drums are sacred, and humans have a spiritual and emotional connection to them. In some settings, drums are considered to be living spiritual entities. They are given names and offerings; they are ritually fed and purified with the smoke of sacred plants. Drums are often painted or decorated with symbols of significance to the people who use the drum. A person is sometimes given the responsibility of caring for the drum, and individuals and families sometimes own drums that they pass along from generation to generation.

Native American drums are made from many different materials, including wood, clay, and even modern synthetic materials. Some drums have two heads and some have one, usually made of animal hides. Most drums are played by one person, but some of the big drums are played by many individuals at the same time.

The flute is the primary wind instrument of Native peoples. Probably the best-known flute comes from Great Plains and Eastern Woodland cultures. Made of cedar and other types of wood, this flute was used often for courting. A man would make his own flute based on the measurements of his arm and hand. Cane and bone flutes were also common in California wand Southwestern tribes. The flute has seen a revival today in contemporary music.

Singer, songwriter, musician, actor, and playwright Arigon Starr (Kickapoo/Creek) in her one-woman play, *The Red Road*. National Museum of the American Indian, August 5, 2006. Washington, DC.

Rattles, bells, striking sticks, rasps, and whistles also can be an important part of social dances and religious ceremonies. Rattles are made of hollowed-out materials such as turtle shell, animal horn, gourds, rawhide, and elm bark. The hollowed vessels are filled with seeds, gravel, or pebbles to create the rattle sound. Other materials, such as deer dewclaws, buffalo hooves, animal knucklebones, or seashells can be strung together to create a rattling sound. Handles are made of wood or bone, and many rattles are decorated with beads, porcupine quills, feathers, and horsehair.

The rasp consists of a stick of hard wood notched like a saw, or a grooved dried gourd, over which a smaller stick is rubbed back and forth, creating a rhythm. Some tribes have stringed instruments such as fiddles. The Seri of Mesoamerica have a one-string, box-shaped fiddle, and the Apache a one- or two-stringed violin, also called a fiddle. The Apache fiddle is played with a bow made from the century plant stalk and one or two horsehair strings. The Quechua and Aymara people of the Andes have an instrument called a *charango*, which is similar to a guitar and made from the armor of an armadillo.

Depending on the region, trumpets or horns were made from materials such as bamboo, conch shells, clay, wood, the tail of an armadillo, or tree bark. Some instruments were used for hunting. A horn made from bark was used by Northeastern tribes to attract moose, and whistles made from wood or animal bone were used to call game.

Some whistles were created specifically to scare birds away from vegetable gardens.

In addition to playing these traditional instruments, contemporary Native people—as classical, jazz, hip hop, rock, folk, and pop musicians—play many other kinds of instruments. Some Native American communities have also adapted non-Native instruments and musical styles, making them part of their own contemporary cultural expressions. In southern Arizona, for example, musicians of the Akimel O'odham and Tohono O'odham tribes perform a style of music known as *waila*, or chicken scratch music, which originated when a European priest brought an accordion to the local mission. Chicken scratch is performed by ensembles that include instruments such as violins, accordions, guitars, bass guitars, drums, saxophones, and trumpets. This distinct style features Native American adaptations of Latin American polkas, two-steps, and *cumbias*, a folk dance that originated in Colombia.

The Native American Music Awards is the first national awards program for North American Indigenous music. In recent years Native musicians, including singer/songwriter Bill Miller and flutist Mary Youngblood, have earned Grammy awards for their talent.

—MARY AHENAKEW AND EDWIN SCHUPMAN

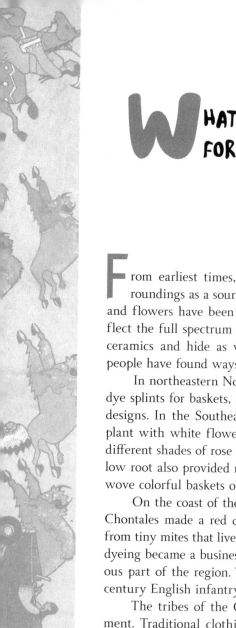

WHAT DID INDIANS USE FOR PAINT AND DYE?

From earliest times, Native Americans have used their surroundings as a source of color. Indigenous rocks, clays, plants, and flowers have been transformed into paints and dye that reflect the full spectrum of natural hues. By creating paintings on ceramics and hide as well as dyeing yarn and grasses, Indian people have found ways to decorate everyday and ritual objects.

In northeastern North America the Mi'kmaq used pollen to dye splints for baskets, and the Mohegan used potatoes to stamp designs. In the Southeast the Cherokee used bloodroot, a tiny plant with white flowers that grows in wooded areas, to make different shades of rose and reddish brown. Walnut root and yellow root also provided natural dyes. The Choctaw of Mississippi wove colorful baskets of native river cane.

On the coast of the Mar del Sur, in present-day Mexico, the Chontales made a red dye called cochineal, or grana cochinilla, from tiny mites that live on cacti. After the arrival of the Spanish, dyeing became a business for the Native people in the mountainous part of the region. The famous red coats of the eighteenth-century English infantry were dyed with cochineal.

The tribes of the Great Plains were the masters of adornment. Traditional clothing included shirts, leggings, moccasins, dresses, and buffalo robes. From clothing to tipis, hide objects were decorated with meaningful, often personal, designs and pictographs. Hide painting was done on buffalo robes, tipi covers, and clothing. Iron-laden earth clays yielded rich paints of brown, red, and yellow. Scoops of black earth were used for dark colors. The clays were pulverized in stone mortars and then made sticky with glue from plants. Both men and women were artists. Men

A bloodroot flower growing in the forest landscape at the National Museum of the American Indian. The roots and stems of the bloodroot are used to create a reddish-brown or rose-colored dye.

painted robes, shirts, shields, and tipis. Women painted geometric figures and did quillwork and beadwork.

In southwestern North America local flora provided a wealth of color possibilities. The Navajo weave beautiful rugs and blankets, using different colors of wool from various breeds of sheep. For dyes, they use indigo (the oldest of all dye plants) to create a deep blue, rabbitbrush to make yellow, sagebrush to produce a muddy green or off-brown, and mahogany roots to yield orange-red, deep purple, or lavender. Soil, climate, and rainfall all affect the colors that the plants produce. Many weavers today use dyes available in stores, but some still work with indigenous plants, which they harvest, soak, ferment, and dry until they are exactly the right color for their yarn, clay, grasses, or hide.

—NEMA MAGOVERN

WHAT ARE KACHINA DOLLS? WHAT ARE THEY USED FOR?

Kachina, or katsina, dolls are not toys. They are intended for young people, but unlike toys, these special objects are a serious and important part of a young person's education in the Hopi, Zuni, and other Pueblo communities of the Southwest.

For the Hopi people of Arizona, katsina dolls—three-dimensional carved and painted cottonwood figures—are seen as physical representations of the katsinam, deities that traditionally come to stay in Hopi villages for six months of the year. Parents, grandparents, and other relatives give katsinas to children as part of their training so they can learn about the different katsinam, which the Hopi and other Pueblo people recognize in many ceremonies and dances. There are literally several hundred katsinam—and all are central to Hopi social and ceremonial life.

It is believed that some of the katsinam came to the Hopi people from other pueblos in the Southwest—in particular, the Pueblo of Zuni in New Mexico. Katsinam, who may embody male or female characteristics, represent the beings that make up the natural world, such as plants (corn), insects, animals (deer, wolf, antelope), and birds (eagle, owl). Some display human traits, such as humor, leadership, and discipline.

The Hopi people believe that the katsinam arrive in their villages in human form at the solstice in late December and stay until July. During this time the katsinam serve as messengers between the temporal and spiritual worlds, carrying the prayers of the Hopi people to the gods. They also are said to have supernatural powers—for example, they can control the weather by bringing rain for crops. During social dances and ceremonies, the katsinam, embodied by men in masks, guide various community

Scott Secakuku (Hopi) carves a katsina doll.
A finished doll stands beside him, 2001.
Phoenix, Arizona.

© 2003 John Harrington (Siletz) and the
National Museum of the American Indian

activities. All Hopi people belong to either the Katsina or Powamuy ritual societies.

One of the most famous of the katsinam is the Kokopelli, a Hopi fertility god whose present-day form is that of a carefree, playful, humpbacked flautist. One sees Kokopelli in many advertisements, on signs, and emblazoned on commercial sale items in the American Southwest. Other katsinam well known to non-Natives include the Koshari and Mudhead, who have the role of clowns.

In the book *Meet Mindy, a Native Girl from the Southwest* (2003), Mindy Secakuku, a contemporary Hopi girl who spends a lot of time on the Hopi Reservation, explains, "The katsinam bring gifts to children who have been good. These gifts can be fruit or other food, or musical instruments like rattles, drums, or dancing sticks. A katsina may give a girl a very special gift of a miniature doll that looks like it, called tihu. You know you've been good when you get a katsina doll!"

—LIZ HILL

DID ALL TRIBES HAVE TOTEM POLES? DOES ANYONE STILL CARVE THEM?

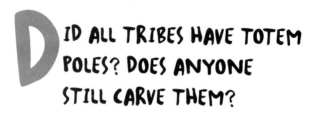

Native people along the North Pacific Coast from present-day Washington State to Alaska have a long history of intricately carving cedar logs with images of people, animals, and characters from oral narratives. The carvings are most often clan symbols—Raven, Bear, Eagle, or Killer Whale, for example—and they tell of supernatural events, journeys to other worlds, and community or family histories. In relating its story, a finished pole can reach a height of 40 or more feet. There are many kinds of totem poles: poles for the entrance of a house, poles that honor a person who has died, poles that tell stories, and poles that welcome people to a school or community center.

Over time, totem poles eventually disintegrate and return to the earth. As a result, no one knows when the practice of carving them began. The estimated ages of the oldest existing poles are between 100 and 150 years. Figures similar to those carved on the wood poles also have been found on stone surfaces. This finding suggests that the practice of carving has persisted on the North Pacific Coast for several millennia.

When a potlatch is held, the sponsoring family may have a totem pole erected to commemorate the occasion. A potlatch is a celebration that can take many forms, but usually the hosts invite a large group, provide an abundant feast, and give each participant gifts. The more the hosts give away, the more honor they bring to themselves. In the 1880s, Canadian church and government officials interpreted the potlatch as a negative influence that encouraged wastefulness, so the potlatch was outlawed in Canada from the 1880s to the 1950s. Although potlatches were still held in many communities during the ban, the tradition—together with totem-pole carving—suffered a decline. Today

Native communities along the North Pacific Coast have revived potlatches, seeing them as an integral connection to their ancestors.

Among the many contemporary Native totem-pole carvers along the North Pacific Coast, a group from the Lummi Nation of Washington State called the House of Tears Carvers believes that totem poles can be a means of national commemoration and healing. One carver suggests that carving brings out both happiness and sadness. When a tree is cut, it is sad, and the carvers offer gifts to honor and thank the cedar. When the carvers are finished, they cry with joy at what they have brought forth from the spirit of the tree.

In 2002 the Lummi carvers erected a totem pole called *The Healing Pole* in the Sterling Forest, about 60 miles north of Manhattan. It was named to help bring about resolution to the grief of families and communities following the attack on the World Trade Center towers on September 11, 2001.

Although totem poles today are carved almost exclusively by the people of the North Pacific Coast, the practice of carving figures in trees and stone has a long history in Native cultures throughout the Americas. The Lenni Lenape, Piscataway, Powhatan, Haudenosaunee (Iroquois), and many other eastern and southern tribes carved what were called "living faces" in trees. And the pre-Contact cultures of Mesoamerica and South America carved entire stories on the walls of their stone palaces and temples.

Kaats totem pole, in the National Museum of the American Indian, tells the story of Kaats, the Bear Hunter. For more information on this totem pole, see page 218. Nathan P. Jackson (Tlingit), Stephen P. Jackson (Tlingit), and Dorica R. Jackson, 2004. Saxman, Alaska. NMAI museum commission, 2004.

26/3856

> While most people believe that the "lowest person on the totem pole" is the least esteemed, totem carvers know that the figure at the bottom of the pole holds a position of great honor.

Totem poles have differing purposes and hold complex meanings. Many people think that totem poles are religious objects, but the communities that carve them have never worshipped them. Rather, totem poles tell stories of family, clan, and community, linking people with their ancestors and their origins.

—RICO NEWMAN

DO INDIANS MAKE ART?

Like all other cultures, Native peoples create art in all its forms, from their ancient artistic traditions to contemporary art, and often a mixture of the two. But there are reasons many people ask this question. A common saying claims that there is "no word for art" in Native American languages. In a sense, this is true. The European and Western definitions of art do not apply to Native artistic expression. Navajo artist and educator Harry Walters described Native art this way: "Art is not seen as separate from other cultural components like music, philosophy, religion, or history. To study Navajo art, one must study the whole culture. Any attempt to study Navajo art by itself would fail." While not always essential to artists from Western schools of art, cultural context and influence is typically important to Native artists. In some cases, Indigenous belief systems require artists to respect particular traditions in order to practice their craft. By European definitions, art is separate from daily life. This is generally not true for Native Americans.

This question also addresses the stigma of Native American art as being primitive and, by extension, the idea that all art by Native Americans should resemble pre-Contact art in order to be considered authentic. This fallacy is fueled by a belief that if Native art is influenced by contemporary or other artistic movements, then its traditional values are somehow compromised. In fact, Native art has always had outside influences, and it has changed and evolved through time; this was true before contact with Europeans, and remains so today.

One of the major influences on Native art was the tourist trade. Although the timing was slightly different depending on tribe and region, sales of Native art to non-Natives became most

Roxanne Swentzell (Santa Clara Pueblo, b. 1962) *Don't Shoot*, 1990. Indian Arts and Crafts Board Collection, Department of the Interior, at the National Museum of the American Indian, Smithsonian Institution.

26/1351

popular in the nineteenth century. Notably, the railroad brought tourists to destinations that were inaccessible before, such as the Southwest. As a result, Native people created works specifically for sale to tourists. In many communities, art sales meant income—and survival. While it may seem like that would cheapen fine basketry or pottery work, it did the opposite; the tourist market sparked creativity and innovation within Native arts and in some cases elevated the status of individual artists, such as Hopi/Tewa potter Nampeyo (1859–1942).

A notable example of the tourist trade inspiring art occurred in California basket making. The Pomo of Northern California traditionally made baskets to carry food, infants, and household goods and to collect and store food. Some were even filled with water and used for cooking. Intricate feathered baskets were made as special gifts for important occasions. By the 1890s, American Indian baskets were popular collector's items, becoming fashionable household decorations and museum pieces. As a result, basket making became a major source of income for Pomo people. The new market sparked friendly competition between basket makers for buyers and thereby inspired innovative new forms such as tiny baskets made to wear as stick pins. Pomo people also collected their own baskets. During the 1940s, basket maker Annie Burke noticed that all the finest baskets had left her community through trade. Burke bought baskets from her family members to start her own collection and displayed them at her basket-making demonstrations, educating non-Indian people about basketry. Her daughter, Elsie Allen, kept the collection after her mother's death and continued to educate people for many years. Today Pomo baskets are known throughout the world as among the finest baskets ever made.

Yet Native artistic expression is still not held in the same esteem as Old World art traditions such as painting. Why is that? Many art historians argue that because most art is measured by European standards, the West has control over how the world's art is judged. For similar reasons, many Indigenous contemporary artists have difficulty breaking through into the mainstream contemporary art world. Likewise, viewers have trouble seeing Native contemporary art—painting, sculpture, installation, and digital art—as "authentic" Native art, believing that only pre-Contact expressions (e.g., pottery, basketry) are authentic. As art historian Laura E. Smith has observed, Native artists are judged only in relation to how they follow modern trends in mainstream Western art, not as modernists in their own cultural context. Nonetheless, there are many Native contemporary artists working and innovating today in all types of media.

—ALEXANDRA HARRIS

How do I know if something I purchase is really made by an American Indian artist or tribe?

Cultural appropriation practiced by individuals and companies choosing to misrepresent their products as Native American is an age-old problem in the United States. The introduction of e-commerce has exacerbated the issue and increased systemic fraud. Machine-made or handmade counterfeits produced cheaply in countries like Mexico, Pakistan, India, Thailand, and the Philippines account for much of the merchandise fraudulently marketed as having Indigenous origins. In addition to defrauding the consumer, fake products drive down prices and put legitimate artisans and Native stores out of business.

The Indian Arts and Craft Act 25, U.S.C. §305e (IACA), initially passed in 1935, revised in 1990 and 2000, and then amended in 2010, was enacted by Congress to curb fraud and protect consumers from purchasing artworks that are advertised as Indian made but are not produced by Indian people. In addition to protecting the consumer, the IACA seeks to protect American Indian artists whose livelihoods depend on their ability to compete in the marketplace against mass-produced imitation goods from foreign countries, as well as individual artists who are not American Indian.

The IACA grew out of the historic need to recalibrate the Native American tourist-trade market that had economically marginalized Native artisans since its inception in the eighteenth century. As tourists, anthropologists, merchants, and writers began to visit and engage with Native communities, Indian artists and artisans found a growing market for their own cultural products.

Joseph Coriz (Santo Domingo Pueblo) Storyteller Bracelet, ca. 1990. Silver metal overlay. Angie Reano Owen (Santo Domingo Pueblo) Bracelet, ca. 1988. Shell base, mosaic herringbone of jet, coral, and turquoise. Jesse Monongye (Navajo/Hopi) Bracelet, ca. 1983. Silver metal with inlay of coral, pink and gold mother of pearl, lapis lazuli, turquoise, and malachite.

25/6290, 25/7427, 25/6299

In the late nineteenth century, Native Americans began to rely heavily on the production of art and cultural merchandise for sale to travelers visiting Indian Country, spurring a vast tourist-trade network, overhauling traditional tribal economies. The art forms produced during this time reflect the cross-pollination of cultures intrinsic to the tourist trade, dovetailing Indigenous techniques like quillwork, moose hair embroidery, birchbark, and basketry with European styles. As the tourist market expanded, so did competition, ushering in a new culture of fraud that further disenfranchised Native artisans. With the introduction of railroads, Native artists had to contend with an influx of American settlers producing goods that they would dishonestly market as Indian made at trading posts and cultural heritage sites.

The problem of fraud eventually became so cumbersome that legislation like the IACA was enacted to deal with gross disempowerment of Native artisans and vendors. Designed to empower Native artists, the IACA has succeeded in offering a measure of protection. However, the act continues to generate controversy and has led to other problems, namely raising the question, "Who is an Indian artist?" Under the law an Indian artist or craftsman must be a member of a federally or state-recognized tribe or certified by either as an artisan. The imposition of rigid definitions of Indian identity along with ongoing fraud adversely affect Native artists and craftspeople, who find it exceedingly diµcult to keep pace in a marketplace stymied by misappropriation.

To support Native artisans and protect themselves, consumers should purchase directly from certified artisans or established dealers who present a written guarantee or verification of authenticity. This helps to ensure that products are marketed eµciently for fair compensation and without sacrificing the artistic principles of craftspeople. To learn more about the Indian Arts and Crafts Act and related state laws, visit the Indian Arts and Crafts Board's website, or call the Board's toll-free number, 1-888-ART-FAKE.

—BETHANY MONTAGANO

WHY ARE THERE DIFFERENT SPELLINGS FOR WORDS— SUCH AS TIPI AND TEEPEE— IN NATIVE AMERICAN LANGUAGES?

While there were thousands of different Indigenous languages in the Americas, only a few were written down before contact with Europeans, and those were composed of glyphs or pictographs rather than letters as we use today. At the National Museum of the American Indian, we always defer to the tribal preference for spelling Native words. But how do we know what their preference is?

Many tribes have their own oцcial dictionaries. Often, early tribal dictionaries were created by and with missionaries who desired to translate religious texts and hymns into the local language. The first dictionary printed in the New World was *Vocabulary in Castilian and Mexican Language*, created between 1555 and 1571 by Alonso de Molina, a Franciscan priest who grew up with Nahuatl-speaking children in the Aztec capital of Tenochtitlán as it was becoming Mexico City and so became a fluent speaker of the language. He worked alongside other grammarian Franciscan priests Bernardino de Sahagún and Andrés de Olmos, who both documented the Aztec language and culture through their missionary work and translated many religious texts into Nahuatl. Scholars today still consult the work of these three priests.

Some Native people developed their own writing systems. Most notably, the Cherokee syllabary (a system of writing in which each syllable has a symbol) was the first instance of a Native person—a Cherokee man named Sequoyah—singlehandedly creating a written language. Within a year the Cherokee Nation

Sioux hymnals (left) decorated with porcupine quills, ca. 1900. Sioux bible (right) decorated with glass beads, ca. 1920s.

23/8300, 25/3885, 23/6809

was literate in its own language. Another Indigenous writing system, Cree syllabics, was co-created by Cree community member Mistanaskowew (Badger Calling) and English missionary James Evans, and is now used to write different dialects in First Nations communities throughout Canada. In the territory of Nunavut, similar Inuktitut syllabics have oµcial status, which means that many government documents must be published using both Inuktitut syllabics and the Latin script. While syllabic use is strong in some First Nations communities in Canada, others spell their language with the Latin alphabet. Original scripts are not otherwise common in writing Indigenous languages; most base their writing on the Latin alphabet with accents and other linguistic diacritical marks.

Numerous Indigenous languages are endangered today for many reasons, including English (or Spanish, in Latin America) being the dominant language. The current movement by tribes to revitalize their languages has resulted in increased standardization in how each language is written (and therefore spelled). *Tipi*, once popularly spelled as teepee, is now spelled to correspond to the Siouan language. *Inka*, as in Inka Empire, instead of Inca, is currently the accepted spelling because the "k" more accurately represents the sound made in Andean languages. Tribal citizens have often hired linguists to develop dictionaries for their language. Immersion schools and language programs operated by tribes seek to halt the rapid decline of Indigenous languages. Some tribes have even changed their oµcial names from those given by colonial powers to one in their own language. There is no easy answer to the question of "correct" spelling as languages are continuously evolving and being standardized, but the tribe itself is the most reliable source.

—ALEXANDRA HARRIS

What is a Powwow?

The word powwow comes from the Algonquian term *pau-wau*; it refers to curing or healing ceremonies. The word was quickly adapted to the English language to refer to any Indian gathering, or it is used as a verb, meaning "to confer in council." To Native people, however, the word powwow came to signify important tribal or intertribal gatherings, fairs, and celebrations, featuring singing and social dancing for people of all ages.

Powwows are most often large, intertribal celebrations, yet they represent much more to Native people: they are a dynamic way of life that connects communities; they provide a sense of identity and pride; and offer a creative outlet for dancing, singing, cooking, beadwork, regalia making, and more. Although some community-based powwows are strictly traditional, most are large, intertribal, competition events that draw hundreds of dancers and thousands of spectators over two or three days and nights. Most powwows in the United States and Canada are held in the summer months. Traditionally powwows were held outdoors, but today many are held in large gymnasiums or sports arenas. Some of the largest include Schemitzun in Connecticut, Gathering of Nations in Albuquerque, New Mexico, and the Canadian Aboriginal Festival Powwow, held each year in Toronto's Rogers Centre.

Although powwows have changed over time, many aspects of powwows today have origins in the ceremonial war dances of the Great Plains. Sacred ceremonies of the Osage, Ponca, Kaw, Omaha, and Pawnee tribes, which are practiced today, form the basis of a powwow. Created in the 1950s, many of the Head Staff positions in the powwow arena today can be traced to the ceremonial ouces held by tribal warriors. The role of the Arena

Grand Entry at the National Powwow, August 14, 2005. Washington, DC.

Director, for example, evolved from that of the traditional Whip Men of Plains dance societies. The Whip Men were the first to respond to the call for dancers, encouraging others to rise and, when necessary, using their ceremonial whips on dancers' legs to get their attention.

As its origins show, a powwow can be viewed as a gathering of leaders. Contemporary powwows do bring together tribal leaders and tribal council leaders as well as many Native color guards and veterans, all of whom have proven their bravery and leadership by serving their country. These highly respected people often lead Grand Entry, the colorful procession of Native color guards, veterans, tribal leaders, pageant princesses, and dancers that takes place every morning and evening.

A powwow today is many things. It does bring together Native leaders, but it is largely a celebratory gathering where Native people can express themselves. Perhaps most importantly, powwows represent cultural survival and the ability to maintain Native identity into the twenty-first century.

—TANYA THRASHER

DID AMERICAN INDIANS INVENT LACROSSE?

The origin of contemporary lacrosse is attributed to the six nations of the Iroquois Confederacy (Cayuga, Mohawk, Oneida, Onondaga, Seneca, and Tuscarora), also known as the Haudenosaunee or "People of the Longhouse."

Many of today's sports fans think of lacrosse as a tough, competitive game, but for Native people from Southeastern, Eastern Woodlands, and Great Lakes tribes, it's the "Creator's Game," a divine gift that serves the people in many ways. Southeastern Native peoples play stickball, a double-stick version of the game. Jesuit missionaries gave the game its French name (*crosse* means "stick"). The Mohawk word for the game, *tewaarathon*, is known widely today; the Tewaaraton Award is given annually to the most outstanding male and female American college lacrosse players.

Lacrosse is often referred to as the "Little Brother of War." One of the traditional goals of lacrosse was to resolve territorial disputes between neighboring tribes or clans. Haudenosaunee people played lacrosse on a field that could be as short as 100 yards or as long as 2 miles. Teams could have from a handful to hundreds of players.

Lacrosse is a way of life for the Haudenosaunee people of the Northeastern Woodlands, and is practiced as a "medicine game" that teaches health, strength, unity, and the continuance of traditional values within Iroquoian culture. When a respected or revered tribal member becomes ill, medicine men may call for a lacrosse game to be played in order to instill the sick person with the energy and vitality of the game. In this way, Haudenosaunee people reaffirm their connection to the Creator and the spiritual aspect of the game they play.

Today, the Iroquois are the only Native American nation authorized to compete in any sport on an international level. The Iroquois Nationals team is composed mainly of Haudenosaunee tribal members, but also accepts players from other tribal nations. They are the only Indigenous member nation in the International Lacrosse Federation, the governing body for international play. While traditionally only men were allowed to play lacrosse, the Iroquois now have a women's team.

Stories involving the sport are common among lacrosse- and stickball-playing tribes. One story told among Southeastern tribes recounts a game played between the birds and animals that began as a dispute between the crane and the bear, each claiming superiority over the other. Ultimately, they decided that a lacrosse game should decide. In preparation for the game, they divided themselves into two teams, the crane leading those with wings and the bear leading those with teeth.

Because he had both teeth and wings, the bat did not know where he belonged. He first approached the bear, but was refused because of his wings. The bat then spoke to the crane, but the birds laughed at him because of his small size. The bat had teeth, they said, so he must belong to the animals. The bear finally took pity on the bat and accepted him, but believed that the bat neither belonged to the animals nor benefited his team.

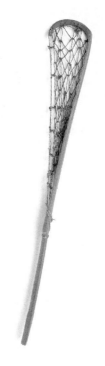

Iroquois lacrosse stick, ca. 1890. Carved and bent wood, hide.

00/8792

As the sun began to set on the game, the bear and the animals were tired and unable to see clearly in the dusk. The birds pulled ahead because they could see to catch the ball in the air and score. Adept at navigating in the darkness, the bat sprang into action, capturing the ball and showing his ability to quickly dart between the animals and birds. The birds could not catch or block him, leaving the bat free to score the winning point.

As a reward, the bat was accepted as an animal and allowed to decide what penalty the birds would suffer as the losers. He told the birds they must fly south each year during the winter. To this day, the bat appears at dusk to see if the animals need his help.

[Creek version as told by Justin Bruce Giles, Muscogee (Creek) Nation of Oklahoma]

—ALEXANDRA HARRIS

WHAT WAS THE FIRST GAME EVER PLAYED WITH RUBBER BALLS?

A precursor of the modern game of basketball was the first game ever played with rubber balls, which were invented in Mesoamerica thousands of years ago. Along with other games, it was played among the Olmec people—whose civilization flourished in Mesoamerica between 1700 BC and AD 400—and among the Aztec (who called their game *tlachtli*), the Maya, and other Indigenous peoples of the region. Today's soccer, baseball, football, and the modern game of basketball (which was invented in 1891 by James Naismith, a teacher in Springfield, Massachusetts) all have their origins in Mesoamerican ball games.

The Mesoamerican ball game was for boys and men of all social classes. Teams played against one another during feast days. The object of the game was for the player to hit a rubber ball with his hips or buttocks into the opposing team's end zone or into one of the stone or wooden hoops that protruded from the sides of the courts. The game was so popular that remnants of hundreds of ballcourts have been found from Bolivia to Arizona and in parts of the Caribbean.

Rubber was a significant invention of the Indigenous peoples of the Americas. The Olmec—who were even known as the Rubber People by other tribes—were the first people in the world to produce rubber from latex, a sap that comes from the native *Hevea brasiliensis*, or rubber tree, found in Mesoamerica and along the Amazon River in South America. Latex was collected from the rubber trees, cleaned, and then cured with smoke from a fire made with palm nuts. After the latex was mixed with sulfur, the naturally bad odor of the latex disappeared, its stickiness was eliminated, and the final product became like the rubber we know today: hardy and impervious to moisture. Centuries

Maya bas-relief depicting a ball player, AD 600–750. La Corona, Department of El Petén, Guatemala. Limestone.
24/457

later, in 1839, the process, known as vulcanization, was rediscovered by the American inventor Charles Goodyear.

The Maya people of Central America and the Quechua people of South America were also known for their use of rubber products. Rubber had a role in a variety of domestic and utilitarian items, including food and water containers, rubber ropes, and clothing, such as raincoats and footgear.

During his second voyage to the Americas in 1493–1496, Christopher Columbus reputedly became the first European to see rubber balls, a fact that was documented by Antonio de Herrera y Tordesillas, a historian serving in the court of King Phillip II of Spain. Ironically, the use of rubber was not at all popular in Europe until the invention of rubber tires in the late 1890s. For the first explorers in the Americas, rubber was easily overlooked in their insatiable quest for precious metals, such as gold and silver, and cash crops such as tobacco.

—LIZ HILL

DID EARLY MESOAMERICANS PRACTICE HUMAN SACRIFICE DURING THEIR BALL GAMES?

Mesoamerica includes the present-day countries of Mexico, Belize, Guatemala, Honduras, and El Salvador. Various games involving rubber balls, unique to that region but extending as far north as Arizona and east to the Caribbean, were played from approximately 1500 BC until the Spanish Conquest 3,000 years later. The Olmec people developed rubber from the sap of the *ulquahuitl*, or the rubber tree.

For the early Mesoamericans, a ball game was not merely a game by contemporary definitions, but rather a sacred rite practiced to maintain cosmic balance between life and death. It had symbolic associations with celestial movements—particularly those of the sun and moon—and with agricultural fertility. In addition, it served as a method of conflict resolution within and between communities, maintaining sociopolitical categories and replacing high-casualty warfare.

A description of a ball game as a ceremonial rite tied to celestial bodies and transformation through death and rebirth is found in the *Popol Vuh*, a Maya creation story. The Maya gods created humans in their present form, the first of whom were the skilled ballplayers Hun Hunahpu and Vucub Hunahpu. Their raucous ball playing so enraged the lords of the Underworld, the Xibalba, that they tricked the brothers into playing a game in which they were killed and buried under the ballcourt.

The sons of Hun Hunahpu, known as the Hero Twins, grew up to become even more highly skilled ballplayers than their father and uncle, but their talents quickly got them into trouble with the Underworld lords, too. They are challenged by the lords of the Underworld to a ball game and a series of tests. The twins cut off their own heads and yet came back to life, fooling the Xibalbas into not demanding as much death. Conquering the Xibalba lords, the Hero Twins disinterred the bodies of their father and uncle, placing them in the heavens to become the sun and moon. Most important, the twins gained for human beings the right to replace the "heart" sacrifice with the ritual burning of the "heart" of copal, a sacred tree resin.

From this creation story, the Mesoamerican ball game can be seen primarily as a battle between the darkness and the light, the death of the sun as it enters the Underworld and its rebirth each morning as it ascends into the sky. The life-sustaining sun is intimately tied to the cycle of the seasons and, thus, agricultural fertility. Whether human sacrifice was as prominent in Mesoamerican society as Spanish explorers made it out to be is still unknown. Exaggerating violence made the nasty business of conquering easier. Evidence, such as imagery depicted in stone carvings and on ceramic vessels, suggests that certain individuals, possibly members of the losing team, were sacrificed upon the outcome of some Mesoamerican ball games. Scholars suggest that ritual sacrifice may relate to the movement of celestial bodies, which in turn impacts the growth of crops, or serve as part of a reenactment of mythological battles, but the exact role human sacrifice played, and its extent, is still under speculation.

—ARWEN NUTTALL

DID ANY INDIANS PRACTICE CANNIBALISM?

Some Indian people apparently engaged in cannibalism—the eating of humans by other humans—as a part of their religious and cultural beliefs. In this, Native Americans were no exception among cultures worldwide. But, generally speaking, cannibalism was feared and abhorred by most Native people, much as it is today by Native and non-Native people everywhere in the world.

In his book *The Indian Heritage of America* (1968), Alvin Josephy Jr. offers a number of accounts of cannibalism, particularly among pre-Columbian tribes of Central and South America, including some of the peoples of the Caribbean region. In many cultures, such as the Maya and the Haudenosaunee (Iroquois), however, basic cultural teachings opposed cannibalism, creating a dynamic both for and against the practice. According to Josephy, cannibalism occurred, "here and there on both continents, although the reasons for its practice differed considerably among various tribes."

In his book *In the Hands of the Great Spirit: The 20,000-Year History of American Indians* (2003), Jake Page also takes up the issue of cannibalism. While not denying that some ritualistic cannibalism did take place among some groups, Page also notes the lack of evidence for most accounts of cannibalism: "European accounts of cannibalism among various groups of American Indians would accompany virtually all of the movements of Europeans into Indian territory, and the subject is (as can be imagined) one of the most emotionally laden in Indian history and, of course, one of the most painful to discuss in any context."

—LIZ HILL

WHAT DID INDIANS REALLY SMOKE IN THOSE PEACE PIPES?

Pipes and tobacco are sacred to Native peoples throughout North America. For American Indians, pipes are the instrument, or conduit, through which smoke and prayers are carried to the spirits. Each tribe has its own ceremonies and occasions for using pipes and tobacco.

Many Native people mix other dried plant materials with tobacco leaves. For example, the Chippewa add the dried inner bark of the dogwood tree to the tobacco mixture. The combination of tobacco and other ingredients is commonly called *kinnikinnick*, an Algonquian word of the Chippewa and Cree that means "what is mixed." There is also a plant that the Chippewa/Cree of Montana call kinnikinnick. Leaves of this plant are mixed with tobacco and act as a natural preservative to keep the tobacco fresh.

The two most abundant types of tobacco that grew in the Americas before contact with Europeans were *Nicotiana tabacum* in the Caribbean and South America and *Nicotiana rustica* in North America. By the first millennium AD, Native peoples had started cultivating them. In addition to being smoked, tobacco was used as a laxative, to dress wounds, and to relieve toothaches. The Maya of Central America and the Taíno of the Caribbean rolled tobacco in tobacco leaves to form cigars. The Aztec filled reeds with tobacco, creating an ancient version of a cigarette.

By the early 1600s the Spanish of the West Indies had imported the more fragrant *Nicotiana tabacum* to Europe, where it became wildly popular. The harsher *Nicotiana rustica* was introduced (along with the white potato) to England in 1586 by members of Sir Walter Raleigh's failed expedition to Virginia,

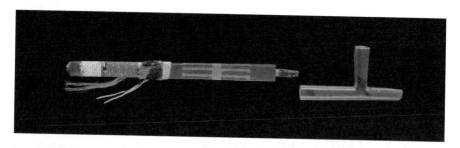

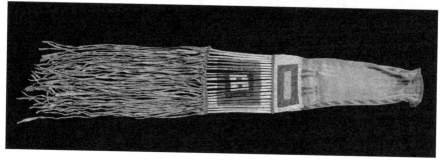

Eastern Shoshone pipe owned by Chief Washakie, ca. 1850. Wind River Reservation, Wyoming. Wood, pipestone, feathers, lead, horsehair, porcupine quills, dye, cotton yarn, and bird skin.
Shoshone pipe bag, ca. 1870. Idaho. Hide, glass beads, pigment, wool fabric, porcupine quills, dye, and sinew.

20/3667, 2/3294

but it was not until colonist John Rolfe began experimenting with Caribbean tobacco seed in 1612 that the Virginia colony had a viable cash crop and a means of survival.

For European colonists, tobacco was a recreational pleasure and an economic mainstay. But for Indigenous Americans, the plant has always played a more meaningful role. Integrated into Native cultures for millennia, tobacco leaves and tobacco smoke remain an important part of Native ceremonial life.

—MARY AHENAKEW

WHAT IS "COUNTING COUP"?

For the Sioux, Crow, Cheyenne, Mandan, and other Plains Indian groups, "counting coup" meant successfully challenging an enemy in one of four specific ways. Touching a live opponent, taking an enemy's weapon during face-to-face combat, capturing a tied horse from an opponent's camp, and leading a horse raid against an adversary—all were generally recognized as counting coup. The four feats were not only displays of courage but also the basis of a system of gaining political and social prestige.

A warrior did not distinguish himself by accumulating goods. Although his most treasured possessions probably were the weapons or horses he had captured from enemies, he often gave away these prizes to someone older or otherwise to be respected. It brought extra merit to distribute an enemy's possessions among one's kinsmen.

The value of the coup lay primarily in the tremendous skill and daring that it took to draw close enough to one's opponent to acquire the coup. For some, ermine skins worn on a shirt and wolf tails attached to moccasin heels—emblems of the number of coups achieved—were worn with pride. At any public gathering, such as a feast or dance, warriors recounted their exploits. Here, too, they distributed some of their captured possessions, demonstrating generosity.

A man could be acknowledged for his hunting or storytelling abilities, but only in counting coup was he recognized as a "good man." A man who had never gained a single coup was a "nobody." If he had at least one, he was honored. In some cultures, performing one coup of each type might make him a chief—an example of generosity, honesty, skill, and bravery.

—NEMA MAGOVERN

Kiowa drawing of a mounted warrior counting coup on a Mexican or white man, 1875–1877. Fort Marion, St. Augustine, Florida.

National Anthropological Archives,
Smithsonian Institution 08547604

Do Indians Do Rain Dances?

> We give thanks to all the waters of the world for quenching our thirst and providing us with strength. Water is life. We know its power in many forms—waterfalls and rain, mists and streams, rivers and oceans. With one mind, we send greetings and thanks to the spirit of water.
>
> —Excerpt from *Ohen:ton Kariwahtekwen:*
> *Greetings to the Natural World,*
> the Iroquois Thanksgiving Address

Yes, some tribes maintain the tradition of rain dances. Like all humans, Native peoples of the Americas have always understood the connection between rain and life. Traditional Native American views include a recognition that rain at the right times and in the appropriate amounts is a vital component of a well-functioning natural world. This knowledge is deep, based on the collective experiences of thousands of years. All people depend on rain to fill the rivers, to help plants grow, and to nurture life. Among groups that practice traditional agriculture, the connection to rain is even more critical. Native cultures conceptualize and participate in these relationships with the natural world in a wide range of ways. Ceremonies, prayers, ritual art, songs, and, yes, dances are among the many ways that Native people acknowledge and help to maintain the delicate balance in nature.

These spiritual and culturally important activities are not practiced randomly. They are part of complex religious cycles that occur throughout the year, year after year. Native peoples of the southwestern United States nurture their crops from the time they prepare the fields through harvest. Over the centuries,

Hopi people in northeastern Arizona have adapted their planting and plant breeding techniques to the arid desert climate. Most of their ceremonies are dedicated to the successful raising of crops.

> Anything that Hopis do, it's for the rain; any kind of dances, even your social dances, they still have to pray for the rain or a good summer or good days ahead. . . . It's all connected. The ceremonies are for all the people . . . throughout the world; not just for themselves; but throughout the world, for every- body . . . [to] live in harmony. . . . That's what it's all about.
>
> —Clifford Lomahaftewa (Hopi),
> *Rain: Native Expressions from the Southwest*

The importance of water is reflected in many Native cultural expressions besides dance. Among the Navajo (Diné), water symbols can be found in sandpaintings, which are created for ceremonies and destroyed upon their completion. The value of water is also evident even in Diné social structures, with clan names such as Tábaꞏaꞏhí (Water's Edge Clan), Tóʼahaní (Near to Water Clan), and Toʼtsóhnii (Big Water Clan) calling attention to places and lineages related to water. Across the hemisphere, water-related images are found on pottery, beadwork, carvings, weavings, and hide paintings.

In addition to supporting life, the appearance of water is also seen as a blessed cleansing of the earth. Traditional Hupa people of northern California perform an elaborate ceremony called the Jump Dance every two years to ward off disease and other disasters. At the end of the ten-day dance, they watch for rain, a sign that the Kixunai, or spirits, approve of the ceremony and that the earth is renewed.

It is hard to know when or why these important activities were first caricatured, joked about, and denigrated in American society and media. Inaccurate and stereotypical images often misrepresent Native cultures. The reality of cultural practices such as rain dances is, of course, much more meaningful and humanly rich than the popular images portray.

—EDWIN SCHUPMAN

ARE DREAM CATCHERS AN AUTHENTIC TRADITION?

Yes. Dream catchers are an authentic tradition for the Ojibwe people of the Great Lakes region. Frances Densmore (1867–1957), an ethnomusicologist who did exhaustive fieldwork among the Ojibwe (sometimes known as Chippewa or Anishinaabe), describes dream catchers as one of three types of objects that families hung from a baby's cradleboard. Each had a specific purpose: as a protective charm, as a toy, or as a diversion to keep a baby occupied. Dream catchers fell into the first category.

In her book *Chippewa Customs* (1929), Densmore wrote,

> Two articles representing spider webs were usually hung on the hoop of a child's board, and it was said that "they catch everything evil as a spider's web catches and holds everything that comes in contact with it." These articles consist of wooden hoops about three-and-a-half inches in diameter, filled with an imitation of a spider's web. In old times, the web was made of nettle-stalk twine and colored dark red with the juice of bloodroot and the inner bark of the wild plum.

In *Chippewa Child Life and Its Cultural Background*, originally published by the Smithsonian Institution's Bureau of American Ethnology in 1951, anthropologist Sister M. Inez Hilger (1891–1977) also describes similar objects hanging from baby cradleboards among the Ojibwe of Nett Lake and Vermilion, Minnesota—lands that are part of the present-day Bois Forte Reservation.

Ojibwe doll in a toy cradleboard with a dream catcher attached. Velvet panels are decorated with Ojibwe floral beadwork, early 20th century.

12/2180

Because of the dream catcher's popularity today, it can be found throughout Indian Country and beyond, as people from many different tribes make them. It seems that everyone—especially children—appreciates the legend of the dream catcher. Who among us likes to be bothered by bad dreams? Dream catchers capture the bad dreams and prevent them from entering the person being protected. Only good dreams are allowed to go through the dream catcher's web.

Traditional dream catchers were not made to last a long time. Thus, they represented the fleeting nature of childhood. Traditional Ojibwe dream catchers (which are still found today) were made with a piece of wood worked into a small circle—though the dreamcatcher frame is often an irregular teardrop shape, rather than completely round. Today, however, dream catchers are made of different materials—for example, a circular metal frame can be wrapped with colored leather or suede and decorated with a variety of objects, such as colored beads and feathers.

—LIZ HILL

WHY ARE MOST INDIAN CEREMONIES AND DANCES OFF-LIMITS TO NON-NATIVE AUDIENCES?

Ceremonies, which often include dances and music, abound in Native communities across the Western Hemisphere. These ceremonies are personal and communal, private and public. They are the deepest expressions of Native American religious and spiritual beliefs. They help heal people—spiritually, emotionally, physically, and mentally. They seek to establish and maintain order in the universe. They are offered to ensure the well-being of the earth and provide for the favorable outcome of human endeavors, such as hunting, building and dedicating a new home, or planting crops. Ceremonies are solemn and important events, and, as such, they are generally not intended for observers or an audience. Practitioners, beneficiaries, and those who participate according to cultural protocols are allowed to attend. According to many Native American traditions, the presence of casual observers, no matter how respectful their intentions, could negatively affect the outcome of the event, and could conceivably do harm to the observer as well.

Many Native American cultural events, however, are shared with the public. At such events, it is acceptable to observe and occasionally participate. Sometimes, even portions of ceremonies are opened for public attendance. On these occasions, visitors are welcomed, and, often, someone from the community explains the activities for guests.

Powwows are a type of Native American social event that observers are encouraged to attend. Powwows occur in many parts of North America. They are not shows or performances, but rather intertribal cultural events that feature dances, music, and other activities. Some of the individual powwow dances are only for participants who dress in the correct regalia and know the dances. Other dances, however, such as "intertribals," are open to anyone in the audience who wants to join in. They are dances of welcoming and fellowship, and it is appropriate to participate.

Native American communities set their own rules and regulations about opening their events to the public. If one wishes to attend a ceremony or other event, it is important to find out in advance if outside observers are acceptable. Many tribes and organizations now provide publications, websites, and other sources of information about which events are open. "When in doubt, ask" is a good axiom to keep in mind when visiting Indian Country. It is important to observe the protocols, such as asking before taking pictures, sitting or standing in the right places, and learning what portions of the event may or may not be open for public participation. It is also important to remember that American Indian reservations are tribal lands, and the laws of those communities must be obeyed. Visiting a Native American community to observe a ceremony or dance can be a profoundly enriching activity, but it must be done with measured respect for the community's values and beliefs.

—EDWIN SCHUPMAN

WHAT IS THE NATIVE AMERICAN RELIGION?

No one Native American religion exists or ever did, although many Native cultures are imbued with common spiritual principles. Each tribe has its own beliefs, cosmology, creation stories, songs, ceremonies, and worship practices for keeping balance between the physical and spirit worlds. For Native people, religion traditionally has been deeply integrated into daily life. Ceremonies and prayers complement activities such as harvesting corn, collecting medicines, hunting game, and waging war. Certain animals—Raven or Bear, among others—represent different aspects of the spiritual world. The phases of an individual's life—birth, naming, coming of age, marriage, and death—may be honored in ceremonies unique to each culture. From baby-naming ceremonies to puberty rites to clan, band, and nation ceremonies such as the Lakota Sun Dance, Native spiritual practices remain vibrant today.

Europeans brought to the Americas a heavy dose of Christian missionary fervor. In the North American colonies, Christian Indian "praying towns," established in 1646 by John Eliot, began the process of forcing Native people to give up their cultures. Even if a Native community did not fully accept Christianity, the newcomers' religion influenced traditional practices. For example, before European contact, the Chickasaws called their supreme being Ababinli, which can be translated as "sitting-above" or "dwelling-above." After Contact, this being was sometimes called Abainki, or "father-above."

Today, many Native people combine traditional practices with Christianity, many are members of various Christian denominations, and an estimated 250,000 people in the United States and Canada are members of the Native American Church.

Rebecca Brady (Cheyenne/ Sac and Fox, b. 1969) Cheyenne three-hide dress and accessories with symbols representing the Native American Church, ca. 1995.

26/5186

The Native American Church has ancient roots among the Huichol people of Mexico and the tribes of the Rio Grande Valley. In the late 1800s some of these tribes were removed to Oklahoma, where they shared their religious beliefs and practices with other tribes. Formally established in 1918, the Native American Church advocates brotherhood, love, family values, self-reliance, and abstinence from alcohol. Central to the church's ceremonies is peyote (part of a small, spineless cactus called mescal), which is used as a sacrament, analogous to the bread and wine that are used as sacraments in the Catholic Church. Peyote, which may only be used by members of the Native American Church, is said to be a powerful, spiritual plant, a telescope through which one can experience God as well as the powers of fire, cedar, and other elements of creation.

Until at least the 1920s, the US government ocially discouraged many traditional Native religious practices—such as pipe ceremonials, sweatlodges, vision quests, and Sun Dances. In 1883 Secretary of the Interior Henry M. Teller established Courts of Indian Offenses on reservations, which investigated, convicted, and punished Native people who followed tribal religions. It was not until 1994, after the US Congress had passed the American Indian Religious Freedom Act Amendments, that Native Americans could feel protected enough to fully exercise the freedom of religion guaranteed to all citizens by the US Constitution.

—MARY AHENAKEW

How can I find a shaman (or medicine man) who will teach me?

It is unlikely that you will. The knowledge possessed by medicine people is privileged, and it often remains in particular families. One is initiated into medicine knowledge as one grows older or is initiated into a particular society that "owns" specific ceremonial wisdom, rites, and accoutrements. In some tribes medicine knowledge is considered a spiritual gift, but a disciplined apprenticeship of many years is also necessary. According to the late Mathew King, a Lakota spiritual leader, "The forbidden things . . . must be learned, and the learning is very diµcult. . . . For someone who has not learned how our balance is maintained to pretend to be a medicine man is very, very dangerous."

Originally condemned as heathenish by European invaders and missionaries, Native religious beliefs and traditions have been usurped since the 1970s by a number of people claiming to have insight into the deepest recesses of Native spiritual wisdom. These pseudo-shamans prey upon susceptible people who are in search of either a quick spiritual fix or something more fulfilling than their own belief systems have provided. The embezzlement of Native spirituality has been a long-standing problem that jeopardizes the survival of Native cultures. For example, the authority of traditional spiritual leaders is diminished when information provided by impostors passes for "Indian" because it fits widely held stereotypes.

Knowledgeable elders may sometimes be willing to school someone outside their tribe in the spiritual ways of their people. Non-Natives may even be allowed to participate in certain ceremonies. Sun Dances and sweatlodge ceremonies are held by various tribes all over the country. Non-Natives or members of other tribes may be invited to join them, as long as the guests have been properly introduced and behave with respect. Certain ceremonies in the Southwest are open for public viewing but not for participation. Others, such as the Hopi Snake Dance, have been closed to outsiders for many years because of aggressive attempts to profit from the sacred ceremony. An inquiry to a Native person about religious beliefs or ceremonies is often viewed with suspicion. It is better to wait until he or she volunteers the information. If you insist on asking, be polite and respectful, and do not take offense if the answer is no.

—ARWEN NUTTALL

Do Indians Have Funerals?

Today, with the influence of many religions, individual beliefs differ from person to person, but all tribes traditionally had some form of afterlife as part of their belief system. In the traditional Native view, death was not an end, but rather a transition. It was an inevitable turning point at which a person emerged into a new plane of being. Beliefs about what happened when a person left this world and traveled to the next differed across tribes, as did the ritual practices and ceremonies that accompanied the newly deceased.

For most Native communities, certain codes of conduct were in place for handling the deceased and preparing the body for the soul's journey into the next world. For Zuni people, it included dressing the body in certain clothes or covering it with cornmeal. At San Juan Pueblo, relatives placed cornmeal under the arm of the deceased as sustenance for the journey. Some believed that only certain people or members of a particular group or society could handle the body. Some tribes, such as the Lakota, prescribed a specific period of mourning and the cutting of mourners' hair. For the Haudenosaunee (Iroquois), the ceremonies surrounding interment might have included feasting and gaming. Other communities practiced weeping, which ranged from silent crying to agonized wailing. Some Amazonian tribes created a drink from plantain juice and the ashes of the deceased, consuming it as a way of keeping their loved ones near them. While many may find this rite disturbing, there are cultures who think placing loved ones underground is equally unsettling. Certain rules also had to be followed so that the spirit of the dead would journey in peace. The Navajo destroyed or gave away all the belongings of the deceased. Other tribes avoided speaking the

The night of Día de los Muertos (Day of the Dead) family members pay tribute with candles, flowers, and offerings to loved ones who have passed, 1998. Huatulco, Mexico.

Photo by Roberto Ysáis.

dead person's name. Placement of the body also differed among tribes. Some buried their dead, while others cremated the bodies. Several Plains tribes placed the dead on scaffolds above the ground or in trees.

The influence of Christianity has had a profound effect on the traditional beliefs of Native people. Many were converted to Catholicism or other Christian religions. Today most Native people bury their loved ones in coμns in cemeteries or have them cremated. Many still engage, however, in certain traditional funeral rites. Specific prayers may be recited, certain articles placed on or with the body, or rules of mourning maintained. A special group or society may prepare the body or lead specific rituals associated with encouraging the spirit along its journey. While funeral rites among Native people are diverse, they are all accompanied by deep respect and wishes to their loved one for a safe journey into the next world, whatever form it may take.

—ARWEN NUTTALL

Was Tonto a Real Indian?

When *The Lone Ranger* hit the radio waves in 1933, audiences of all ages could feel the drama. Even without visual cues, it was easy for listeners to picture the characters. The advent of television in the late 1940s reinforced what had been imagined. The Lone Ranger was white, self-assured, quick to act, and gave orders like a field marshal, while Tonto, his submissive Indian sidekick, loyally followed instructions. Tonto and the Lone Ranger projected the personalities and images expected of them.

The character of Tonto marked a decisive break with the literary and cinematic stereotype of Indians as bloodthirsty savages forever on the warpath. Although Tonto was just as one-dimensional as his movie predecessors, he was a peaceful, dutiful, loyal pal who spoke pidgin English and wore clothes—headbands, feathers, fringed leather, moccasins—that could only belong to an Indian. This stereotype pervaded movie and television westerns of the 1950s and 1960s, remaining unchanged even when the actor playing it was not Native American.

Jay Silverheels (Mohawk), the most famous of several actors who played Tonto, was born Harry Smith in 1912 on the Six Nations Indian Reserve in Ontario, Canada. He played the role in the long-running *Lone Ranger* television series (1949–1957) as well as in two feature-length films. Silverheels's acting career began as a stuntman in 1937. After serving in World War II, he played lacrosse and boxed. As an athlete, he adopted the last name "Silverheels." Having had a taste of acting, he set his sights on Hollywood and, as fortune would have it, he and Clayton Moore worked together before their long association as Tonto and the Lone Ranger. In 1949, while appearing with Gene Autry in the film *The Cowboy and the Indians*, they caught a producer's

Tonto (Jay Silverheels [Mohawk]) and the Lone Ranger (Clayton Moore) hard at work in their familiar television show, ca. 1949–1957.
Bettmann/Getty Images

attention. From this meeting came *The Lone Ranger* series, in which Silverheels became the first American Indian to play an American Indian on television.

In later years, Silverheels became a spokesperson for Indian rights. He was opposed to having non-Indians playing Indian roles, and he became a respected teacher within the Indian acting community. He appeared on talk shows and variety shows. It is said that when he went on *The Tonight Show*, the audience was in stitches after he told Johnny Carson he had married an Italian woman to get even with Columbus. At the age of sixty-seven, he suffered a stroke, and succumbed on March 5, 1980. His ashes were buried at the Six Nations Indian Reserve.

However stereotypical Tonto may have been, the actor who played him ultimately opened doors of opportunity for future American Indian actors. Many American Indians today have played historical Indian figures, and many land dramatic roles that rely solely on their ability to bring a complex, multidimensional character to life on the screen. Harry Smith/Jay Silverheels had a long and successful career in Hollywood in many roles. He will be remembered, however, for the role he brought to life and legend, Tonto.

—RICO NEWMAN

WHY DID CARVED WOODEN INDIANS STAND OUTSIDE CIGAR STORES?

The stereotyping of ethnic groups has always been a part of American culture. Stereotypes are harmful because they reduce complex human beings to mere caricatures who are then ridiculed as inferior. American Indians have been stereotyped continuously ever since the first Europeans wrote and illustrated their accounts of the "New World." Beginning with these early, often-inaccurate depictions, Europeans have cultivated an intense fascination for Native peoples.

For centuries the cigar-store Indian has illustrated prevailing stereotypes. Made of carved wood or cast iron, the nearly life-sized statues of Native Americans can be found today in antiques and "western" shops around the United States. Their original location, however, was outside tobacco and smoke shops.

Why was this depiction of a Native American an appropriate way to announce to the public the location of a smoke shop? The answer is quite simple. Tobacco was a plant first cultivated by the Native peoples of the Americas thousands of years ago. Europeans got their first taste of it when Christopher Columbus accepted it from the Taíno people three days after he made landfall in the Americas in 1492. From that time on tobacco and the New World's Native peoples were connected.

Cigar-store Indians appeared as early as the 1600s in Europe. In those days much of the general population was illiterate, so advertising to reach the masses was most easily accomplished through the use of visual images. American Indians and tobacco represented a connection that many people—Europeans and, later, Americans—could understand; thus, the popular use of Native figures outside smoke shops. From the time of their first encounters, Europeans have tended to romanticize Native peoples,

Wooden statue of an American Indian man in front of a New York cigar, book, and novelty shop, ca. 1895.

Bettmann/Getty Images

and one sees that romanticism in some of the earliest cigar-store Indians. The majority of the European public had never actually seen an Indian person face-to-face; what they knew of American Indians was from explorers' illustrations. Some of the early cigar-store Indians looked more like African enslaved peoples than they did Indigenous Americans. Figures depicting Native females were extremely popular, and some of the woman figures included Indian infants. Later, the carved figures looked more like the Native peoples of the Great Plains, replete with feathered war bonnets and the clothing common among those tribes.

Although cigar-store Indians are rarely seen today outside cigar and smoke shops (their presence declined in the late nineteenth century owing to increased restrictions on the use of sidewalk space), they are still manufactured. Many sources for purchasing cigar-store Indians can be found on the Internet, proving that antique—and newly made—cigar-store Indians remain highly collectible pieces of Americana.

—LIZ HILL

How Authentic Are Contemporary Movies That Try to Tell Stories from a Native Perspective?

There is no real consensus among critics on the accuracy of fictional movies telling a story from a Native perspective. For some, the mere fact that such movies exist is positive in and of itself, but others take a more critical stance, particularly toward movies written, directed, or produced by Native people. While there have been admirable attempts by non-Natives to create films from a Native perspective, such as *Powwow Highway* (1989), Native filmmakers bear a much greater responsibility to tell accurate stories that do not build upon existing stereotypes. How they break down false imagery differs from film to film.

The rise of Native filmmaking was inspired by the civil rights movement and the emergence of Native political consciousness. Beginning in 1966, organized attempts to train Native people in the art of filmmaking as well as the rise of independent film and the video format gave many Native filmmakers, for whom the door to commercial success had been closed, a viable outlet for expression. Since then numerous Native film festivals—including the NMAI's biannual Native American Film and Video Festival—have been developed.

The content of Native films is diverse, focusing on political or social issues, culture and history, environmental degradation, and tribal or familial relationships. Native people have produced documentaries for decades, but commercial studios often argue that most American audiences will be unable to relate to a film composed of Native actors telling a Native story. The 1998 film *Smoke Signals* proved the movie moguls wrong. A land-

Movie still from *Smoke Signals* (1998), directed by Chris Eyre (Cheyenne/Arapaho).
United Archives GmbH/Alamy Stock Photo

mark in film history, *Smoke Signals* was not only written, directed, and coproduced by Native people, but it also achieved modest success among mainstream US audiences. The film, directed by Chris Eyre (Cheyenne/Arapaho) and based on a screenplay by Sherman Alexie (Spokane/Coeur d'Alene), consists almost entirely of Native actors speaking from a Native perspective. Critic Amanda J. Cobb has argued that the success of *Smoke Signals* is in its creation of widely accessible yet uniquely Indian characters and its ability to draw upon the geography and residents of the Coeur d'Alene reservation to present a specific tribal experience. At the same time, the film turns politics on its head by allaying with humor the potential guilt of its white, mainstream audience. Director Chris Eyre tries to convey Native concepts of time, relationships, and storytelling to create complex, multilayered characters that contrast sharply with the one-dimensional caricatures of earlier films. The popularity of *Smoke Signals* allowed Eyre's second full-length feature film, *Skins* (2002), to go straight to commercial distribution.

Some Native people, however, feel that *Smoke Signals* is only a small step forward in the portrayal of Native people in film. The dozens of false images depicted on screen for more than a century cannot be discredited by just a few movies, nor will all Native viewers be satisfied just because a Native person is guiding the filmmaking process. While most people in the early twentieth century learned about American Indians almost exclusively from the movies, the ability to break down the stereotypes the medium helped create is not something one or even a dozen movies by Native filmmakers can be expected to achieve. But that the ranks of Native filmmakers are growing, and that they are continuing to take back the ways in which Native people are portrayed in popular culture is a good start.

—ARWEN NUTTALL

SE-QUO-YAH.

TIME, CONTINUITY, AND CHANGE

WHERE DID INDIANS COME FROM? HOW DID THEY GET TO THE AMERICAS?

For thousands of generations, Native communities throughout the Americas have affirmed the creation of each nation on its land. According to a creation story told in the Northeast, the world began when Sky Woman fell from her home in the heavens. Birds flew under her to prevent her fall, and they placed her on the back of a great turtle, giving her a safe landing. Mud brought by the muskrat became the entire world, providing Sky Woman's descendants with a place to live—the Eastern Woodlands. In the Northwest, Raven coaxed little people to come out of their hiding places in the earth, while in southeastern North America, Crow pecked at shells and, in opening them, released people upon the earth. The stories vary in their details, but all convey the idea that Native people have always lived in the Americas. Oral histories give meaning to beliefs in a way that can be memorized and retold, and they emphasize the presence of a creative force that permeates humans, animals, and the land.

In contrast, the long-held scientific theory focuses on migration. Popularly called the Bering Strait theory, it asserts that ancestors of American Indians gradually came to North America from Asia between about 12,000 and 60,000 years ago. According to this school of thought, nomadic peoples journeyed from Asia to North America at various times during the last ice age, when sea levels were lower and the land underneath what is known today as the Bering Strait (a narrow body of water between Siberia and Alaska, near the Arctic Circle) was exposed. This 1,000-mile-wide "land bridge" probably supported migrations in both directions. Similarities in the spear points used in Asia and those found in the southwestern area of North America and similarities in the physical traits of Asians and American

Indians have been the primary pieces of evidence that support this theory. More recently, geneticists have been tracing DNA markers, which tend to indicate various waves of migration. Over many generations, it is postulated, nomadic hunters followed game animals such as mammoths, elk, moose, and caribou across the land bridge, eventually (once the longer-lasting inland glaciers had receded) fanning out to settle the entire Western Hemisphere.

In 1996 the oldest known skeleton in North America—Kennewick Man—was discovered near the Columbia River in Washington State. The region's Native people advocated an ancestry claim to the almost 10,000-year-old remains, with the goal of reburying them. In April 2016, DNA testing conducted by the US Army Corps of Engineers (the Corps) revealed that the ancient skeleton known as Kennewick Man is related to modern Native American tribes. This finding opened the process for returning one of the oldest and most complete set of human remains ever found in North America to tribes in the Columbia Basin region for burial. The Corps, which owns the remains, said the skeleton is covered by the Native American Graves Protection and Repatriation Act (NAGPRA). The legal and ethical principles of NAGPRA—the federal law that allows tribes to reclaim human remains and cultural items from museums and other institutions—prompted the decision to return the remains. President Barack Obama signed a bill on December 19, 2016, with a provision requiring the ancient bones known as Kennewick Man be returned to a coalition of Columbia Basin tribes within 90 days. On February 23, 2017, the coalition—composed of the Confederated Tribes of the Colville Reservation, the Confederated Tribes and Bands of the Yakama Nation, the Nez Perce Tribe, the Confederated Tribes of the Umatilla Indian Reservation, and the Wanapum Band of Priest Rapids—laid the remains to rest.

Open to further study is the possibility that North America was populated by migration from Mesoamerica and South America. Corn cultivation, textile skills, rubber ball games, and other sociocultural developments in the Western Hemisphere began in Mesoamerica and the Andes. For instance, it is known that squashes were being cultivated by about 8700 BC in Mexico and by 2500 BC in eastern North America. Although the crop may have been developed separately by two Indigenous groups, the seeming migration of squashes and other cultivated plants suggests the gradual northward migration of humans. Still, the question remains: Where did South Americans themselves originate? Modern archaeological discoveries in the Andes suggest humans may have inhabited South America far earlier than previously thought, more than 30,000 years ago.

Many American Indians reject the various migration theories, wary that they could be used to portray Native people as immigrant settlers who happened to arrive earlier than their European "counterparts." By dismissing as unscientific the creation stories that spiritually bind Native communities to the land, non-Native scholars and educators reinforce the idea that Europeans were simply another wave of immigrants who had the right to displace the Americas' previous inhabitants. In 1995 the late Vine Deloria Jr. (Standing Rock Sioux) wrote, "By making us immigrants to North America, [non-Indians] are able to deny the fact that we were the full, complete, and total owners of this continent. They are able to see us simply as earlier interlopers and therefore throw back at us the accusation that we had simply found North America a little earlier than they had."

The scientific quest for knowledge about the origins of the earliest inhabitants of the Western Hemisphere is far from conclusive. Some researchers in the new science of geomythology are turning to Native traditional tales as a source of knowledge about climatic and geologic events of the distant past. As scientific theories continue to be refined, however, Native people will likely also continue to provide the same answer to this question as have generations of their ancestors: "We have always been here, from time immemorial."

—RICO NEWMAN AND GEORGETTA STONEFISH RYAN

How Many Indians Lived in the Western Hemisphere When Columbus Arrived?

Nobody knows the exact population of the Western Hemisphere at the time Europeans first arrived, but the question has been keenly debated by historians for nearly a century. The first scholarly estimate of an Indigenous population was made in 1910 by James Mooney, a Smithsonian ethnographer who, relying on historical documents, concluded that the population of America north of Mexico in 1491 was about 1.15 million people. This number now appears exceedingly low.

In 1966, Henry F. Dobyns published an article in the journal *Current Anthropology* that pieced together the devastating effect on Native people of the diseases unleashed by the arrival of Europeans in North and South America. Beginning in 1525, smallpox wiped out more than half the population of the Inka Empire. During the following century, typhus, diphtheria, and measles added to the toll. The diseases spread inland, even to communities that had never been visited by white people. Dobyns estimated that in the first 130 years after Contact, Native America lost about 95 percent of its population. When the French, the English, and the Spanish arrived in parts of the Americas, they were mystified by empty villages. In other regions the land seemed untouched by human inhabitants.

From his evidence, Dobyns concluded that the Indian population of North America in 1491 was about 18 million and the hemisphere's population about 90 million, but the figures continue to be disputed. More recently, Russell Thornton, in his book *American Indian Holocaust and Survival* (1987), surveys the estimates of other anthropologists and demographers and offers an estimate of approximately 75 million for the Western Hemisphere in 1492. No one can be certain of the death toll exacted by the initial waves of disease, but succeeding epidemics, warfare, forced relocations, and harsh living conditions continued to reduce Indian populations over the next 400 years. Many historians believe that the Native population of the United States reached its lowest point—about 250,000—at the end of the nineteenth century. In the past hundred years, it has rebounded to about 6.6 million.

European explorers and settlers who first arrived in the "New World" wanted to believe it was just that: new not only to them but to all humankind. With their diseases preceding them, diminishing complex Native civilizations, Europeans readily assumed that the Americas were, and always had been, a barely populated wilderness. This view, which justified hundreds of years of European land theft and mistreatment of Indians, has been slow to die. As late as 1987, a standard high school textbook described American history as "the story of the creation of a civilization where none existed."

—STEPHANIE BETANCOURT

IS IT TRUE THAT INDIAN LANGUAGES ARE NOW EXTINCT?

Not all Native languages are extinct. While the exact number of languages in the Western Hemisphere before 1492 can never be known, at least 300 different languages were spoken in North America and possibly as many as 1,800 spoken in Mesoamerica and South America. Fewer than 125 Indigenous languages remain in North America. The Navajo language remains the most vital, with more than 100,000 speakers. Other fairly robust languages include Cree, Cherokee, and Yup'ik.

Mesoamerican and South American languages have generally fared better than languages farther north, although many are extinct and others are endangered. Approximately 50 million Indigenous people (about 10 percent of the population) in Latin America speak between 400 and 700 Native languages. The Quechuan language family is the largest, with some 8 to 10 million speakers. Approximately 25 percent (7.7 million) of Peruvians speak some variation of Quechua. In three countries an Indigenous language, together with Spanish, is the oцcial language: Quechua in Peru, Aymara in Bolivia, and Guaraní in Paraguay. While the overall numbers of speakers of Indigenous languages might seem large, the Native peoples of Latin America are nonetheless under enormous pressure to adopt the predominant national language (either Spanish or Portuguese, depending on the country) as their one and only tongue.

Government policies and pressures from the dominant society are the root causes of language loss. The goal of government policies in the late nineteenth century switched from the destruction to the assimilation of Native North American societies. Missionaries and, later, the US government forcibly

Julianna Coté (Osage) in her Osage language class, writing the word for the color blue, September 2006. Skiatook, Oklahoma.

removed children from their families and placed them in government-run boarding schools. When they arrived at the schools, teachers and administrators cut their hair, made them wear European clothing, and replaced their Native names with English names. Children were punished, often severely, for speaking their Native languages. Outside the schools, fear and ridicule compelled some Native parents to stop teaching their traditional languages to their children, while others saw the exclusive use of English as the only way to survive economically. The heartbreaking result was that many who went through the boarding-school system and then returned to their communities could no longer communicate with their own people. Well into the late twentieth century, the humiliation many adults had faced in the boarding schools kept them from attempting to relearn their lost tongues or encouraging their children to speak them.

Before relatively recent developments in formulating written Native languages, Native speakers passed their languages to others only through speaking and listening. A great deal of the knowledge of a people—cultural, spiritual, medicinal, cosmological—is carried in that people's language. With the loss of language comes the loss of an immense accumulation of cultural knowledge, history, and beliefs. The US government's assimilation policy was effective in diminishing the strength of Native languages, but it did not wipe them out completely.

A strong language revitalization movement is under way today. The emphasis on language as the bearer of culture has encouraged many tribes to introduce their languages to children at earlier ages and to continue language education for older kids. Some tribes have programs whereby traditional speakers work in daycare or Head Start programs, while other communities have developed language-immersion programs and even entire language-immersion schools. Many tribes are working with linguists to create a written version of their language to preserve it. Others have taken advantage of different technologies to maintain and pass along their language. The Cherokee Nation of Oklahoma, the Blackfeet Nation, and Native Hawaiians are just a few of the tribal groups that maintain repositories of print and digital language materials.

Colonization and contemporary influences have done much to erode Native languages, but the resilience that characterizes Native societies can be found in their struggle to ensure that traditional languages are spoken for generations to come.

—ARWEN NUTTALL AND LIZ HILL

DID INDIANS HAVE ALPHABETS AND WRITING BEFORE CONTACT WITH EUROPEANS?

The answer to this question may depend on how broadly one defines "writing." The narrow definition preferred by academics describes writing as a visible record based on sound and language structure, which can be interpreted by someone outside the language. Native people did not have alphabets, the basic symbols that stand for a sound, before European contact. Some Native peoples, however, especially in Mesoamerican cultures, had pictographic forms of written communication that relayed complex narratives with subtlety and detail.

In the Maya system, words as well as full sentences could be represented. At the time of Spanish invasion the Mexica (Aztec) relied heavily on a pictographic system. Pictographs illustrate ideas, not words, but Mexica artisans depicted some words and sounds. Writing in Mesoamerican cultures, which was reserved primarily for the elite, centered on genealogies, political history, and the calendrical system.

Forms of visual communication existed in North America, but none that a non-Native academic would call "writing." Petroglyphs and pictographs carved and painted on rock surfaces, for example, could convey messages, ideas, stories, or events. Many Plains tribes used pictography on buffalo hides—called winter counts—to maintain historical records. Each year, a writer added a new image that depicted the most memorable occurrence since the previous winter. Northeastern historians sealed treaties, recorded events, or communicated messages with wampum (valuable beads made out of the shell of the quahog clam).

Native people have strong oral traditions. Histories, stories, and religious rites were passed from the memories of one generation to the next through the spoken word. The world view of

Native people is intricately woven into the fabric of language and ways of speaking. The oral tradition connects past, present, and future and tightens tribal and familial bonds. Before European contact, the need for writing did not exist except in Mesoamerica, where the populations in certain areas were much greater and the leadership was organized more hierarchically than in North America. Development of written Native languages after Contact was both a Native adaptation to the dominant society and a technique by which non-Natives tried to convert Native people to Christianity.

The first instance of a written Native language developed by a Native person in North America was the Cherokee syllabary, created in 1819 by a Cherokee man named Sequoyah. While he borrowed the concept of writing from Europeans, Sequoyah's accomplishment is all the more impressive because he could neither read nor speak English. His writing system was not an alphabet but rather a set of symbols, each of which stood for the sound made by one or two consonants and a following vowel. Within a year, thousands of Cherokee people learned to read and write with the syllabary, and Cherokee scholars translated several English texts. In 1828 the first American Indian newspaper, the *Cherokee Phoenix*, was published.

Language loss was part of the systematic destruction or assimilation of Native peoples. Some languages have vanished completely, while many others are weakened. Elders believe if the language is lost, the people will be, too. Teachers, elders, and linguists have been working to capture Native speech in written form as a way to pass on the languages—and cultures—to younger generations.

—ARWEN NUTTALL

Sequoyah with the Cherokee syllabary he invented. Engraving of an oil painting by Charles Bird King, 1828. Reproduced in Thomas Loraine McKenney and James Hall's *History of the Indian Tribes of North America*, Philadelphia: 1837–1844.   P27706

Did Indians Really Help the European Settlers?

From the early days of European contact, historical documents record many accounts of assistance given by Native peoples to explorers and colonists. In his journals, Christopher Columbus often commented (albeit mockingly) on the generosity and gentleness of the people he encountered, such as Guacanagarí, *cacique* (Taíno word for chief) of Hispaniola Island, and his community. Columbus observed the generosity as "so artless and so free with all they possess, that no one would believe it without having seen it." Records from his subsequent voyages confirm that Columbus and his crew of more than a 100 men survived only thanks to an entire year's hospitality by the people of Jamaica.

Early colonial governments found alliances with Native nations key to negotiating conflicts with other colonial powers and the myriad tribes in the region. In turn, Native individuals and tribes strategized for their own survival. Often, this meant offering aid through goods and forging military alliances, which allowed them to retain greater autonomy. Over the past five centuries, countless Indigenous communities helped and guided Europeans and European Americans by providing food, shelter, and military aid. Think of the stories of the first Thanksgiving, of Squanto, of Pocahontas, and of Malinalli in Mexico—these and other stories have become mythologized, woven into the histories of an entire continent.

Pocahontas is perhaps the most famous of these early legends. Her abduction by the English and marriage to John Rolfe had great political implications for the success of the Jamestown colonists and her own Pamunkey people. Daughter of Powhatan, the chief of a regional confederacy of tribes, Pocahontas's marriage to an Englishman forged an alliance that resulted in a period of peace between warring powers. She was presented to the court of James I as the daughter of the emperor of Virginia. The alliance, coupled with her husband's burgeoning tobacco business, turned a failing colony into a successful enterprise.

Tisquantum (popularly called Squanto) and the aid he gave the English separatists who arrived on the *Mayflower* has also become American legend. Tisquantum was abducted in 1614 by the British and transported to Spain and England, where he learned English. This would later enable him to act as liaison and diplomat between the English and Native peoples. He returned to New England in 1621 to find that disease had wiped out his tribe in his absence. Ironically, the colonists who arrived on the *Mayflower* had settled Tisquantum's former village of Patuxet, which they renamed Plymouth. He lived with the Plymouth settlers for twenty months, teaching them the skills needed for survival in his homeland. Tisquantum demonstrated how to find eels from the river and instructed the colonists in Native horticulture and how to fertilize weak soil using fish. Colony leader Edward Winslow documented, "We set the last Spring some twentie Acres of *Indian* Corne, and sowed some six Acres of Barly and Pease; and according to the manner of the *Indians*, we manured our ground with Herings or rather Shadds, which we have in great abundance, and take with great ease at our doores. Our Corn did prove well, & God be praysed, we had a good increase of *Indian*-Corne . . . ." Most significant, Tisquantum brokered an alliance between the English colonists and the Pokanoket tribe. He carved out a space for himself as a shrewd advisor and diplomat during a time of great change.

Although she is not well known in the United States, Malinalli (also called Malintzin, Doña Marina, and La Malinche) is a famous and controversial figure in Mexican and Latin American history. Like legends involving Pocahontas, stories of Malinalli's life are often fictionalized, making her true story difficult to establish. Daughter of the cacique of Paynala, she was sold into slavery after her father's death and mother's remarriage to another cacique. Sold to the Spanish in 1519, she eventually became Hernán Cortés's intermediary, advisor, interpreter, mistress, and mother to his child. Because of the latter, she is often portrayed as the mother of the Mexican people—people of both European and Indigenous heritage. She was fluent in the Nahuatl and Mayan languages, and often spoke for Cortés in negotiations. In Aztec codices she is depicted both as accompanying Cortés and alone, suggesting that she could also direct events independently. Historians credit her diplomatic skills as critical to the success of the Spanish Conquest. As a result, many today see her as a traitor to

Indigenous people; others see her as the mother of a nation.

These stories of interactions between the first peoples of the Americas and the colonists are examples of the conflicted understandings that run throughout Native histories. Some criticize the aid given by Indigenous people to colonists as hastening the demise of Native nations. Others have a more nuanced view, recognizing that these historic figures faced excruciating choices as they fought for their homelands, their lifeways, and their very survival.

—ALEXANDRA HARRIS

IS IT TRUE THAT POCAHONTAS SAVED JOHN SMITH FROM EXECUTION?

Historians disagree, but the general consensus is that John Smith's story about his rescue is probably not true.

"Pocahontas" was actually a nickname, one of four names that the famous Indian girl had throughout her life. Although known today as Pocahontas, meaning "mischievous one," her given name was Amonute. Yet she also kept the secret spiritual name Matoaka, and when baptized and married she took the name Rebecca. She was never able to tell her own story, but Pocahontas's legend endures 400 years later and grows stronger with each new generation. As an eleven- or twelve-year-old girl in the early 1600s, and one of the many children of the ruling chief Powhatan of present-day Virginia, Pocahontas lived during a time of great change for her people—a time of war and struggle with the English colonists of the Jamestown settlement.

Although little is known about her, aside from that provided by English sources, there is still much more to the story of young Pocahontas than today's films and storybooks tell. These dramatic (and largely false) versions usually describe Pocahontas as a mature woman in her twenties, who fell deeply in love with colonist John Smith and heroically saved his life. In truth, she was a much younger girl when she met Smith, and her connection to him was likely not a romantic one. Facts that remain important milestones in the young woman's life are her abduction by colonists and her life as a captive aboard an English ship; her eventual conversion to Christianity, her marriage to Englishman John Rolfe and the birth of a son named Thomas; and her celebrated visit to the court of King James I in England—all before her death at the tender age of twenty-two.

Unknown artist, probably after a 1616 engraving by Simon van de Passe (1595–1647). Pocahontas (ca. 1595–1617).

National Portrait Gallery, Smithsonian Institution; gift of the A. W. Mellon Educational and Charitable Trust. NPG.65.61

The details of Pocahontas's life are still actively debated among scholars and historians, the most frequently discussed question being whether Pocahontas threw herself across John Smith at his execution, pleading for mercy. Interestingly, the first person to recount the details of Pocahontas's life was Smith himself, when he began writing a "Generall Historie" of his experiences in America. Although he had published other accounts much earlier, the story of his "rescue" in AD 1607 from certain death by Pocahontas did not appear until 1624. Since its publication, Smith's vivid rescue story (by his account, Chief Powhatan would have smashed in his head with a stone ax if Pocahontas had not begged her father to spare him) has been vigorously challenged and doubted by many. But the story was adopted by other writers, who often romanticized it to appeal to eighteenth- and nineteenth-century readers.

No one knows for certain whether Smith's legendary rescue by Pocahontas actually occurred. Some scholars believe that Smith might have misunderstood what was happening to him, asserting that the elaborate ceremony taking place was actually a traditional adoption ceremony, bringing him into the tribe. But some historians maintain that the event could have taken place as Smith recalled it, and that he may well have been killed if Pocahontas had not intervened.

A more romanticized engraved portrait of Pocahontas, wearing a shawl, feathered headdress, and European-styled necklace.

Kean Collection/Archive Photos/Getty Images

Although the details of her rescue of (and relationship to) John Smith are not fully understood, it is widely accepted that Pocahontas was an important figure in American history who, despite her youth, contributed greatly to the early survival of the Jamestown colony.

—TANYA THRASHER

Is it true that Indians sold Manhattan for twenty-four dollars worth of beads and trinkets?

The "sale" of Manhattan was a misunderstanding. In 1626 the director of the Dutch settlement, Peter Minuit, "purchased" Manhattan for sixty guilders worth of trade goods. At that time Indians did everything by trade, and they did not believe that land could be privately owned, any more than could water, air, or sunlight. But they did believe in giving gifts for favors done. The Lenni Lenape—one of the tribes that lived on the island now known as Manhattan—interpreted the trade goods as gifts given in appreciation for the right to share the land. We don't know exactly what the goods were or exactly how much a guilder was worth at that time. It has been commonly thought that sixty guilders equaled about twenty-four dollars. But the buying power of twenty-four dollars in 1626 is not known for sure.

To Europeans, ownership of land was synonymous with wealth, power, and prestige. To purchase land meant that the purchaser had the exclusive right to own and use it. The Lenni Lenape did not realize that the Dutch meant to hold the land for their exclusive use. In 1653, Dutch colonists put up a wall across lower Manhattan to protect the north side of their settlement from attacks by Indian tribes and the British. By 1700 the British had taken over the Dutch colony, torn down the barrier, and built in its place a paved lane called Wall Street.

At the time the Lenni Lenape (which translates as "the people") occupied lands now known as the states of Delaware, New Jersey, lower New York State, lower Connecticut, and the western tip of Long Island. Not long before the supposed sale of

An artist's rendition of a scene in which Peter Minuit (1580–1638), the director of the Dutch colony of New Netherland, offers a group of Native villagers a variety of goods from a chest in exchange for Manhattan Island, May 24, 1626.

Archive Photos/Getty Images

Manhattan, a man named Captain Samuel Argall found a large bay on the Atlantic Coast north of the Chesapeake Bay. He named it in honor of Sir Thomas West, 12th Baron De La Warr, who was the governor of the Virginia colony. The bay, the river, the governed territory, and the local Indians all became known by the name Delaware.

—GEORGETTA STONEFISH RYAN

Did Europeans Purposely Use Smallpox to Kill Indians?

There is no clear evidence that the US government ever used the smallpox virus to conduct a systematic, intentional extermination of Native peoples, but some tribal histories describe how some Europeans tried to wage war by accelerating the disease's spread. For example, the Crow Indian Tribe Resource Report issued on April 15, 2002, states that in 1843 "The United States used army blankets and rations festered with the smallpox germ and distributed [them] at Fort Parker." British soldiers, in one well-documented case at Fort Pitt, Pennsylvania, during the French and Indian War, discussed the notion of spreading smallpox intentionally. With the approval of their commanders, soldiers gave to two chiefs some blankets and a handkerchief from a smallpox hospital. In 1763 Captain Simeon Ecuyler recorded the event in his journal, adding, "I hope it will have the desired effect."

Everywhere the Europeans landed, smallpox and other diseases quickly followed. Smallpox arrived as early as 1507 on the island of Hispaniola in the Caribbean, and the disease devastated the Taíno people of the Greater Antilles. In the mid-1520s 200,000 Andean Indians died. From 1616 to 1619 the disease hit coastal New England, decimating the population; in 1633 a smallpox epidemic struck the Narragansett peoples farther north along the eastern seaboard and quickly spread throughout the colonies. More than 10,000 Huron people of Ontario died. From 1780 to 1782 smallpox traveled through the Great Plains, affecting the Shoshone, Ojibwe, Blackfeet, Cree, Assiniboine, and many others. Around 1834 thousands of Chumash people in California died from the disease. In 1837–1838 smallpox almost entirely decimated the Mandan, Hidatsa, and Arikara tribes along the

Missouri River in present-day North Dakota. In 1840 the Crow were swept by the first of three smallpox epidemics that reduced the population from an estimated 10,000 to approximately 2,000 in 1850. By 1853 the Makah people in Washington State had also been hit by the virus, as had a number of other Northwest Coast tribes.

In 1803 measures were already being taken to protect the U.S. military from smallpox and other infectious diseases in the Indian territories. Indians began to be provided with vaccinations against the smallpox virus in 1832, but the early vaccines may have caused more disease than they prevented.

As historian and Smithsonian curator Herman J. Viola notes in his book *After Columbus: The Smithsonian Chronicle of the North American Indians* (1990):

> Little wonder, then, that the Native Americans had no love for the European intruders. From North to South, East to West, the Indians shared the same tragedy, the same heartaches, the same feelings as the unknown Maya who lamented, "There was then no sickness; they had no aching bones; they had then no high fever; they had then no burning chest; they had then no abdominal pain; they had then no consumption; they had then no headache. At that time the course of humanity was orderly. The foreigners made it otherwise when they arrived here."

—LIZ HILL

Was Sacagawea Really All That Important to the Lewis and Clark Expedition?

Sacagawea, a young Shoshone woman who had been captured by the Mandan/Hidatsa people and was living among them, is often seen as a pivotal figure in the Lewis and Clark Expedition, which took place between 1804 and 1806. Sacagawea, who was about sixteen years old at the time, together with her husband—a French Canadian fur trader named Toussaint Charbonneau—and her infant son accompanied the American explorers Meriwether Lewis and William Clark on a journey ordered by President Thomas Jefferson that would take them from Fort Mandan on the Missouri River (land that became North Dakota) to the Pacific Ocean and back again. The primary purpose of the expedition was to find a western link in the (ultimately nonexistent) Northwest Passage, thought to be a waterway between the Atlantic and Pacific. Another purpose was to learn about the natural resources and Native tribes of the territory so that trade could be established.

Over time Sacagawea's importance to the Lewis and Clark Expedition has taken on legendary proportions. It is true, however, that she was a valuable member of the party, identifying landmarks in her Shoshone homelands and helping to communicate with her people. Without Sacagawea, her brother Cameahwait would probably not have provided the expedition with goods and horses, taken them through Lemhi Pass, or saved them from a dangerous winter in the Rockies. In addition, her presence, and that of her baby, signaled to other tribes that Lewis and Clark's group was not a war party. She also had knowledge of a great variety of indigenous plants, which were useful sources of medicine and food.

The head and tail sides of the U.S. dollar coin, 2000. The head side shows the likeness of Sacagawea and her infant son, Jean Baptiste. A bald eagle in flight surrounded by seventeen stars (the number of states in the Union at the time of Lewis and Clark's expedition) is featured on the tail side of the coin.

Hulton Archive/Getty Images

The only written record of Sacagawea's life is in the journals Lewis and Clark kept during their expedition, and very little is known about what happened to her after 1806. The date of Sacagawea's death is debated. Not only is her actual year of birth unknown—it is recorded as either 1786 or 1788—but also two death dates, years apart, are disputed. According to oral traditions, Sacagawea is said to have returned home to her Shoshone people, with whom she lived until her death in Wyoming in 1884. Another, more plausible, story reports her dying of a fever in 1812 at Fort Manuel in present-day South Dakota. Today Sacagawea remains among a handful of Native men and women who continue to fuel the popular imagination of many Americans for their courage and fortitude during one of the most important times in this country's history. To commemorate Sacagawea's bravery in a period when women were not recognized for their accomplishments, the first US coin of this millennium featured her face and that of her baby.

—LIZ HILL

What Happened to White People Captured by Indians?

Since the 1700s stories have abounded of the terrible fates that befell innocent white maidens or courageous white frontiersmen and soldiers who were captured by American Indians supposedly hell-bent on rape, murder, and scalping. Catering to eighteenth- and nineteenth-century European stereotypes, the stories created romanticized legends of good (white settlers) versus evil (Indians). The stories—which appeared in newspapers, books, and popular journals, and later became staples of Wild West shows, movies, radio, and television—represented the righteous colonizers against the wild "other." What actually happened to white people captured by Native people varied from tribe to tribe, but the image of the murderous savage became a national myth that supported the theft of Native lands and the destruction of Native cultures.

Captivity stories are a documented part of North American history. Many are biased, however, overemphasizing or misinterpreting perceived negative aspects of Native society. Many books and the entertainment industry ignore the numerous accounts of white people who were captured by Indians, adopted into a tribe, and then wrenched unwillingly from their new families by their relatives or government soldiers. James Axtell, in his discussion of "white Indians," notes the case of John McCullough, a fourteen year old who had lived among the Shawnee in Ohio since the age of six. In 1764, while trying to forcibly remove McCullough from his community, the English "had his legs tied 'under the horses belly' and his arms tied behind his back with his father's garters, but to no avail." At first opportunity, McCullough escaped and returned to his Indian family, only to be recaptured a year later. When given the option to leave and return to the

Geronimo's band of Chiricahua Apaches abducted Santiago McKinn from his family's ranch in the Mimbres Valley, New Mexico, in 1885. Well treated, the boy assimilated to his new life, speaking Apache fluently and joining the other children in sports and games. When finally "rescued" in March 1886, he acted, according to Fletcher Lummis, a *Los Angeles Times* reporter, "like a young wild animal in a trap. . . . He bawled badly when told that he was to be taken back to his parents, and said he always wanted to stay with the Indians."

Camillus Sidney Fly. Santiago McKinn with Apache children,
Canyon de los Embudos, Sonora, Mexico, March 1886.
National Anthropological Archives, Smithsonian Institution
SPC BAE 4605 01604807

white world, even many older adoptees preferred to stay with the tribe, shunning the entrapments of Anglo-European life.

White people came into the hands of Native people by several means, among them capture, adoption, marriage, and voluntary exchange. Some captives, usually the men, were killed for the violation of agreements, as retribution for the killing of tribal members, or to prevent the disclosure of settlement locations. Haudenosaunee (Iroquois) warriors sometimes forced their captives, en route to the victor's

85

village, to run through a double row of hitting and kicking villagers from allied tribes along the way. Native tribes might eventually adopt their white captives, especially women and children. Adoption established ties of kinship and bestowed upon the captives membership in the community. A non-Native could then marry into a tribe and opt to follow the ways of his or her spouse's people. Stories also exist of lost children who were found and adopted by Native people.

Sometimes white people were captured for the express purpose of prisoner exchange. Other times, Native headmen and government or military leaders would voluntarily exchange members to learn each other's language and customs. These volunteers could act as intermediaries during negotiations.

—ARWEN NUTTALL

IS IT TRUE THAT WHITE PEOPLE INVENTED SCALPING, OR DID THE PRACTICE ORIGINATE WITH NATIVE AMERICANS?

While a few tribes took enemy scalps as trophies of war, many Native peoples considered the practice repugnant. But thanks to early frontier literature and, later, Hollywood westerns, scalping has become part of the American Indian stereotype. Certainly the practice was not exclusive to American Indians. In the *Handbook of American Indians North of Mexico* (1959), Frederick Hodge states that the practice was noted among Scythians (Persian warriors who lived in the fifth century BC) as far back as the time of the Greek historian Herodotus. Archaeologists believe they have found evidence of scalping on pre-Columbian skulls in North America, at sites both east and west of the Mississippi River.

Scalping by North American Indians was first recorded by Europeans in the mid-1500s. In the *Encyclopedia of North American Indians* (1996), historian James Axtell documents some of these encounters: "On his voyage up the St. Lawrence in 1535–36, Jacques Cartier was shown by the Stadaconans at Quebec 'the skins of five men's heads, stretched on hoops, like parchment.' In 1540, two of Hernando de Soto's men, the first Europeans to reach west Florida, were seized by Indians. The killers of one 'removed his head, or rather, all around his skull . . . and carried it off as evidence of their deed.'"

Europeans manipulated Indians by encouraging warfare between tribes, arming them with guns and knives through trade, and offering bounties to Indians for Indian scalps. The practice of scalping turned into the practice of murder during the 1600s, when English colonial governments began offering scalp bounties. Indian "enemies" were hunted and killed for their scalps, which became more valuable than beaver, otter, or any of the other animal pelts in demand at the time. This systematic murder for profit spread westward with European settlement, continuing until about 1800.

In 1694 the first Massachusetts colonial proclamation to encourage volunteer hunters offered bounties "for every [hostile] Indian, great or small, which they shall kill, or take and bring prisoner." The act was renewed in 1704, but the General Court, deciding to follow a more "Christian practice," established a scale based on age and sex. Scalps of "men or youths capable of bearing armes" were worth one hundred pounds; women and children in their teen years and above were worth only ten pounds; and no reward was given for killing children under ten years old. Any captured children were instead sold as slaves and sent out of the colonies.

For colonial governments in North America, scalping appears to have been a favored technique, no matter who the supposed enemy. In 1688 the French governor of Canada became the first to encourage Indian scalping of whites. In his proclamation, ten beaver skins were offered to Indians in northern New England for every enemy scalp, "Christian or Indian." And in 1696 the New York Council resolved "for the future, that Six pounds shall be given to each Christian or Indian as a Reward who shall kill a French man or Indian Enemy."

—MARY AHENAKEW

PEOPLE, PLACES, AND ENVIRONMENTS

WHAT IS THE RELATIONSHIP OF NATIVE AMERICANS TO THE ENVIRONMENT?

In the 1970s, America's imagination was captured by the "Keep America Beautiful" television ad, which featured a purported Native American dressed in traditional regalia with a tear running down his cheek at the site of polluted land and water. While that vivid image has some basis in traditional values, it is overly simplistic.

Traditional Native American sensibilities regarding the earth and the human relationship with it are elucidated in these words of the writer, actor, and chief Luther Standing Bear from his book, *Land of the Spotted Eagle* (1978): "The Lakota was a true naturist—a lover of Nature. He loved the earth and all things from the earth. . . . From Wakan Tanka there came a great unifying life force that flowed in and through all things—the flowers of the plains, blowing winds, rocks, trees, birds, animals—and that was the same force that had been breathed into the first man. Thus all things were kindred and brought together by the same Great Mystery."

As people who see themselves as part of the natural world—not separate from it—Native Americans come from cultures that value balance and strive to live in a way that respects and preserves it. When things become imbalanced, sickness, unhappiness, and confusion are the results. Then it is the human responsibility to take steps, including conducting ceremonies, to restore the balance and harmony necessary for the appropriate functioning, not only of humans but also of all things.

Like all people, Natives have traditionally obtained food, clothing, tools, transportation, homes, and medicines from the environments in which they have lived. Because Native Americans are tied philosophically and spiritually to their resources,

A gathering place for traders and salmon fishers for thousands of years, Celilo Falls, on the Columbia River in Oregon, was submerged by the opening of The Dalles hydroelectric dam on March 10, 1957. Today the Columbia River is broken up by fourteen hydroelectric dams, and the 14 million wild salmon that inhabited the river in 1855 have dwindled to fewer than 100,000. Native fishers spearing salmon from wooden scaffolds at Celilo Falls, ca. 1940.
MPI/Archive Photos/Getty Images

however, they treat them with respect. Native Americans express veneration not only in ceremonies but also in the careful management of certain resources.

Before the arrival of Europeans, many Native Americans used their knowledge of the environment in the practice of agriculture. With fire and tools they cleared trees and brush to make room for fields of corn, beans, and squashes. Companion-planting the three crops helped rejuvenate the nitrogen in the soil, keep insect infestations down, and maintain moisture in the soil. According to a USDA Forest Service report issued in 2013, Native Americans across North America also cleared vast tracts of land with fire. "Native Americans used fire for diverse purposes, ranging from cultivation of plants for food, medicine, and basketry to the extensive modification of landscapes for game management or travel."

Many modern Native Americans feel these traditional connections to the earth. Communities still practice their traditional arts, agriculture, and ceremonies related to the environment. In response to modern challenges, many tribal governments are addressing environmental issues that affect their communities. The Karuk Tribe of northern California is one of many that have fought to preserve salmon spawning runs in the rivers of the Northwest. Power-generating dams built on rivers in the mid-twentieth century severely depleted salmon runs. That encroachment not only interrupted the ancient cultural connection to the salmon but also affected the diet of tribal members, such as the Karuks, who believe that epidemics of obesity, heart disease, and early onset diabetes are related to the dams. In another example, the Colville tribal members of Washington State recently rejected an opportunity to open a molybdenum (a metal used to harden steel and dye plastics) mine on their reservation. While the mine would have offered some economic opportunities, it was rejected on the basis of its impact on the reservation environment and traditional culture.

The late Native American scholar and philosopher Vine Deloria Jr. (Standing Rock Sioux) described the difference between Western and Native American understandings of the universe in an interview published in 2000:

> I think the primary difference is that Indians experience and relate to a living universe, whereas Western people— especially scientists—reduce all things, living or not, to objects. The implications of this are immense. If you see the world around you as a collection of objects for you to manipulate and exploit, you will inevitably destroy the world while attempting to control it. Not only that, but by perceiving the world as lifeless, you rob yourself of the richness, beauty, and wisdom to be found by participating in its larger design.

—EDWIN SCHUPMAN

WERE THE AMERICAS A VAST, UNTOUCHED WILDERNESS WHEN EUROPEANS ARRIVED?

By the time Europeans arrived in the Americas, Indigenous peoples—thousands of cultures, each with different languages, belief systems, and lifeways—had occupied all regions of the Western Hemisphere for millennia. Far from being a virgin landscape, the Americas were home to an estimated 72 million people who expertly and sustainably managed their environments through agriculture and engineering to produce food, medicine, shelter, tools, and more. Some peoples used the land lightly; others established vast cities, roads, and empires.

All aspects of Native peoples' lives—food, clothing, architecture, language, social structure, and spirituality—evolved from their local environments, whether that was the icy Arctic, the Southwestern deserts, or expansive plains. Native peoples engineered their homes to suit the landscape: adobe pueblo homes of the Southwest insulated against the intense heat and cold, portable tipis allowed Great Plains tribes to travel to hunt bison, and building homes on stilts allowed people to stay dry in the riverine floodplains of Peru. The environment also determined peoples' food sources. People in the desert Southwest perfected dry farming, while tribes in what is now California farmed very little because of the abundance of food sources, from river and ocean fish to acorns and animals in the mountains. Lack of large agriculture didn't mean lack of land use, however. California peoples, for example, regularly managed their environments using controlled burning. One of the main food staples in the region was acorns from oak trees. Seasonal controlled burning removed undergrowth that competed with oaks for water and nutrients, encouraged grasses that attracted game, served as a

The Tovvne of Secota in *A briefe and true report of the new found land of Virginia* by Thomas Hariot (1560–1621). This engraving by Theodor de Bry (1528–1598) depicts Secoton village, possibly in North Carolina. Buildings of pole-and-mat construction are dispersed in the landscape and surrounded by fields of corn, tobacco, sunflowers, and pumpkins. Also shown are people hunting deer, guarding a field, tending a fire, and eating and dancing.

© John Carter Brown Library, Box 1894,
Brown University, Providence, R.I. 02912

nonchemical pest control, and reduced the impact of catastrophic wild-fires. Native peoples managed their environments using controlled burning, erosion control, fish and waterway management, and other inventive techniques to optimize the resources that were already there.

Several factors contribute to the myth of the American wilderness. It was in the interest of European colonists to justify taking land by asserting that the Indigenous people weren't using or improving it, in spite of the evidence of extensive Native occupation and large-scale farming. The fact that disease was wiping American Indians out via trade routes before some Native communities even came into contact with Europeans was proof to colonists that God was making way for their settlement. As scholar David E. Stannard observed, according to English colonists, "God was making a place for his Christian children in this wilderness by slaying the Indians with plagues of such destructive power that only in the Bible could precedents for them be found. His divine message was too plain for misinterpretation." Instead of the garden that Indigenous people meticulously cultivated, the landscape was used as a backdrop for manifest destiny.

Indigenous peoples and Europeans thought about nature in drastically different ways. While the Native peoples had been using the environment in ways that would sustain their communities, the Europeans who arrived sought to exploit the Americas for wealth. Journals written by early observers—including Columbus himself—included few descriptions of nature beyond how it could be commodified and sold in Europe. As scholar Kirkpatrick Sale observed, English colonists wrote of their fear of nature: "To this terror of the wild the European mind opposed the serenity of the garden: nature tamed, nature subdued, nature, as it were, *denatured*." Once settlements were established, settlers began to clear-cut forests and overhunt game (such as the beaver) to the point of near extinction. Elimination of nature and game led to widespread degradation of the environment, including erosion and pollution. Defining nature by commodities—how much wood can be cut down, how many beaver pelts can be sold, etc.—was a very different world view from that of the Native peoples and was a fundamental reason why Europeans saw the Americas as uninhabited, despite the civilizations that already occupied the continents. Rather than the mythical wilderness that settlers imagined occupying, the Americas were home to millions of people who had been conserving, cultivating, and managing the landscape for millennia.

—ALEXANDRA HARRIS

Did Native Peoples and European Colonists Have Different Perspectives About Land?

During initial encounters with each other, Native peoples and Europeans had very different ways of thinking about land. Europeans viewed land ownership as an expression of personal independence and economic self-sufficiency, which wasn't possible to attain in Europe at the time. They based their property rights on deeds, surveys, and written documents. The young colonies, their towns, and individual colonists all purchased land from Native peoples and recognized the Indian ownership of land. At the same time, they saw Native people and their land as wild, savage, and chaotic. Their European definitions of land imposed order on what they saw as a wilderness.

Native peoples had a deeper relationship to the land. The land was the foundation of their existence and at the center of their creation stories. It was the origin of their sovereignty, identity, spiritual practices, and cultures. For many tribes, the plants, animals, and forces of nature were all equally important actors in the living universe. Tribes had territories that they defended against invaders; families and individual tribal members owned rights to certain tracts of land for hunting, farming, and fishing. They didn't sell these rights to each other, but asked permission for use or to cross another tribe's territory. Villages relocated periodically for different reasons, so land rights were inherently temporary. When fields were depleted, for example, a village might temporarily rotate off that land or move location entirely, changing a tribe's territorial boundaries. Ecologist M. Kat Anderson described a California Indian concept of ownership as *usufruct*, meaning to use but not possess. "Under the usufruct system," she wrote, "each family had a combination of exclusive rights to certain resources and communal rights to other resources." Individual oak trees might be privately owned, while another area of oaks might be owned by the tribe in common. Additionally, Native people didn't accumulate wealth in the same way Europeans did, so there was no reason—or need—to buy and sell land.

Early agreements between colonists and Eastern Native Americans show evidence that these differences led to misunderstandings, the most famous being the sale of Manahatta, or Manhattan Island. When approached by Europeans to sell land, Native peoples likely viewed these transactions as the purchase of rights to use the resources in a specific area, just as fellow members of the tribe would do. In this way, the same plot of land might be sold repeatedly to different buyers, a tendency that colonists complained about frequently.

Native people learned quickly, however, that land sales meant something very different to the colonists and that the newcomers did not share traditional Native conceptions of land. After initial encounters (and the clashes that resulted from misunderstandings), Indians began to reserve rights, such as the right to fish, hunt, or gather wood, from the sale of territory. The fact that these rights are named and included in land sales documents implies that Indians well understood the necessity to negotiate continued rights; without them, the English would think they had the authority to evict Indians from the land.

Notably, Northeastern Native peoples who achieved literacy with their languages began conveying land to one another via written contracts as early as the fifteenth century. Nantucket people began writing their own deeds in the 1660s, separate from the English deed-title system. Indians who spoke the Massachusett language, who may have been more literate than nearby colonists in the eighteenth century, confirmed oral agreements between tribal members with written contracts.

Today many tribes still recognize family and tribal territories, formally and informally. During powwows and formal gatherings, organizers invite a local tribal leader to welcome visitors to their territory. In many cases on the tribal level, family territories are still recognized and custom requires that other families ask permission to use that parcel of land.

—ALEXANDRA HARRIS

DO ALASKA NATIVES REALLY HAVE HUNDREDS OF WORDS FOR SNOW?

It is true that the Yup'ik and Iñupiaq peoples of northern Alaska and the Inuit people of northern Canada have a seemingly unlimited number of words and phrases that describe types, textures, and amounts of snowfall. Many other words describe different conditions that exist when snow is on the ground. Yup'ik and Iñupiaq are only two of Alaska's eleven culture groups, but in those languages single words can often express detailed descriptions.

The vast array of snow descriptions in Yup'ik and Iñupiaq is possible largely because the languages are polysynthetic, meaning that entire sentences can be formed by a single word. Many different suffixes also can be added to a root word, such as snow, making it possible for the Yup'ik and Iñupiaq to say in one word what an English speaker would need several words—perhaps even an entire sentence—to say.

Types of snowfall include such simple conditions as lightly falling snow, heavy wet snow, blowing snow, and others. Because Native peoples have always had to understand the land on which they live with an eye toward communal survival, it makes sense that weather would be closely monitored by Indigenous peoples, particularly those in climates where changes in weather can be extreme. Describing a weather condition in detailed language—and adapting one's behavior to more easily live with it—is a practice common to many other Native peoples, including Native Hawaiians, who have countless words to describe rain (for example, rain that sweeps over the ocean to the islands; misty, cool rains of the valley regions; torrential downpours in the rain forests), an important feature of their tropical environment. Because snow is an important part of many Native Alaskan people's environment (in northern Alaska, snow covers the ground for most of each year), the ability to describe the various kinds of snow was—and continues to be—crucial to their survival on the land.

Here is a list of a few of the different types of snow that have been described by Inuit people, in just one dialect, the Copper Inuit: *aniu* (good snow to make drinking water); *apiqqun* (first snow in autumn); *apun* (fallen snow); *aqilluqaq* (fresh soft snow); *mahak* (melting snow); *minguliq* (falling powdered snow); *natiruvik* (snow blowing along a surface); *patuqun* (frosty sparkling snow); *pukka* (sugar snow); *pukaraq* (fine sugar snow); *qaniaq* (light soft snow); *qanik* (snowflake); *qanniq* (falling snow in general); *qayuqhak* (snowdrift shaped by the wind, resembling a duck's head); and *ukharyuk, qimuyuk, aputtaaq* (snowbank).

—LIZ HILL AND NEMA MAGOVERN

DID INDIANS REALLY USE SMOKE SIGNALS? DO THEY TODAY?

Yes. Some Native peoples living on the Great Plains and in the Southwest used smoke signals hundreds of years ago. For example, the Navajo and Apache transmitted smoke signals as a military tactic to warn of the approach of enemies. But the use of smoke to convey messages has been greatly exaggerated—and even ridiculed—in twentieth- and twenty-first-century mainstream popular culture, particularly in Hollywood movies, advertisements, and cartoons.

The image is now deeply ingrained in the public consciousness. Think of it: a Native man, dressed in the style of the Great Plains cultures, long hair in braids with a headband and feather, sits on the edge of a cliff (of course in the "Indian style," with his legs crossed in front of him). The Indian man is fanning a fire with a blanket, from which smoke billows upward. His smoke "signals" are received and interpreted by another Native man, perhaps miles away.

American popular culture also has distorted the rudimentary character of smoke signals and would have the average person believing that an entire language has been built around their use. Native peoples did not use smoke to spell out entire words, as is often depicted in the media. Neither did all tribes use smoke to communicate. Today, when someone mentions smoke signals, the image of an Indian immediately comes to mind. When asked by *Cineaste* magazine about the title of his film *Smoke Signals* (1998), author Sherman Alexie (Spokane/Coeur d'Alene) said, "On the surface, it's a stereotypical title; you think of Indians in blankets on the plains sending smoke signals, so it brings up a stereotypical image that's vaguely humorous. But people will also instantly recognize that this is about Indians."

Indian people no longer use smoke signals as a mode of communication. News and information that travel from one Native American person to another—and to others around the country—are sometimes said jokingly to travel on the "moccasin telegraph" (or, in the case of Native Hawaiians, on the "coconut wireless"), which is a way of acknowledging the speed at which news travels to Native communities no matter how far apart they are located.

Native people today communicate by cell phone, email, social media, telephone, and text.

—LIZ HILL

DID NATIVE AMERICANS USE SIGN LANGUAGE?

Many tribes in North America used sign language from before European contact through the twentieth century. Sign language was common throughout the Americas, although its use has been most frequently documented from northern Mexico all the way into southern Canada.

Although sign language was used in tandem with everyday speech—and still is today in some communities—it is a method of communication completely independent of any one language. It is a fully functional language unto itself and enables an individual to communicate varied and complex ideas just as spoken languages do. All tribes didn't necessarily use the same signs. Just as speakers of the same language have different dialects, so do practitioners of Indigenous sign language, sometimes referred to as American Indian sign language or Plains Indian sign language. As linguist Jeffrey E. Davis observed, sign language is a "universal linguistic phenomenon," but that doesn't necessarily mean that all signs used by different peoples are mutually intelligible. Regional differences in sign language gestures can be compared to regional differences in a spoken language—vocabulary as well as speed and style of delivery may differ depending on the tribe. These differences do not prevent the individuals using sign language from understanding one another. Likewise, American Indian sign language instructor Shawn Ware (Kiowa) recalled what older generations have told him: "As long as there is communication and clear understanding, there is no wrong sign." While American Indian sign language is still practiced, it is not used as frequently today as it was in previous generations. Nonetheless, new signs continue to be created, especially to address technological advances.

Portrait of Tendoi (Shoshone) demonstrating sign language, ca. 1800s.

Photo by C. M. (Charles Milton) Bell. National Anthropological Archives, Smithsonian Institution NAA INV 00866700

Historically, sign language has served many different purposes. In addition to providing a means of communication for deaf people, it enabled the exchange of information between those who spoke completely different languages. It was also used in hunting and war situations, where stealth and secrecy were required, and for communication from a distance when speech wasn't possible. Trade was likely a major factor in its development. The Americas are home to hundreds of Native nations, many of whom have mutually unintelligible languages. Sign language served as a lingua franca, or a common language, that allowed speakers of different languages to communicate.

Sign language was probably also used during treaty negotiations between the United States and American Indian nations and to recount historical events. Treaty scholar and anthropologist Raymond DeMallie observed, "What we don't see referred to in the record, and I think it's important to realize, is that traditionally when Plains Indians spoke in council, they said everything that they had to say in speech also simultaneously in sign. The sign language was universal throughout the plains, and it was tremendously valuable. . . . So I think probably the substance of what the white commissioners had to say was very well communicated. The meaning is another question." Jeffrey Davis further reflected on the capacity for sign language to be used to recount histories. He noted that one of the best-known eyewitness accounts of the Battle of Little Bighorn was originally told by Lakota Chief Red Horse in sign language, then translated into English.

As a lingua franca for many American Indian peoples, sign language was a way to facilitate communication across linguistic and tribal boundaries. Signs were shared between people and communities, and users creatively devised the signs they needed. While English is the present-day common language, sign language endures and is still used inventively in many Native communities.

—ALEXANDRA HARRIS

WHAT KINDS OF FOODS DO INDIANS EAT?

Who hasn't experienced the enticing smell of popcorn upon entering a movie theater or enjoyed a big bowl of potato chips and guacamole while watching the Super Bowl game? These are just a few of the sumptuous foods that have their origins among Native Americans of the Western Hemisphere. At the top of the long list of plants grown or processed by American Indians are corn, beans, squash, pumpkins, peppers, potatoes, sweet potatoes, tomatoes, peanuts, wild rice, chocolate, pineapple, avocado, papaya, pecans, strawberries, blueberries, cranberries, and sunflowers. More than half the crops grown worldwide today were initially cultivated in the Americas.

American Indians hunted, herded, cultivated, and gathered a vast variety of species. The sciences of plant cultivation and food preparation were highly developed in the pre-Columbian Americas. By the time of the Spanish invasion in 1492, Indians in the Andes had developed more than a 1,000 different species of potato, each of which thrived in distinct growing conditions. Native Americans throughout the hemisphere developed at least as many varieties of corn to suit climates ranging from the northern woodland areas to the tropics. Today corn grows over a larger area than does any other cultivated food in the world.

The people of northeastern North America were among those who recognized the symbiotic relationship between corn, beans, and squash: the bean climbs the natural trellis of the corn stalk, while the squash shades the ground below, discouraging other plants from spreading and choking the corn roots. Each plant also gives and takes different nutrients from the soil. The people of the Iroquois Confederacy called these crops the Three

Sisters, or the sustainers, because of their importance to the well-being and survival of the people.

Many foods and food techniques have changed little from those developed by Native people. Modern manufacturers ferment, dry, and roast cacao beans to extract chocolate in much the same way as did Maya and Aztec growers. Along the North Pacific Coast, salmon is dried and smoked using processes that have existed for millennia. On the Great Plains, buffalo was the fundamental food source—entire cultures developed around communal buffalo hunts. Today Native breeding programs are restoring buffalo populations, making the meat available as a healthy alternative to beef.

Since reservations were first established in the late nineteenth century, many American Indians have depended on nontraditional, government-issued food commodities, from which has arisen one of the most delicious and least healthful "Native" foods: fry bread. Made with flour, yeast, and lard, fry bread is served warm with powdered sugar or syrup, or loaded with meat, cheese, shredded lettuce, and tomato to make another familiar treat: the Navajo (or "Indian") taco.

Most Native people today eat the foods that other Americans do, but traditional foods such as salmon, venison, wild strawberries, varieties of beans and chilies, and especially corn remain integral to seasonal ceremonies, dances, and other special occasions throughout Indian Country. Increased nationwide interest in fresh, local foods has led to renewed cultivation of Indigenous ingredients and the creation of nontraditional dishes that bring out their flavor.

So, when you dig into a bowl of chili, a pile of mashed potatoes, or a piece of pumpkin pie, remember that such seemingly modern dishes depend on ingredients that were first cultivated, cooked, and given to the world by Native Americans.

—STEPHANIE BETANCOURT

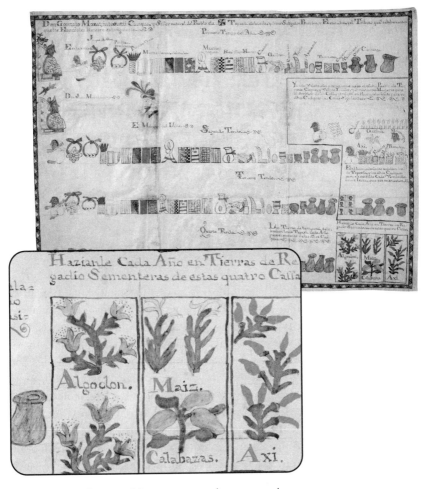

A record of tribute paid by Native people to Spanish overlords. Items pictured include slaves, gold, precious stones, fine feathers, textiles, cacao, chickens, sandals, woven chairs, rattles, gourd vessels, bowls, pots, and pitchers. A detail from the painting shows some of the principal crops grown by Native people in the region: cotton, corn, squash, and peppers.

Painted tribute record of Tepexi de la Seda, 18th c. copy of ca. 16th c. original. Puebla, Mexico. 8/4482

BEFORE CONTACT WITH EUROPEANS, DID INDIANS MAKE ALL THEIR CLOTHING FROM ANIMAL SKINS?

No, not all clothing was made of animal skins, furs, or other animal parts. Many American Indians made their clothing from plant materials, including cotton and yucca, and from wool. Between 3500 BC and 2300 BC, Native people in Mesoamerica and on the eastern slope of the Peruvian Andes domesticated many varieties of cotton, a plant that is indigenous to the Western Hemisphere. Archaeologists have found 7,000- to 8,000-year-old mummies wrapped in cotton textiles, and it is possible that wild cotton was used for clothing in Peru as early as 10,000 BC. American Indians in southwestern North America began growing cotton shortly after 1500 BC, and the earliest textile found in present-day New Mexico dates back to AD 700. As early as AD 300, ancestral Puebloans were gathering other plant fibers, such as yucca, willow, and juniper bark, processing them, and weaving them into sandals, blankets, leggings, socks, belts, and other articles of clothing.

Today, Native people wear all kinds of modern attire, just like everyone else. Almost all tribes, however, continue to wear traditional and dance clothing, which is customary for social and ceremonial occasions. Ceremonial wear is made of modern textiles in addition to other materials—including animal skins—that predate the arrival of Europeans.

—MARY AHENAKEW

Nazca poncho (detail) made of camelid fiber and plant fiber, AD 1000.

18/946

BEFORE CONTACT WITH EUROPEANS, DID INDIANS MAKE ALL THEIR CLOTHING FROM ANIMAL SKINS?

Is it true that Native people used all parts of the animal?

Native peoples used as many parts of the animal as they could. Native communities were keenly aware of the resources they needed for survival and the methods they could use to ensure a food source. They were subsistence hunters, as opposed to hunting with the intent to sell or trade, and they knew that overhunting meant less food in the future. As a result, they endeavored to sustainably manage their environments to protect the plants and animals consumed. For example, controlled burning was widely used to regulate animals' food sources and to corral or flush out game. Native peoples took great pains to nurture and control hunting territories both to attract game and to remove obstacles.

Once game was captured, it only made sense to figure out how different parts of the animal could be used. Having lived in their homelands for hundreds of years, Native peoples became experts in how to derive benefits from the flora and fauna. They tested, experimented, and refined their resources. Animal skins were used for everything—homes, clothing, bags, drums, and more. Sinew was used to sew and tie objects together and for bowstrings. What could you do with a buffalo's shoulder blade? Attached to a stick, it worked well as a shovel. And its horns? Whole horns could be fashioned into a cup; halved horns could be carved and bent into spoons. Deer toes became rattles or glue while teeth were used as decoration for clothing. Bladders were dried and used to carry water. For the Blackfeet, a northern Plains tribe, the buffalo provided more than 100 different items of material culture. In short, in a subsistence economy where resources were not always plentiful, inventiveness was essential for survival.

Hand-colored lantern slide of Uliggaq (Ella Pavil, Yup'ik), dressed in a seal-gut parka and standing next to a dip net full of tomcod, 1935. Kwigillingok, Alaska.

L02290

At the same time, it was not always possible to use all of an animal and there were undoubtedly situations where resources were wasted. Survival sometimes required people to butcher an animal where it fell and transport what they could to their village or camp. The Great Plains tradition of a buffalo jump is one example of hunting where it may only have been possible to butcher lightly rather than taking everything. A buffalo jump typically occurred when hunters—men and women—encouraged buffalo over a cliff, where they fell to injury or death. Dozens and possibly hundreds could be killed at once. While at times all edible parts of the animal would be taken back to the village for consumption or preservation, at other times the unused buffalo remained where they died. The demand for meat determined how much was used.

It bears mention that wise use of hunted animals was not just for practical purposes. In many tribes, traditions teach and require giving thanks to the animal that has died so that people may eat. Many of those traditions dictate that the animals are relatives. Some Pueblos in the Southwest believe that their ancestors return as deer—a belief that necessitates expressing appreciation during a hunt and discourages waste. This tradition endures today.

So while all parts of the animal may not have been used after every hunt, Native peoples devoted much energy to ensuring the survival of their community by working to sustain wildlife populations. Overhunting may indeed have occurred before European contact, but it was only after European settlement and the introduction of game and fur (mainly buffalo and beaver) to the colonial and European market economy that Natives and non-Natives caused the decimation of species and ecosystems.

—ALEXANDRA HARRIS

IS IT TRUE THAT NATIVE AMERICANS HUNTED A GREAT NUMBER OF LARGE ANIMALS TO EXTINCTION?

There continues to be a debate in scientific circles about whether or not Paleo-Indian peoples living on the American continent during the thousands of years before and during the Pleistocene epoch (1.8 million to about 10,000 years ago—this was also known as the period of the ice ages) contributed to the extinction of the great variety of animals that were known to have inhabited the land. The existence of an incredible array of plant, animal, bird, and other nonhuman life in the Western Hemisphere during the ice ages is not in doubt. What is less certain is exactly how all of these living beings disappeared during a relatively short period about 10,000 years ago. Did the ancestors of today's Native peoples hunt and kill large numbers to extinction? One theory suggests that they did. Another argues, however, that climatic and environmental changes caused by retreating glaciers wiped out many North American creatures, both large and small.

Most scientists believe that it was also during the Pleistocene, approximately 15,000 years ago, that waters receded in the strait that linked Siberia and Alaska, thus creating a "land bridge" that made it possible for people to make their way onto the North American continent. This theory—which is vigorously debated by scientists and Native peoples, many of the latter believing their ancestors have always been on the continent—contends that successive generations of northern nomadic peoples, traveling in small bands, made their way from Alaska to southern South America. Their numbers grew along the way—some scientists believe that the population could have grown relatively quickly into the millions. Certainly, when one looks at the population estimates for the Western Hemisphere just before Columbus's arrival, with Indigenous peoples perhaps numbering more than 70 million, the idea doesn't seem farfetched.

There is no doubt that the array of animals living on the American continent was at one time significantly more diverse than it is today. In *1491: New Revelations of the Americas before Columbus* (2005), Charles C. Mann describes the scene as an "impossible bestiary of lumbering mastodon, armored rhinos, great dire wolves, saber tooth cats and ten-foot-long glyptodonts like enormous armadillos." He continues, "Beavers the size of armchairs; turtles that weighed almost as much as cars; sloths able to reach tree branches 20 feet high; huge, flightless, predatory birds like rapacious ostriches—the tally of Pleistocene monsters is long and alluring."

Then, suddenly, all of these beasts were gone, rapidly disappearing from the earth around 10,000 years ago. Today's relatively small Indigenous population may make it difcult to imagine a late-Pleistocene continent teeming with humans, but one theory raises the possibility that the animals could have been killed off by human overhunting. The other argument—equally convincing—is that the end of the last ice age killed off the animals. Lending more weight to the second theory is the simultaneous disappearance of plants and other nonanimal species during that time of great climatic disruption.

Some evidence, however, supports the theory that some Native cultures, such as the Maya of Central America, may have depleted their natural resources—including animal life—thus contributing to their own eventual collapse. But more recently it was Europeans and Americans who nearly exterminated the North American buffalo, and commercial whalers—not Indigenous people—who drove whales to the brink of extinction.

—LIZ HILL

WHY DO INDIANS WEAR FEATHERS? WHY ARE EAGLE FEATHERS SO IMPORTANT TO INDIANS?

Known as the Thunderbird in many Native American cultures, the eagle is said to be the messenger between humans and the Creator, flying higher and seeing farther than any other bird. The feathers of the eagle, which help send messages to the Creator, represent prayers. Eagle feathers are used in ceremonies, worn as part of powwow regalia, or given away as honoring gifts—all to show respect to the eagle and maintain a spiritual and physical connection to this sacred creature.

Greatly prized, eagle feathers are often handed down from one generation to the next, both individually and as part of a person's regalia. The feathers are either obtained naturally—from eagles that have died or molted—or from the National Eagle Repository in Denver, Colorado, a government facility where members of federally recognized tribes can legally acquire them. Recognizing the ceremonial value of eagles to American Indians, lawmakers granted this important exception to the Bald Eagle Protection Act of 1940 (amended in 1962 to include golden eagles), which makes it illegal for anyone to possess eagle feathers or eagle parts.

Powwow dancers consider eagle feathers to be the most important item of their dress, and any part of an eagle used by a dancer—the beak, talons, and bones, for example—are treated with respect and honor. Eagle feathers are treated with great care throughout the powwow in many ways. If an eagle feather accidentally falls off a dancer's clothing during a powwow dance, a war veteran or the Arena Director will stand next to the feather

William H. Rau. Portrait of a Sioux man, entitled *Chief Iron Tail—Sinte Maza*, ca. 1901. North or South Dakota.

P27530

to protect it. At the end of the dance, the powwow arena is cleared and a ceremony is held to retrieve the feather. In addition, feathers are often given away to dancers formally entering the arena for the first time, or to celebrate an individual achievement.

In the past, tribal warriors earned eagle feathers when they demonstrated bravery, either in battle or on the hunt. Sometimes a feather would be painted or cut in a certain way to tell the story of how the feather was earned. For many non-Native people, the image of an elder or tribal leader wearing a long eagle-feather war bonnet is powerful and familiar. Plains Indian leaders and warriors did wear these beautiful headdresses—and still do today for ceremonial purposes. Wearing eagle feathers in such a way indicates rank or personal achievement.

Today as in centuries past, Native people use feathers of all kinds to decorate their dance wear, stabilize arrow shafts, weave elaborate robes and cloaks, and adorn baskets or jewelry. Tribes in certain regions honor hawks, kingfishers, ravens, woodpeckers, and hummingbirds. For many, these unique creatures of the air have great spiritual significance; by using and wearing the feathers of these birds, one can access their powers and honor them.

—TANYA THRASHER

How Did Native Americans Acquire Horses?

Scholars generally agree that Native Americans initially acquired horses from the colonial Spanish herds brought to present-day New Mexico. Some horses were captured in raids, but most were apprehended during the Pueblo Revolt of 1680. In August 1680 the Pueblo Indians of northern New Mexico mounted an uprising against Spanish colonizers and drove them from Native lands. The strategic move to steal the Spaniards' horses guaranteed the success of the revolt and introduced the horse as a permanent fixture in Native life and culture. This horse population of Spanish origin then expanded rapidly across North America, moving north and east along established Native trading networks. The horse quickly gained popularity and prominence throughout Native society, particularly with Western tribes, such as the Nez Perce and Blackfeet of the far Northwest, the Kiowa and Comanche of the southern Plains, and the Arapaho, Crow, Cheyenne, and Sioux of the northern Plains.

The introduction of horses to Native peoples opened up new possibilities. Tribes could hunt more efficiently, travel farther, and transport items from camp to camp with ease. Horses became such a central component of Native culture that definitions and ideas about what constituted wealth began to shift. Mass herds increased Native peoples' leverage and power in trade networks, territorial expansion, and warfare. While horse culture increased mobility and became a symbol of wealth, prestige, and honor, it also introduced new problems. Intertribal warfare, conflicts with white settlers, and the overharvesting of buffalo were negative aspects of the horse revolution in Native society.

Horses changed life most profoundly on the Great Plains and became integral to Plains cultures. Horses allowed these

Pretty Beads, a Crow girl, carries her doll and cradleboard fastened to the pommel of her horse's saddle.

N41420

tribes to better defend themselves as settlers and soldiers encroached on tribal lands. Attacks carried out by the US military and vigilante groups forced Plains tribes to adapt and transform their approach to warfare, placing horses at the center of Plains peoples' survival. Horses made fighters swift in battle and were considered comrades in arms. Horses became so prized that many Plains tribes began the practice of painting and decorating their horses. Horse masks made of buffalo skin and then painted with pigment were decorated with pony beads, brass buttons, and a mixture of horse and human hair. These elaborate masks signaled strong spiritual overtones and intimidated enemies.

Today the horse remains extremely important to Plains Indian life. The Crow Fair, for instance, held during mid-August at Crow Agency, Montana, speaks to the continued centrality of the horse to Native life and culture. The event attracts skilled Native horsemen and horsewomen from as far away as Pine Ridge in South Dakota to Fort Hall in Idaho and includes competitions in sprint races, team roping, and women's calf roping. Without a doubt, however, the horses are the main attraction at Crow Fair. They debut with great pageantry in finest dress, adorned with elaborately beaded masks and accoutrements. Plains tribes continue to manage their own herds today and also help to protect wild horses, symbols of Native pride, healing, and spiritual wealth.

—BETHANY MONTAGANO

WHERE DID NATIVE PEOPLE GET GLASS BEADS TO DECORATE THEIR CLOTHING?

Before the introduction of glass beads by European colonists in the mid-1700s, Native peoples depended on materials derived from their environment to decorate clothing. Some of the earliest dresses and shirts were painted with natural materials, known as earth paints. Minerals and clays were frequently used and would often be combined with buffalo fat and mixed in bowls made out of turtle shells to make paints. In addition to paints, Native people used other natural materials like porcupine quills, elk teeth, bone, bird or bear claws, and shells that were most often acquired through trade. The glass beads, easier and more flexible to use than unforgiving porcupine quills, quickly replaced other materials.

Not only were the beads more practical to use but the people who introduced them also brought their own influential style of decorative arts, opening new creative outlets for Native artisans. Scholars posit that Ursuline nuns of Italy, who arrived in northeastern Quebec as early as the seventeenth century, introduced silk embroidery and beadwork floral motifs to young Huron and Iroquois girls. From there, European needlework and Indigenous design forms gradually converged into designs that Native artisans fused and embellished.

Trade between and with Native peoples initiated a diffusion of cultures that enriched Native adornment practices. Prior to contact with non-Native peoples, American Indians established vital networks of trade. The evidence of these exchanges often surfaces in material culture. For instance, the Hohokam tribe, centered in present-day Arizona, traded seashells acquired from

This lavishly beaded dress would have been worn by a young Sicangu Lakota girl on a very special occasion.

16/2518

the Mojave, near the California border, for buffalo hides from various southern Plains tribes. From first contact with Europeans and their abundant trade goods, Native peoples made artistic use of these new materials to ornament their ritual objects and possessions. Examples of nineteenth-century Tlingit body armor, for instance, demonstrate the convergence of Northwest traditions with two other cultures: the crafted armor is covered in Chinese coins the Tlingit received in trade from Boston sea merchants in exchange for sea otter pelts.

While glass beads from Europe became a prominent fixture in Native life and culture, beadwork grew into a distinctly Native art form, full of meaning. Native artisans developed intricate beaded designs to pass down stories and histories from generation to generation and reinforce tribal identity. It is a cherished practice that continues today. For instance, the elaborately beaded dresses that Plains women made—and still make and wear—became canvases upon which women expressed their creativity, marked significant events (such as marriage or a family member's military service), and displayed family pride.

—BETHANY MONTAGANO

DO NATIVE AMERICAN PARENTS STILL PUT THEIR BABIES IN CRADLEBOARDS? ARE THE CRADLEBOARDS COMFORTABLE?

Yes. Many Native people still use cradleboards to secure their babies. While they may not be as common as they were 200 years ago, you can still see children all over Indian Country wrapped in blankets and packed in their cradleboards. The cradleboards reflect a wide variety of tribal styles, and the materials used to make them range from wood, hide, and plant fibers to canvas and other fabrics. Most cradleboards have a protective arch made from a willow branch, reeds, or carved wood above the child's head.

While not all tribes use them, those that do have a name for a cradleboard or baby carrier in their own language: *pá:jol* for the Kiowa, *tihkinaakani* in the Myaamia language, and *xe:q'ay'* for the Hupa. No Native American people call a cradleboard a papoose, however. So how did the word become associated with Native American baby carriers? The word papoose seems to have entered the English language around the 1630s, and comes from the Narragansett word *papoos*, meaning child, or a similar New England Algonquian word that literally means "very young." Either way, papoos refers to the baby and not to the baby carrier. In 1643 Roger Williams, a Puritan who interacted with the Narragansett and Wampanoag peoples as a missionary, wrote *A Key into the Language of America*, which introduced and popularized several Algonquian words that were adopted into English. Among them were papoose, quahog, moccasin, and moose. Today the word papoose is often considered pejorative and stereotypical.

Crow woman and baby in a cradleboard, ca. 1900.
P09352

Traditionally, cradleboards were highly utilitarian; a mother could carry a child on her back by a strap attached to the back of the cradleboard. The strap went across the mother's upper chest and upper arms or across her forehead. This arrangement freed the mother's hands to work. The mother and other family members could hang or prop up the cradleboard providing visual contact with the baby.

The cradleboard protects the infant physically and emotionally, allowing the baby to feel secure. Some cradleboards have bindings that attach the child directly to the backboard; other styles have a sack attached. The sacks (some tribes call them moss sacks because moss was used as a diapering material years ago) have binding to secure the infant. Some people use only the moss sacks, without a backboard. The flat back of the cradleboard keeps the infant's spine aligned, and the binding helps strengthen the baby's muscles by creating resistance when the baby pushes against it. Some types of cradleboard include additional cushions and supports for the crown of the head, neck, and feet. Most babies stay in cradleboards until they can walk and/or work their way out of them.

The Haudenosaunee (Iroquois) people of the Northeast have always made cradleboards from wood and have carved beautiful designs on the backboards and protective wooden arches. They sometimes add paintings to enhance the carvings. Cradleboards made by many of the Plains tribes have wooden frames covered with soft hide and elaborately decorated with glass beads and porcupine quills. Other materials used in decoration are sequins, shells, silk- or cotton-thread embroidery, satin ribbon, metal tacks, and horsehair.

Some designs include sacred symbols and colors to bring the child good fortune and long life. Parents in many tribes saved the child's umbilical cord and made it into an amulet, which was carried on the cradleboard as a toy, and kept throughout the person's life. The Western Shoshone had two types of cradleboards made of woven willow reeds: the boat basket, which was used for newborns, and the hoop basket, used once the baby's neck muscles were strong enough to hold up his or her head. A woven willow shade was added to the basket to protect the baby from the sun and keep the cradle upright if accidentally bumped. Some tribes, such as the Pomo of present-day California, used a sitting-style cradleboard, designed so that the child's legs hung over the bottom edge. Today many of the woven cradleboards are covered with cloth, which is cool and also washable. A lot of time and effort are put into making a cradleboard, and its aesthetic beauty reflects the deep love parents and families have for their children.

—ALEXANDRA HARRIS AND MARY AHENAKEW

ARE INDIANS MORE PRONE TO CERTAIN DISEASES THAN THE GENERAL POPULATION? WHY?

Statistics show that considerable health disparities exist between American Indians and the general population of the United States. With a life expectancy of 71.1 years of age, Indians live on average 4.7 years less than the rest of the nation. Poverty, unhealthy eating habits, inadequate housing, poor sanitation, uneven quality of and access to medical care, and resistance to seeking treatment all contribute to the current health peril.

Indians face grim statistics for most diseases, with rates that are 4.9 times higher for liver disease and cirrhosis, more than 7 times higher for death due to alcoholism, 3 times higher for accidental deaths, and more than 6 times higher for tuberculosis, a disease often thought to be a plague of the past. Although drastic differences between Indians and the general population are evident for most diseases, the gap narrows for the leading causes of death, which for both groups are cardiovascular disease and malignant tumors. If there is one disease that Native Americans are more prone to than the rest of the population, it is adult-onset diabetes, and it is presently a threat that looms large.

Type 2 diabetes is on the rise for all Americans but significantly so for Native Americans, who have seen a 93 percent increase within their population since 1981 and currently suffer a diabetes death rate that is 3.5 times greater than the rest of the nation. One of the most important factors increasing the risk of diabetes for anyone is unhealthy weight, and, unfortunately, 37 percent of Native Americans are overweight, while 15 percent are obese. Through European contact, federally issued commodity foodstuffs, and poverty, contemporary Indians have developed a diet that is substantially different from that of their ancestors, one that often leads to the weight conditions conducive to diabetes.

The second critical factor that increases diabetes risk is genetics. Over centuries in a harsh and often unreliable land, Native Americans evolved metabolic genes that allowed them to eµciently store fat and survive famine. With the quantity and types of food available today, these genes are no longer beneficial. Nobody knows this better than the Tohono O'odham people of Arizona. Once a desert tribe whose meals were often few and far between, the Tohono O'odham now have the highest rates of diabetes in the world—approximately 50 percent of the tribe is aɗicted. Ongoing medical research in the community is now establishing valuable knowledge about the genetic predisposition to diabetes. Meanwhile, the Tohono O'odham are joining tribes from across the country to actively confront the disease through diabetes prevention campaigns. As for all Americans and many other health concerns, regular exercise and a healthy diet are paramount in the battle against diabetes.

—JENNIFER ERDRICH

WHAT ARE THE RATES OF ALCOHOLISM, DRUG ADDICTION, AND SUICIDE AMONG AMERICAN INDIANS?

There is no doubt that alcohol abuse is a significant concern for Native American communities, but many misconceptions obscure the reality of this complicated situation. According to the most recent statistics published by Indian Health Service in *Trends in Indian Health, 1998–1999* the alcoholism death rate for American Indians and Alaska Natives is more than seven times the rate for the general population of the United States. In addition, alcohol is implicated in three-fourths of all traumatic American Indian deaths. It is a major factor in the high rates of suicide, homicide, automobile accidents, crime, family abuse, and fetal alcohol syndrome in Native American communities. These numbers, however, do little to explain the history, the present reality, and the confusion over American Indians and alcohol.

Researchers have proposed different theories about why alcoholism is still a scourge to the Native American population. Historical explanations describe how past laws making it illegal for Indians to possess or consume alcohol led to a consumption pattern of binge drinking. For those less inclined to historical arguments, many researchers have sought a genetic explanation for the disease. Some studies have focused on two candidate genes associated with alcohol metabolism that sometimes have a different form in American Indians. To date, no report has conclusively confirmed that the gene variants do indeed cause American Indians to process alcohol any differently than the rest of the population or cause them to be more prone to alcoholism. Scientific literature is careful to state that there may be a link, but that important qualification is often overlooked. Meanwhile, the idea of possible genetic susceptibility can be misconstrued into myths of "genetic weakness" that misled both non-Indians and Indians themselves. Lost in the mythmaking is the fact that individual tolerance levels vary among individuals.

Amid the controversy and confusion, the risks and causes of alcoholism have yet to be clearly identified. Many focus on the critical role that socioeconomic, cultural, and psychological factors play in the disconcerting rates of Native American alcoholism. Poor education, alarming poverty, family and community instability, and low occupational status increase the prevalence of alcoholism in any family. Sadly, these conditions are all too real for many American Indians.

As for drug addiction and suicide, the rates are elevated in the Native American population as well. The drug-related death rate for American Indians and Alaska Natives is 65 percent higher than for the rest of the general population of the United States, while the suicide rate is 72 percent higher. Again, the historical and current causes of these perplexing and diμcult situations must be considered just as seriously as the numbers themselves to better understand the existence of the disparities.

—JENNIFER ERDRICH

DO ALL INDIANS LIVE IN TIPIS?

Most American Indians live in contemporary homes, apartments, condos, and co-ops, just like every other citizen of the twenty-first century. Some Native people who live in modern homes do erect and use tipis in the summer for ceremonies and other community events. But most Indians in the Americas, even those who live in their community's traditional dwellings, have never used tipis at all.

Tipis are the traditional homes of Plains Indians, but in other regions of the Western Hemisphere Native people lived in many different kinds of dwellings. Whether a tribe lived in a buffalo-hide tipi, an adobe hogan (dwellings made of adobe and supported by rocks or timbers), a birch-bark wigwam, or an igloo made of ice, the home's structure and materials were suited to each tribe's needs and environment. Some Diné (Navajo) people, for example, still live in hogans because the structures are well adapted to the desert, which can be extremely hot during the day and cold at night. During the day the hogan remains cool inside as the adobe absorbs the sun's heat. At night the structure releases the heat, keeping everyone inside comfortable.

The Great Plains at one time sustained millions of buffalo, and the Plains Indians depended almost entirely on the buffalo for their basic needs—including shelter. Their larger tipis were each made of as many as eighteen buffalo hides. Pueblo people of the Southwest live in homes made of adobe, which were the first apartment-style structures in North America.

American Indians have traditionally lived in structures that took best advantage of their individual resources, environment, and location. Inuit people constructed domed structures called igloos, which were made from blocks of snow. The coastal Inuit

A Paipai mother and four children sit outside a house made with brush siding, 1926. Baja, California.
Photo by Edward H. Davis. N24649

used igloos as temporary hunting shelters, but the interior Inuit lived in them year-round. An igloo could be built in about an hour and easily repaired or replaced. They are still used as temporary hunting shelters.

The people of the Haudenosaunee (Iroquois) Confederacy built long houses made from logs, saplings, and bark, all of which were abundant in their forested environment. Each long house could shelter several families and, if needed, could be expanded to accommodate more people. During World War II, when US troops needed inexpensive and easily constructed housing, military architects modeled what came to be known as Quonset huts on the long house design. Today not only long houses but also many other traditional Native dwellings are used primarily as places for social and ceremonial gatherings.

—STEPHANIE BETANCOURT

INDIVIDUAL DEVELOPMENT AND IDENTITY

What is the Correct Terminology: American Indian, Indian, Native American, or Native?

All of the above terms are acceptable. The consensus, however, is that whenever possible, Native people prefer to be called by their specific tribal name. Native peoples in the Western Hemisphere are best understood as thousands of distinct communities and cultures. Many Native communities have distinct languages, religious beliefs, ceremonies, and social and political systems. The inclusive word *Indian* (a name, used by the Spanish to refer to much of southern Asia, given by Christopher Columbus, who mistakenly believed he had sailed to India) says little about the diversity and independence of the cultures.

In the United States, *Native American* has been widely used and grew out of the 1960s and 1970s political movements. It is falling out of favor with some groups, and the terms *American Indian* or *Indigenous Americans* are now preferred by many Native people. Today *Native American* and *American Indian* are used interchangeably in legislation. Legally, it refers not only to the Indigenous people of the lower forty-eight states but also to Native people in US territories. As an adjective, many people now prefer to use simply *Native* or *Indian*.

Canadians, too, have addressed the question of names—many Native Canadians, especially Métis (people of Indigenous and French descent) and Inuit people, reject the designation *Indian*. Similarly, the Inuit, Yup'ik, and Aleut peoples in Alaska see themselves as separate from Indians. Canadians have developed a range of terms, including *aboriginal*, *First Nations*, and *First Peoples*.

"We've thought and thought, but we're at a loss about what to call ourselves. Any ideas?"

J. B. Handelsman, The New Yorker Collection/
The Cartoon Bank; © Condé Nast

In Central and South America the direct translation for *Indian* has negative connotations. As a result, Spanish speakers use the word *indígenas*.

—MARY AHENAKEW

SHOULD I SAY *TRIBE* OR *NATION*?

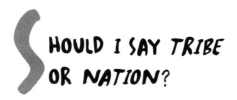

Tribe, nation, community, pueblo, *rancheria*, village, band—American Indian people describe their own cultures and the places they come from in many ways. Often, the words *tribe* and *nation* are used interchangeably, but for many Native people they can hold very different meanings. Each community has a word or phrase in its own language that identifies it, as well as an official name recognized by the federal or state government. When being introduced to a Native person, it is appropriate to ask what community the person comes from and how he or she likes to be described. For example, many members of the Navajo Nation of Arizona (the largest tribe in the country) refer to themselves as Diné, the Navajo word meaning "the people." In this instance, you would refer to a Navajo person as being Diné, or a member of the Navajo Nation. Similarly, members of the Comanche Nation of Oklahoma refer to themselves as Nʉmʉnʉʉ, which also translates to "the people."

Although many tribal groups are known by official names that include the word *nation*, like the Navajo Nation or the Comanche Nation, typically the US government uses the word *tribe* when referring to Indian communities in the United States. Of the approximately 567 federally recognized tribes in the United States alone, many refer to themselves in completely different ways. The nineteen Pueblo communities in New Mexico, for example, have distinct names such as San Juan Pueblo and Zia Pueblo. California is home to more than forty *rancherias*, or Indian communities located on small parcels of land, such as the Berry Creek Rancheria in Oroville and the Dry Creek Rancheria Band of Pomo Indians in Geyserville. Rancherias, like reservations in other states, are government-designated lands over which one or more tribes maintain sovereignty. Farther north, many Native people of Alaska call their communities "villages." Examples are the Traditional Village of Togiak and Skagway Village.

There are many ways to refer to Native communities throughout the United States but even more ways to address the groups living to the north and south. Today Native people throughout Canada refer to themselves as aboriginal or members of First Nations rather than as American Indians or Native Americans. Each First Nation community in Canada has a specific name, such as the Swan Lake First Nation in Manitoba or the Peepeekisis Indian Band of Saskatchewan. In Mexico, Central America, and South America, Indigenous cultures do not like to use the Spanish or Portuguese words for *Indian* or *tribe*, since the direct translations carry negative meanings. As a result, most Native people in these areas use the words *indígenas* ("Indigenous people" or "Indigenous") and *comunidad* ("community") to describe who they are or where they come from.

It is important to remember that each Native tribe or nation has its own distinct viewpoint and culture. When identifying a Native community, first try to learn how members of the community describe themselves.

—TANYA THRASHER

WHY DO MANY TRIBES HAVE MORE THAN ONE NAME?

When Europeans arrived in the Americas, they discovered that Indians had named their particular nations in their own languages, which also specified names for rivers, mountains, trees, animals, plants, towns, and villages. Europeans found these names difficult to understand and pronounce. In time, original Indian personal names and place-names often were replaced by names chosen by the Spanish, German, Dutch, French, and English newcomers.

Thus, the names by which many Indian tribes are commonly known today likewise were not chosen by the tribes themselves. During the twentieth century some tribes cast off the names given to them by the French, Spanish, and English. For example, the Muscogee Nation, originally a confederacy of small tribes who lived in present-day Georgia and Alabama, were identified for several hundred years as the Creek Indians. This name was applied to them by English colonists because abundant waterways flowed through their lands.

Other communities rejected the often insulting nicknames that had originated with other tribes. In 1984 the tribe in southern Arizona formerly called Papago, a Spanish mispronunciation of a Native word meaning "bean-eaters," reverted to its traditional name: "Tohono O'odham," or "desert people." Many Dakota, Lakota, and Nakota peoples prefer these traditional names to "Sioux," or "little snakes," which is a French approximation of the name they were called by the Ojibwe, their tribal enemy. In 1992 the Navajo Nation's president, Peterson Zah, sponsored a resolution to change the official name of his tribe from "Navajo," which derives from a Tewa word that has been interpreted to mean either "people with large cornfields" or "people who steal."

"Diné," the new name, means simply "the people." That name, as well as "Diné Nation," signifies cultural pride.

Sometimes tribal names can become complex for outsiders. Many people mistakenly refer to the Iroquois as a tribe, but they are actually a confederacy of six tribes known as the Haudenosaunee. The nations that comprise the Haudenosaunee are the Mohawk, Onondaga, Cayuga, Seneca, Oneida, and Tuscarora. The Ojibwe people of the Great Lakes region are divided into bands and communities that prefer to be known as either Ojibwe, Chippewa, or—especially in Canada—Anishinaabe. Each of these names can be spelled in different ways. When referring to American Indian tribes, it is best to remain aware that names change and that all names carry meanings and histories that aren't always easily discernible.

—NEMA MAGOVERN AND EDWIN SCHUPMAN

How do I prove my Indian ancestry and enroll in my tribe?

In 2006 each of the 567 federally recognized tribes in the United States had a sovereign government with its own way of identifying tribal members and permitting individuals to become new members. Most tribes today require that members have one-quarter or one-half "blood quantum," which means that at least one grandparent or parent is a member of the particular tribe. Other tribes require very little blood quantum. Still others grant membership based on family lineage—memberships may be passed down only from a mother or only from a father. The Cherokee Nation of Oklahoma determines individual membership by whether a person's ancestor's name was on the Dawes Roll, a census taken at the turn of the twentieth century that listed Cherokee people who were eligible for land allotments. The most important idea, however, is that each tribe establishes its membership in a different way. Tribes have the right—because they are governments—to decide who is and who is not a tribal member. As a result, a lot of Native people today may not "look Indian" or fit the stereotypical image of an Indian.

Before the federal government became involved, membership was determined solely by tribes and not necessarily by the amount of Native "blood" (blood quantum) an individual possessed. Even today, tribes can adopt people who don't have the required blood quantum. But determination of tribal membership by blood quantum has endured since the 1800s mainly because the federal government, in establishing the reservation system, insisted that commodity foodstuffs be issued only to those who could prove they were Native American. As a result, American Indian peoples are the only group in the United States today who require proof (via tribal enrollment cards) of racial identity.

In Canada, before laws were amended in 1985, the federal government oɥcially decided who was and was not an Indian by controlling the membership lists of tribal bands. After 1985 about 250 out of Canada's approximately 600 bands, which are also called First Nations, opted to control their own memberships. The federal government still retains the right to identify individual "Status" and "non-Status" Indians, which in turn determines the government benefits for which an individual may be eligible. To be granted Indian status, a person usually has to be a member of a band that has already negotiated a treaty with the government or been granted a reserve or government funds.

In Mesoamerica and South America, intermarriage between Indigenous and European peoples began soon after Columbus's arrival in 1492. Successive generations became known as mestizos, who now make up a large part of the populations of Mexico, Guatemala, Ecuador, Peru, Bolivia, and other countries. In these nations, being Indigenous has become more a cultural and political than a biological distinction, with the term *indígenas* identifying those who have not abandoned their traditional dress and cultural practices. Oɥcial systems of tribal enrollment have never been established, either by the federal governments or by Indigenous peoples, but in some South American countries Indigenous communities have banded together into strong political federations.

People in the United States who believe they are descended from a particular tribe have many references to consult. American Indians— by virtue of their distinct historical relationship with the federal government—are among the world's most well-documented peoples. One should start by pinpointing the tribe from which one believes he or she is descended. A variety of oɥcial records, such as birth, marriage, and other family documents, can be researched. Schools and churches are also resources for information about ancestors. Government records at the National Archives and Records Administration can be consulted once an ancestor's tribe has been specified. Tribes, which have oɥces that deal with these types of inquiries, can also help, once it has been determined that the ancestor in question was a member of that tribe.

—LIZ HILL

Did Native American Tribes Have Royalty?

Native American tribes did not have royalty by European definitions, such as hereditary titles and dominion over lands and people. When European explorers and colonists arrived in the Americas, they could only understand American Indian governments in terms they knew. While all Native nations had their own words in their languages for their leaders, Europeans used Old World terms—king, queen, prince, and princess—to refer to Indigenous leaders and their children. In reality, many Native nations elected or nominated leaders by more democratic processes rather than by heredity.

The idea of the Indian princess has been pervasive since European contact. As early as around 1500, images of Indigenous Americans—specifically, a man or woman in feathered skirt and stand-up headdress—began to symbolize the Western Hemisphere in European drawings and woodcuts such as maps and diplomatic agreements. Before the outbreak of the Revolutionary War, the British had been depicting their American colonies in political engravings as unruly and weak Indian princesses, calling them the Daughters of Britannia. According to scholar Cécile Ganteaume, Americans—notably Paul Revere and the Sons of Liberty—reimagined the Indian princess as a symbol of "strength, determination, justified rebellion, and, eventually, liberty." The image of an Indian princess or queen was used until the end of the eighteenth century to symbolize the United States.

Arguably the most famous American Indian woman to have been called an Indian princess is Pocahontas. The daughter of Powhatan, leader of the Powhatan confederation of tribes in Virginia, Pocahontas has become part of the mythology of the United States. In 1616, she traveled to England with her husband, John Rolfe, and was received at the court of King James I as an Indian princess. She converted to Christianity, and thereby came to symbolize England's triumph over Native peoples in the colonies. By extension, the image of Pocahontas and the Indian princess were used pervasively by the young country to represent the virgin lands of the Americas, ready to be possessed by white settlers.

Today the term Indian princess has an altogether different association that takes the stereotype and uses it to empower young Native women. Indian princess pageants are held annually on the tribal level, but aren't typical beauty pageants. Competitors must demonstrate cultural knowledge and are judged on how well they represent themselves as a tribal citizen. The national, pan-tribal competition, Miss Indian World, has taken place during the Gathering of Nations Powwow in Albuquerque, New Mexico, since 1983. According to the pageant, "As Miss Indian World, she will be a role model to young and old, help to educate and demonstrate the beauty and diversity of Native American culture as well as represent the Gathering of Nations throughout her travels across the United States of America, Canada, and internationally." Winners of the modern pageants, while not true royals, are certainly regal ambassadors for their culture.

Engraving of Pocahontas, 1793, by Simon van de Passe (1595–1647). Published in *Baziliologia A Booke of Kings*, 1618.

National Portrait Gallery, Smithsonian Institution. NPG.72.65

—ALEXANDRA HARRIS

WHY IS THE WORD SQUAW OFFENSIVE?

Indians of all tribes in the United States and Canada reject the use of *squaw* as the word for an Indian woman. Beginning in the early 1620s, English colonists borrowed the word *squa* from Massachusett, an Algonquian language spoken by the Indigenous peoples of eastern Massachusetts. In that language, *squa* meant simply "female" or "younger woman." In the neighboring Mohawk language, however, the word *ojiskwa'* can be translated as "vagina." In 1973 scholars Thomas E. Sanders and Walter W. Peek argued that *squaw* had evolved from that meaning rather than from the Massachusett.

Over the past 400 years the word has been used in a derogatory manner and has taken on negative meanings. During the nineteenth century, American writers tended to classify Indian women as "princesses" or "squaws," the latter described in James Fenimore Cooper's *Last of the Mohicans* as "the crafty 'squaw' . . . the squalid and withered person of this hag." Today it is not easy to find an Indian woman who accepts being called a squaw.

More than a thousand locales in the United States have the word squaw in their names. One of the best known was Squaw Peak, on the outskirts of Phoenix, Arizona. For six years State Senator Jack Jackson, a Navajo member of the Arizona legislature, repeatedly introduced a bill to rename the mountain but was met each time with strong resistance. In 1998, after several months of public discussion, the Arizona Board on Geographic and Historic Names voted down a proposal to change the name to Iron Mountain but left open the possibility of a future name change. In 2003, when Army Pfc. Lori Piestewa (Hopi) of Tuba City,

Arizona, became the first Native servicewoman ever killed in combat, Squaw Peak was renamed, with nearly no dissent, to Piestewa Peak.

Although similar name changes—such as the transformation of Squaw Lake in Minnesota to Nokomis Lake Pond—have not come as easily, Native protest against the word has intensified. While some American Indians say that they can accept squaw in certain contexts, most feel the word is as offensive as any racist term and should be consigned to linguistic history.

—GEORGETTA STONEFISH RYAN

WHY IS THE WORD *ESKIMO* SOMETIMES OFFENSIVE?

There are eleven different cultural groups in Alaska, so the word Eskimo is used there to refer to all Inuit and Yup'ik peoples who live throughout the world's northernmost regions. But the name is considered insulting in many places outside Alaska because it was given by non-Inuit people and said to mean "eater of raw meat." Linguists now believe that Eskimo is derived from an Ojibwe word meaning "to net snowshoes." The Inuit people of Canada and Greenland, however, prefer other names. Inuit, meaning "people," is used in most of Canada, and the Inuit people of Greenland call themselves Greenlanders, or Kalaallit in their language.

Most Alaskans continue to accept the name Eskimo because, within the state, Inuit refers only to the Iñupiat of northern Alaska. If a person's specific Alaskan cultural group isn't known, however, it's best for outsiders to use the term *Alaska Native*.

—MARY AHENAKEW

WHAT'S WRONG WITH NAMING SPORTS TEAMS INDIANS, BRAVES, ETC.?

Gooooo, Indians! Yay, Redskins! These are just two of the chants one may hear at sports events, when one or both of the teams are identified by Native American names or related terminology. One might also see fans practicing "tomahawk chops" or wearing "war paint" and feathers. You might even see a Muppet-like character dressed in "Indian" garb as the team mascot, whooping, hollering, and jumping around. This in-your-face mockery of Indian identity can easily lead to racist incidents.

Since the arrival of Europeans, Native Americans have struggled for survival. Indian people are often still seen as part of the past and unrelated to the present or future. The approximately 6.6 million American Indians and Alaska Natives in the United States are not a big consideration for politicians seeking votes or corporations marketing to the public. Terms such as *redskins*, *warriors*, *scalping*, *braves*, *squaw*, and *chiefs* belittle hundreds of diverse Indian cultures, reducing them to a single stereotype that can be easily exploited by anyone in search of an identifiable brand. Currently no other ethnic group in the United States suffers from this sort of openly racist treatment.

Many professional and amateur sports teams still use Native American names, even though Native American people have strongly objected. Thousands of people, many of them non-Indians, and more than eighty organizations—including the National Congress of American Indians, the Rainbow Coalition, the American Psychological Association, and the National Education Association—have advocated for change. And change has occurred: since 1970, when the University of Oklahoma became the first school to eliminate its "Little Red" Indian mascot, the

LALO ALCARAZ © 2002 Distributed by
ANDREWS MCMEEL SYNDICATION.
Reprinted with permission. All rights reserved.

majority of the more than 3,000 thousand schools with Indian sports names and mascots have followed suit.

One high-profile sports-team name controversy is that of the Washington, DC, pro football team, the Redskins. Partly because of the team's location in the nation's capital, and partly because the term is considered a racial slur, the Washington Redskins' name has been a particular target of complaint. The most sustained of these protests is a long-standing lawsuit brought by Suzan Shown Harjo (Cheyenne/Hodulgee Muscogee), president of the Morningstar Institute, a Native rights foundation, and six prominent Native co-plaintiffs. A panel of three judges canceled the football team's trademark licenses in 1999, but the decision was overturned in 2003 by a judge who ruled that the plaintiffs should have filed their suit when the team's trademarks were first registered, in 1967. After noting that Mateo Romero, the youngest of the plaintiffs, was only one year old in 1967, the DC Circuit Court of Appeals ruled in 2005 that the case had been prematurely dismissed. Harjo and her co-plaintiffs were given another chance to demonstrate that the Redskins' trademarks do, in fact, disparage American Indians. In July 2015, Harjo and her co-plaintiffs received a break in their case. A federal judge ordered the cancellation of the Redskins' trademark registrations. In June 2017, however, the Supreme Court struck down the law banning offensive trademarks. Harjo will continue her legal battle.

The issue of Indian sports mascots is not always as clear-cut. In August 2005, the National Collegiate Athletic Association (NCAA) ruled that member schools could not use "hostile and abusive" Native mascots at any of the eighty-eight NCAA championship events. The eighteen colleges and universities affected by the decision would either have to change their mascots or use them only during the regular season. Since then, at least four schools, including the Florida State Seminoles and the University of Southern Utah Utes, have won appeals because at least one band of their "namesake" tribe supports the schools' current use of names and logos. Nevertheless, in a poll conducted in 2001 by the newspaper *Indian Country Today*, 81 percent of respondents felt that the use of American Indian names, symbols, and mascots is deeply offensive to American Indians. When a people's identity is reduced to caricatures or mascots, their real concerns can be more easily dismissed.

—STEPHANIE BETANCOURT

What is the origin of the term *Redskin*? Why is it offensive?

Many scholars attribute the term *redskin* to naturalists in mid-1700s Europe who were busy creating classifications for everything and everybody. Carolus Linnaeus, a Swedish naturalist, decided to use primary colors to label the four races of mankind: *Eurpopaeus albus* (white), *Americanus rubescens* (red), *Asiaticus fuscus* (yellow), and *Africanus niger* (black). His labels, described in successive editions of his work *Systema Naturae* (1735), were widely accepted. Another scholar, Alden T. Vaughn, contends that the color red was associated with the red body paint that many Indians wore, and he concludes, "In the middle of the nineteenth century, anthropologist Henry Rowe Schoolcraft's *Oneóta, or, Characteristics of the Red Race of America* (1845) and James Fenimore Cooper's *The Redskins* (1846) symbolically marked Caucasian America's full recognition, in both fiction and science, of Indians as innately red and racially distinct."

An Indian view of the origins of the term *redskin* is expressed by writer Suzan Shown Harjo (Cheyenne/Hodulgee Muscogee), who offers a visual scenario: "Just imagine that it is 1756 and you are being tracked by bounty hunters. But you have committed no crime. A bounty has been placed on you simply because you are an Indian and live on coveted land. The bounty hunter finds you, murders you, and scalps you. Then he turns in your bloody scalp (that's where the red in the term *redskin* comes from) and collects his pay. Decapitated heads were also accepted."

Redskin is offensive to many Indian people, yet it continues to be used today. The name of the Washington Redskins football team is one example.

—MARY AHENAKEW

WHY DO SOME PEOPLE BELIEVE THERE ARE NO "REAL" INDIANS LEFT?

This is a very complicated question and represents a myth that relates to almost all other myths about Native Americans. On the surface, some people believe that there are no "real" Indians left because they expect Native people to look like stereotypical Hollywood images or nineteenth-century photographs rather than contemporary people living modern lives. In effect, this renders actual modern-day Indians invisible. If we dig deeper into this question, we see that this myth—questioning the reality, authenticity, and even the humanity of Native American peoples—has been pervasive since European settlers arrived in the Americas.

Some people believe that only Native American people who look like their stereotype—wearing buckskins and a war bonnet, riding a horse, living in a tipi, with long black hair and dark skin—are authentic, while those who look modern are not "real" Indians. With the exception of a handful of uncontacted peoples in the Amazon, most Native people reflect modern times in dress, language, and material culture (though they may adopt traditional clothing of their own tribe for dances, ceremonies, and other tribal occasions). Also, each of the thousands of tribes in the Americas had their own mode of dress, language, belief system, and material culture, meaning that most Native peoples never resembled the popular stereotype. Another aspect of this myth, the belief that "real" Indians should be full-blooded (and therefore have dark skin and hair to "look" Indian) further questions contemporary Native peoples' authenticity. The diversity of tribes, combined with hundreds of years of marriage between people of different tribes and with non-Natives, results in no single defining American Indian "look." So, why does this myth

Marvin Bradby, chief of the Eastern Chickahominy tribe, at the Six Nations Powwow, which was held in support of the six Virginia tribes seeking federal recognition, May 3, 2003. Charles City County, Virginia.

persist today? And why do people expect American Indians to dress as if they lived in the 1800s?

From the early days of European contact, the notion that Indigenous people and their ways of life were disappearing served colonial interests. The very real disappearances—through violence, disease, and physical removal—fueled the myth of the "vanishing Indian," the belief that Western civilization's manifest destiny was to take over the North American continent, pushing Native peoples out. The fantasy that the "wild" Indian rejected civilization and therefore must be eradicated justified western expansion. Early colonists witnessed Native peoples dying of disease and believed that God was clearing the way for their settlement. Around the turn of the twentieth century, at the lowest point of Native American population, early anthropologists used "science" (rather, scientific racism, the philosophy that physical characteristics determined intelligence and character) to rationalize the "extinction" of American Indian people. Government programs in the United States and Canada removed Native children from families and sent them to distant boarding schools in an attempt to eradicate their languages and cultures. Using the Dawes Act of 1887, the US government integrated the concept of "blood quantum," or how much Native American blood a person has, into Native peoples' legal status for the purpose of breaking up communally held tribal lands and, by extension, communal tribal ways of living. The government further advised tribes on how to base their enrollment on blood quantum instead of on traditional definitions of tribal membership. Despite physical, intellectual, legal, and spiritual attempts to make Indigenous peoples disappear, their diverse cultures endure today. Yet the larger society still defines a "real" Indian as having those qualities the US government actively worked to eliminate—languages, cultures, and living on their homelands.

The vanishing Indian myth serves a political agenda, one that implies that Native people are only in the past, that they are incapable of being both Native and modern. It neglects to recognize that Native peoples have always played an active role in their own change and modernization; they are not victims of progress. People of Native descent likely live in your town, with skin and hair of all shades. They are doctors, teachers, fishermen, business owners—even astronauts! Judgment of the authenticity of Native people happens all the time, from tribal enrollment blood quantum requirements to non-Indians asking, "How much Indian are you?" Native people are constantly required to prove how "real" they are. In truth, there are as many different Native realities as there are Native people.

—ALEXANDRA HARRIS

WHY ARE COMING-OF-AGE CEREMONIES IMPORTANT?

Ceremonies bring meaning, connection, and purpose to transitions in life. We experience rites of passage in American society, although we don't always recognize them as ceremonial: birth, graduation, marriage, death. We treat different life events with honor, recognizing that the person who has accomplished a milestone is not the same person as before. Similarly, Native American cultures recognize life's transitional points through ceremonies that bring meaning, purpose, and a deeper connection to the community with new rights and responsibilities. Before European contact, most tribes held ceremonies to mark rites of passage; after contact, most ceremonies had to be conducted in secret, if at all. Today some tribes are experiencing a cultural resurgence, bringing back puberty ceremonies and honoring these transitions.

Historically all Native tribes recognized rites of passage differently—and some continue to do so today—but most honored several milestones in an individual's life. Many tribes traditionally had instructions for women who were pregnant, nurturing them through a healthy pregnancy and helping them to guide the child through life. Some communities had traditions involving the umbilical cord and placenta after birth. The Diné (Navajo) took special care of the cord after birth; a lost cord could result in a disoriented and antisocial life. Cultures marked an infant's milestones differently: the Diné celebrated the first laugh, the Ojibwe the first steps, and the Mescalero Apache honored the first moccasins, haircut, and solid foods. A child can be named before, during, or after birth, and in some cultures a person acquired additional names throughout his or her life based on additional rites of passage and accomplishments.

Corn pollen, dusted on the face of a young woman, is a symbol of fertility among some southwestern tribes such as the Apache.

Paul Chesley/Getty Images

Puberty ceremonies honored an especially powerful, stressful, and sensitive transition in a person's life. Before puberty, rituals for girls and boys were generally the same. But puberty marks a significant social change, when girls and boys take on gender-linked roles in the community, so often the ceremonies to mark puberty differed between boys and girls. These gender divisions aren't like historical Western divisions where women are subservient; Indigenous cultures recognize the different gender roles as equally valuable and critical to the survival of the community. Although every Native culture's puberty ceremonies were different, they shared common purposes and themes. Scholar Carol A. Markstrom observes that both boys' and girls' ceremonies shared several common features, including separation or seclusion from others, tests of physical endurance, adherence to taboos, mentorship by adults, accomplishment of adult activities, physical manipulations (such as tattoos, ritual bathing, etc.), celebration, and spiritual transcendence.

Girls have a very clear marker of adulthood, the onset of menstruation. At that time, a girl was regarded as having considerable power. Some tribes viewed this as a power of creation, others considered menstruation to be toxic, and still others believed it was a combination of the two. Often at the onset of menses, a girl would be separated from the community and mentored by an older female relative or community member in the skills needed for adulthood. She might also be given spiritual role models, such as Changing Woman for the Navajo or White Shell Woman for the Apache, who represent ideal behavior. Some tribes also sent girls on a vision quest, which involved fasting—and sometimes taking a hallucinogenic medicine such as datura—to achieve dreams. Those dreams would then be interpreted by a spiritual leader or group of elders and had implications for her future life. The training that a girl received during this time prepared her to join the community as an adult and aµrmed the social structure of the tribe. Certain tribes' ceremonies also included a physical aspect, including giving the girl a tattoo to recognize the start of womanhood; rites of strength and endurance, such as running; or, in the case of some Southern California and Arizona tribes, laying the girl on heated stones or sand.

Boys' coming of age ceremonies were generally not as involved—and some tribes didn't have them at all. Since there is no equivalent marker for boys to the onset of menstruation, tribes marked the transition to manhood in different ways. Many California and Great Basin tribes celebrated a boy's first successful hunt. The Atsugewi people in Northern California marked puberty with a ceremony when a boy's voice changed. Similar to girls' ceremonies, boys endured physical training and were taught the roles of adulthood. Vision quests for boys were also common throughout North America.

The transition from childhood to adulthood is one of the most important times, warranting the attention of the community. Coming-of-age ceremonies provided protection and strength to the young person navigating this diµcult time. The belief that behavior at puberty could affect the future and influence the welfare of others necessitated training, testing, ritual, and celebration.

—ALEXANDRA HARRIS

How Have Native Americans Viewed Sexuality and Gender?

Concepts of sexuality and gender among Native cultures are different from those of the Christian Europeans who colonized North America. During colonization, the settlers didn't understand Native gender roles or same-sex relationships. While Native peoples' own cultures included a variety of perspectives on gender and sexuality, settlers' Old World, Christian cultural norms and values did not. After contact with Europeans, many American Indians adopted or were forced to adopt Christianity; as a result, numerous traditionally defined gender roles were suppressed or went out of practice. Today these traditions are experiencing increased attention based on the historical existence of respected gender-variant roles in Native societies. In *Native America in the Twentieth Century* (1996), Lakota anthropologist Beatrice Medicine wrote, "In sum, it is apparent that aboriginal people in North America were more tolerant than many other cultures of gender variation. . . . However, in many Native communities, there seems to be an emerging intolerance which may mirror that of Anglo society. Still, a tolerance is evident. There is a strong respect for persons and their individual autonomy, despite any crossgender orientation."

The Native people who lived their lives as members of the opposite gender were not what contemporary mainstream society might define as lesbian, gay, bisexual, or gender-variant. These are modern terms that focus on sexual behavior and gender difference rather than established roles in Native communities. Before the twentieth century, a number of Native cultures accepted men and women who "crossed genders," effectively taking on the attributes of the opposite sex, most commonly in their style of dress and in their village duties and responsibilities.

Portrait of We'wha (1849–1896) holding a clay ceremonial prayer-meal basket, 1900.
National Anthropological Archives, Smithsonian Institution
NAA INV 02440800

Gender variance was and still is normalized in Native cultures. For instance, many Native cultures have more than two genders. One of the most well-known and documented of these individuals was We'wha (1849–1896), a Zuni biological man who lived out his life as a woman—dressing in women's clothes and performing the daily tasks of a woman. Called lhamana in the Zuni language, this was a socially accepted and respected role in the community, of which We'wha was a much-valued and loved member. In 1886 We'wha visited Washington, DC, as an oµcial representative of the Zuni people. While there, We'wha danced at the National Theater before an audience that included President Grover Cleveland (whom he subsequently met) and demonstrated the weaving techniques of the Zuni people at the Smithsonian Institution. When We'wha died, the Zuni widely mourned. Will Roscoe, author of *The Zuni Man-Woman* has noted that gender-variant people and the acceptance of them were once widespread among more than 155 tribes.

Historically, many tribes had words in their own languages for community members who occupied alternative genders. Jesuit priests living in the Northeast observed Native men in women's dress and used the word *berdache* to describe Native individuals who crossed genders; this word has been used in the anthropological field as a standard label. However, the definition of berdache is considered by many to be insulting. The term "two-spirit," describing a person who possesses both the male and female spirits, has emerged today as a way to reclaim traditions of gender and sexual variance on a pan-Indian level, although not all Native lesbian, gay, bisexual, or transgender people identify with it. Two-spirit differs from non-Indian sexual and gender labels because of the added dimension of Native American spirituality and culture. Two-spirit is a term that allows Native Americans who are gay, lesbian, bisexual, transgender, and queer to unite nationally under a common contemporary identity while recognizing the diverse cultural traditions of their own tribes.

—ALEXANDRA HARRIS AND LIZ HILL

WHY DO SOME NATIVE PEOPLE NOT LIKE HAVING THEIR PHOTO TAKEN?

Photography came of age in a time of great upheaval for Native Americans. By the late 1800s, Native people in the East had endured colonization for hundreds of years, and many already had been forced to move from their eastern homelands across the Mississippi River. Tribes in the West were battling the government to maintain their lifeways and protect traditional lands from encroaching settlers, including the displaced eastern tribes. As the federal government was forcing western tribes onto reservations, photography—which had arrived in North America in 1839—was becoming more accessible and portable. As journalists, anthropologists, documentarians, artists, and tourists invaded Indian Country in pursuit of the newly tamed "wild Indian" or to document the last vestiges of a "vanishing race," Native people became increasingly wary of the ways in which photographers were transforming their lives into spectacle.

In the late 1800s and early 1900s, railroad companies and tour operators set out to entice tourists to the newly "opened" Southwest. One of the features they promoted was a staged version of Indian life that emphasized peaceful artisanship and supposedly exotic rituals. The Hopi Snake and Antelope ceremony, more commonly known as the Hopi Snake Dance, was a particularly popular attraction because non-Indians perceived it as a connection to a wild, primitive paganism. But many people who photographed the Snake Dance abused their privilege. A photographer named George Wharton James, for example, insisted on taking pictures inside sacred underground structures called *kivas*, even after being specifically asked not to do so. He then sold the images of this highly religious ceremony for personal gain. His action led to a total ban on public viewing of the ceremony.

Princess Theresa of Bavaria, photographing Indian performers at the Buffalo Bill Wild West show, 1890. Munich, Bavaria.

Photo by Frank Lehner. P10218

Photography continues to produce mixed emotions among American Indians. The camera's ability to preserve and document has also been used to appropriate images and traditions. Anthropologists and photojournalists remove sacred, privileged knowledge from its context and make it public. Shutterbug tourists show disrespect when photographing without asking permission. Photo-documentarians, of whom Edward Curtis is the most famous, limited by their personal interpretations, often have perpetuated stereotypes.

Native people, however, have been reappropriating their images for decades. Many tribes have closed off their ceremonies to outsiders or placed strict guidelines on photographing events. At powwows the protocol for taking photos of individual dancers requires that permission first be granted by the individual.

In addition to assuming more control of the photos non-Natives take of them, Native people are increasingly becoming professional photographers themselves. Horace Poolaw (Kiowa, 1906–1984) was one of the earliest Native photographers, beginning his occupation in the early 1920s. He documented the lives of Native people as they made the transition from their traditional lifeways into the twentieth century. Another documentarian, Lee Marmon (Laguna Pueblo), began photographing Laguna tribal elders in the 1940s. Some Native photographers use the medium to make cultural and political statements. Jolene Rickard (Tuscarora) uses photographic and digital media to explore her traditional Haudenosaunee (Iroquois) culture, comment on non-Native perceptions of Native life, and illustrate Native peoples' connection to the land. Rather than scrutinize their Native subjects as "others," Native artists create a dialogue between themselves, their subjects, and their audience. Whether as artists or people taking everyday snapshots, Native photographers document the lives and traditions of Native people, convey the power of the sacred landscape, and create social commentary with their cameras. They have a vested interest in preserving the sanctity of ceremonies—by not photographing them—while they "capture" with their cameras the beauty and multidimensionality of Native life.

—ARWEN NUTTALL

INDIVIDUALS, GROUPS, AND INSTITUTIONS

Before the arrival of formal schools, how were Indian children taught?

Traditionally, the entire community was responsible for educating Native children. Parents, grandparents, relatives, elders, clan members, and societies that hold knowledge reserved only for members transmitted the everyday skills, history, beliefs, and social mores of the tribe. Unlike those of Euro-Americans, many Native social structures were matrilineal and matrilocal, meaning that heritage was traced through the mother. In horticultural societies, such as the Pueblo and Haudenosaunee (Iroquois) communities, responsibility for educating and disciplining the children fell to the first male blood relative in the mother's clan, usually her brother, the children's maternal uncle. In addition, tribal elders were highly respected as wisdom keepers and knowledge bearers. They ensured that community history, values, and cultural information were passed to future generations. Elders retain this highly regarded position today. While formal schooling and the nuclear family play major roles in Native education today, clan and community still perform a significant function as teachers.

Before European contact, Native children were taught the skills necessary to fill their social roles as adults. Young boys learned tracking, hunting, fishing, and farming methods, observational skills, and how to increase their physical abilities. The girls learned how to care for the home and children, prepare food, and create utensils such as pottery and baskets. Children would be given small replicas of tools they would need as adults to play and practice with, such as a bow and arrow, a doll, or a

Navajo silversmith at work, with a young girl looking on, ca. 1915. Arizona.
Photo by Carl Moon. N31720

mortar and pestle. Both boys and girls were given religious training in the spiritual beliefs and the cosmological world view of their people. Young people also gained privileged knowledge through induction into certain medicine, warrior, or other societies. Only those who were members of the society were privy to its secrets. A young person could learn through apprenticeship as well. A holy or medicine person would sense that a particular youth was suited—either by temperament, intelligence, or intuitiveness—to bear the medicine, or holy knowledge, of his or her people.

Children learned by listening, observing, and doing. They were instructed to analyze the world around them, the behavior of the animals, the changing of the weather. Their parents and other teachers encouraged them through example and positive and negative reinforcement, but harsh punishment was not a characteristic of Native education. As children grew older, they could seek answers to specific questions through certain rituals, such as vision quests. Learning was a lifelong process. One did not reach the position of an esteemed elder until very late in life.

With the arrival of Europeans came Jesuit missionaries and Protestant ministers, who established mission schools in the 1600s and 1700s to provide training in religion, the English language, and the industrial arts. Newcomers viewed a "proper" education as a way of bringing Native people out of their supposedly primitive and heathenish conditions into the light of "civilization." Schools tended to replace Native values of sharing and cooperation with a European emphasis on individualism and competition, which threatened to fray the fabric of community.

The history of Native education under US and Canadian policies has been a tragic one. Government and religious schools eroded traditional values and greatly contributed to the loss of many Native languages. From the 1880s to the 1920s (to the 1970s in Canada), children who were forcibly removed from their families and placed in boarding schools faced humiliation and despair. The quality of Indian education continues to be an issue today. Since the 1970s, more and more tribes have reclaimed their children's futures by creating tribal education departments, establishing their own schools, and becoming more involved in curriculum development for students both on and off the reservation.

Family and community continue to play a major role in the education and acculturation of children. Hundreds of tribally operated Head Start programs, elementary schools, and high schools teach traditional languages and cultural values together with reading, writing, and math. Native Americans, along with Hispanics, remain statistically unsuccessful: high school dropout rates, around 70%, are high and attainment of college degrees low, less than 20%. But the numbers have improved during the past twenty years, and Native people will continue to battle whenever their children's futures are at stake.

—ARWEN NUTTALL

WHY DID THE US GOVERNMENT FORCE INDIAN CHILDREN INTO BOARDING SCHOOLS?

White missionaries and other reformers in the nineteenth and early twentieth centuries were certain that their way of thinking and being was the one right way. They felt honor bound to "civilize" the supposedly primitive peoples on whose land they had settled, and they knew that they needed to start with the impressionable minds of children. The prevailing concept was "kill the Indian, save the man." So, beginning in earnest in the 1870s, they established boarding schools. Following government policy they took children—sometimes with the parents' consent and sometimes by force—and sent them to boarding schools as far away from their homes as possible, to keep the children from running away. During summer vacations the children were allowed to go home if the parents came for them or sent enough money for train fare. If a child had poor parents, that child often went many years without contact with his or her people.

The boarding-school system, which included schools on reservations as well as day schools, emphasized manual labor and conformity to late nineteenth-century Euro-American values. Boys learned carpentry, blacksmithing, gardening, and farming. Girls worked in the laundry, sewed, and helped cook the meals. Academic courses included history, math, spelling, reading, writing, and geography. Daily schedules were strictly regulated, independent action was discouraged, and children were harshly punished for speaking any language other than English.

Navajo pupils at Albuquerque Indian School, 1904. Albuquerque, New Mexico.

N26622

By the 1930s the efforts of reformers, together with changes in the public education system, had led to the closing of nearly all Indian boarding schools in the United States, but in Canada, most government- and church-run residential schools continued well into the 1970s. On both sides of the border, survivors of the system remember their experiences. At a conference held at Trent University in Ontario in 2003, former boarding-school students told of rapes by adults, beatings given for the slightest infraction of rules, and lack of proper food. In one case, the government took a student named Alan from his family in Oklahoma at the age of four. He was housed in a large dormitory for boys where he was sexually abused nightly by bigger boys. "I used to cry and cry," he said.

—GEORGETTA STONEFISH RYAN

This photo of American Indian students in 1909, dressed for the roles of Priscilla Alden and Myles Standish for the play *Captain of Plymouth* at the Carlisle Indian Industrial School, demonstrates how thoroughly Anglo-European values permeated the school's curricula.

Cumberland County Historical Society,
Carlisle, Pennsylvania

What Distinct Roles Did Men and Women Play in Native Communities?

American Indian cultures had strictly defined gender roles and duties, but most considered men's and women's work complementary and equally valuable. Although it is difficult to generalize for all Native cultures, men's roles typically focused on hunting, defense, and political leadership while women's centered around the home, village, and fields (if they farmed) or processing what was hunted. It bears mentioning that many tribes' social structures included more than two genders. Some individuals from these multi-gendered tribes often took on unique roles in the community, either of the opposite gender or outside the binary gender roles altogether. Even when gender roles were strongly differentiated, Native people were generally tolerant of a woman or man who transcended those roles (e.g., a female political leader or male artisans). With some exceptions, gender roles reflected the social organization of the tribe, whether matrilineal (i.e., names, clans, and possessions passing through the mother's line) or based on a clan structure. Gender roles additionally reflected the spiritual content of tribal cultures, and were inspired by the origins of the first man and woman and the guiding principles outlined in creation stories.

In the Northeast, the Lenni Lenape believed in a gender-neutral god, and male and female creators and spirit beings. They also perceived a version of the world where men and women were created simultaneously (rather than one from the other, as in Christian belief), which created a structure of equality and

Anita Pena (Kumeyaay) winnowing grain,
1904. Mesa Grande Reservation, California.
Photo by Edward H. Davis. N25474

autonomy for both genders. Married men and women gave reciprocally to each other what they produced. All that the husband hunted became the property of the wife. In turn, crops harvested by the wife became the husband's, which he could use as sustenance during the hunt or to do with as he chose. If the wife gave away all the deerskins or meat, or the husband shared corn with hungry friends, this was an accepted part of the reciprocal relationship.

A common duty of women in the East was farming. Women owned the fields and made the decisions about planting and harvesting. Control of goods gave women considerable power. In many tribes, if women disagreed with the men's decision to wage war, for example, they could withhold provisions, disabling the men's mission. Women laboring in fields shocked European observers. They believed that a woman's place was in the home (and subordinate to men). Native women worked hard—but that gave them respect and leverage in the community. When men's roles were suppressed by the colonial impact of overhunting or by territorial limitations (e.g., reservations), women's relative power increased for a time because their roles were still critical to the tribe's survival. In the 1880s, for example, Omaha women in Nebraska still harvested crops and carried the weight of supporting the community, even as men's traditional roles became more and more constrained by the federal government's policies. Once Native people became dependent on European trade goods rather than women's handiwork, the power dynamic shifted again, this time lessening the impact of women's work and making the tribe increasingly reliant on European trade.

Women political leaders were not common but did occur. More typical was a government, such as that of the Haudenosaunee and Cherokee, in which men's and women's councils held equal power. Women's consent in decision making was required, especially as they controlled the provisions men would need for any expedition.

Gaining a deep understanding of historical gender roles can be diμcult. Most first-person accounts of Native American society around the time of Contact were written by Europeans who tended to view the people they saw in terms of European gender norms. As a result, they recorded men's overt power while women's more subtle influence—such as the Haudenosaunee Clan Mothers' political authority— often went unseen. Complicating this is the diversity of tribal social organizations. While many tribes were egalitarian, some were not, such as those in the Pacific Northwest and in the Arctic. The Tsimshian in southeast Alaska, for example, were organized by clan and rank. Although genders were not egalitarian, there was nevertheless opportunity for women to accumulate political and economic power that far exceeded that of nineteenth-century non-Native women, especially by controlling production and distribution of food and supplies. A Tsimshian woman of high ability and rank could become a chief with respected authority.

—ALEXANDRA HARRIS

WHY WAS THE NAVAJO LANGUAGE CHOSEN FOR MILITARY CODE IN WORLD WAR II? WERE ALL INDIAN "CODE TALKERS" NAVAJO?

In 1942, as the United States was entering World War II, Philip Johnston, a non-Native veteran of World War I raised on the Navajo Reservation, suggested that the Marine Corps use the Navajo language as a code. Like most Indian languages, the Navajo language was so intricate and difficult to learn that few people outside the tribe could speak it—and it was a resource unique to the United States. Moreover, with a population of nearly 50,000 at that time, the Navajo offered a large pool of Native American recruits who spoke their language fluently. Using four Navajo volunteers, Johnston gave Maj. Gen. Clayton Vogel of the Marine Corps a brief demonstration of their skills. On the morning of February 28, 1942, at an office in Los Angeles, the volunteers coded, transmitted, and decoded three line messages filled with specialized military vocabulary. The messages were dictated in English, sent in Navajo over a field telephone, and written down in English as received. Impressed with the results, the Marines authorized a program that began with twenty-nine Navajo men.

Initially the Navajo recruits devised and memorized code words for more than 200 military terms (the vocabulary was later expanded to more than 450 words), creating a code that even fellow Navajos could not follow. The Navajo word for eagle, for example, is *atsá*, but in the code it meant "transport plane." *Chaa'* means "beaver," but for Navajo code talkers it meant "minesweeper." During the war, some 380 Navajo Marines serving in the Pacific participated in the classified Navajo Code Talker

Two Navajo Marines operate a portable radio set close behind the front lines, December 1943. Solomon Islands. Photo by US Marine Corps.
USMC/Hulton Archive/Getty Images

Program. They worked mainly in two-man teams, using walkie-talkies and field telephones to call in military maneuvers and report enemy movements. They took part in every Marine assault, from Guadalcanal in 1942 to Okinawa in 1945, changing the code for each island campaign. The complex, month-long operation to capture the island of Iwo Jima was directed entirely by orders communicated in Navajo code. By the war's end thousands of messages had been transmitted, but the Japanese never succeeded in breaking the code.

In the summer of 2001, Congress awarded Congressional Silver Medals—the highest honor Congress can bestow on a citizen of the United States—to the twenty-nine Navajo Marines who originally developed the code.

Choctaws also served as code talkers in World War II, as did seventeen Comanche servicemen. Meskwaki, Sioux, Crow, Hopi, and Cree soldiers also took part. The Comanche men were recruited for the US. Army Signal Corps to devise a top-secret, 250-word code that would be incomprehensible to the German military. On June 6, 1944 (D-Day), they laid communication lines for Allied forces landing on the beaches of Normandy. Over the next eleven months, they participated in four other major campaigns, sending messages on troop movements, strength, and weaponry. These men received commendations from their commander, and in 1989 the French government awarded them the Chevalier de l'Ordre National du Mérite.

—MARY AHENAKEW

HOW DID SOME TRIBES GET A REPUTATION AS WARLIKE AND OTHERS AS PEACEFUL?

Historically, most peoples, when confronted with newcomers who encroached on their lands, stole their food sources, and threatened their families with destruction and death, have sought to protect their lands and loved ones. In general, the Indigenous peoples of North and South America have been no exception. Of course, what appears to be common sense was not the case during the first visits of Europeans to the Western Hemisphere. Initially, a number of Native societies considered light-skinned Europeans to be gods worthy of veneration and even worship and welcomed them with great hospitality.

Typically, first encounters between Indians and Europeans were peaceful, but conflicts would soon develop, and non-Indians would characterize the formerly "peaceful" Indian communities as "warlike." Newcomers stereotyped Taíno and other Caribbean societies—some of the first people whom the Spanish encountered in the late 1400s and early 1500s—as peaceful because they did not immediately attack. Such was also the case when Captain James Cook landed in the Hawaiian Islands in 1778. Cook, believed to be the Hawaiian god Lono—who, it had been predicted, would return on a "floating island"—was warmly received by Native Hawaiians during his first and second visits to their lands. The enthusiastic greeting with which Native Hawaiians met Captain Cook and his crew was unusual, because the Native Hawaiians were known historically as a fierce and warlike people. Their friendly attitude quickly changed, however, during the second sojourn. In a dispute over stolen property, a fight among Native Hawaiians and Cook's men ensued, and Hawaiian warriors killed Cook on February 14, 1779, on the beach at Kealakekua Bay on the Big Island.

The Wampanoag people, who were present at the feast that is commonly known as the first Thanksgiving, also treated the English settlers peacefully. As English hunger for land increased, however, the Wampanoag attitude also changed, culminating in King Philip's War of 1675–1676. This war between Native communities in the Northeast and British settlers proved devastating to the Native peoples. The conflict abrogated the original truce negotiated between the Wampanoag leader, Massasoit, and the governor of the Plymouth Colony.

Tribes also could gain reputations for being warlike or peaceful from neighboring tribes with whom they came into conflict. *Apache*, a word derived from the Zuni language, is translated to mean "enemy" or "fighting men." Apaches were known for their warlike stances toward other tribes and white settlers—although their reputation has perhaps been much exaggerated by the general hostility toward Native peoples. The Maya and Aztec peoples of Mesoamerica, whose civilizations flourished between approximately AD 250 and AD 1550, also were known initially for their warlike practices.

—LIZ HILL

DID ANY INDIAN GROUPS PRACTICE POLYGAMY?

Some groups did practice polygamy, while others did not. Polygamy is usually defined as having more than one wife. Before contact with Europeans, the concept of marriage differed among various Indigenous peoples.

In most Eastern Woodland cultures, a man lived with his wife's family in a large wooden longhouse. When other female siblings married, their husbands moved in with them. The Apache, Navajo, Mi'kmaq, and other tribes across North America followed the same pattern. Men in the community would take responsibility for supporting sisters, daughters, mothers, and other female family members if tragedy struck a male provider. But all the women in one family were usually not the "wives" of the lone man.

Father Andrew White, one of the Jesuit priests who came in 1634 to what is today Maryland, used every available opportunity to convert the Native people he encountered to the Catholic faith. When Kittamaqua, the *tayac*, or tribal leader, of the Piscataway Confederacy, fell ill, his healers were unable to cure him. Father White wrote in his journal that he administered a "powder of known eщcacy" to the tayac, which effected what must have seemed to Kittamaqua and his people a miraculous cure. The tayac submitted to baptism, because his remarkable recovery proved to him the power of the priest's God. As a condition of being baptized, wrote Father White, Kittamaqua "put away all wives but one." Since no mention is made of the tayac's having children by these other "wives," Father White may have mistaken a single wife's female relatives for multiple wives.

In some of the northern Plains and Plateau communities, marriages could be either monogamous or polygamous. It has been estimated that at one time about 20 percent of marriages in these regions included more than one wife. Leading families in a community carried responsibilities of hosting and labor that encouraged the taking of multiple spouses. Most often, sisters would marry one man, who could provide for them both. In contrast, the Haudenosaunee (Iroquois) tribes in the Northeast and the southwestern Pueblo peoples tended to have only one spouse at a time. But no matter what the formal arrangements between individuals, the primary purpose of family alliances was to make sure orphans were cared for and to maintain the strength and stability of the community as a whole.

—RICO NEWMAN

POWER, AUTHORITY, AND GOVERNANCE

WHAT ARE THE INDIAN POPULATIONS OF THE UNITED STATES, CANADA, AND LATIN AMERICA?

According to the US Census of 2000, the American Indian and Alaska Native population totals 2.9 million, less than 1 percent of the total population of the country. But in the 2010 census, people were given the chance to describe themselves as being of more than one race, and 5.2 million people reported themselves as American Indian or Alaska Native in combination with other races. The American Indian in-combination population experienced rapid growth, increasing by 39 percent since 2000. The ten states with the largest American Indian populations were (in order) California, Oklahoma, Arizona, Texas, New Mexico, New York, Washington, North Carolina, Michigan, and Alaska.

Census figures, however, should not be taken at face value, because they do not reflect those who were not counted or did not want to identify themselves as Native American. Some American Indians are suspicious of government representatives. In the past, some reservation communities did not allow census workers to complete their surveys, and independent researchers have concluded that Native Americans were undercounted in 1960 and 1970.

The 2016 Canadian Census enumerated 1,673,780 Indigenous people in Canada, 4.9 percent of the country's total population. Because Native peoples in Mesoamerica and South America don't have the same kinds of relationships with their governments that tribes in the United States have, population statistics about Indigenous groups can be calculated only approximately. The best estimates suggest that about 42 million people (about 8 percent of the total population) in Latin America identify themselves as Indigenous.

—GEORGETTA STONEFISH RYAN

HOW MANY INDIAN TRIBES ARE OFFICIALLY RECOGNIZED IN THE UNITED STATES TODAY? WHY IS RECOGNITION IMPORTANT?

In 2016 federally recognized American Indian tribes numbered 567. That total includes 336 tribes in the lower forty-eight states and 229 Alaska Native village corporations (since 1971, older Alaska Natives have had the option to invest in regional and village corporations rather than to live on reservations set aside for them by the federal government). Numerous other tribes remain unrecognized. A great deal of these tribes located on the East Coast of the United States have been granted state recognition, meaning that the states in which they are located acknowledge prior state government treaties or other state dealings with them. In 2016 the Lumbee made progress in their fight to achieve federal recognition. The US Department of the Interior reversed its long-held position that the 1956 Lumbee Act both terminated rights, benefits, and privileges and prohibited the application of future legislation as an Indian tribe. This opinion does not grant the Lumbee full federal recognition but it does open up additional avenues for them to pursue these efforts.

Federal recognition—or acknowledgment—means that the federal government recognizes a tribe as having certain rights and powers of self-government as well as rights to services that have been granted as a result of the tribe's special relationship with the United States. This relationship goes back to the Indian Commerce Clause and the Treaty Clause of the US Constitution. Today federal acknowledgment is a complex process overseen by the US Bureau of Indian Affairs. Acknowledgment is determined by seven primary factors: proof that (1) the petitioner (or tribe) for federal acknowledgment has existed historically as American Indian, (2) the group (or tribe) has existed throughout history as an entity with a governing body, (3) the group shows evidence that it has governed its members (i.e., demonstrates political influence), (4) the group has a governing document and a statement of membership criteria, (5) the tribal members are descended from a historical Indian tribe, (6) tribal members are members of that specific tribe and not of any other tribe, and (7) neither the group (or tribe) nor its members are the subject of laws that have expressly terminated or forbidden the federal relationship. Federal recognition can also be obtained through acts of the US Congress and federal court decisions. The criteria are still the same.

Federal recognition also is important because with it tribes are entitled to a great number of services that the federal government provides by virtue of the long-standing federal trust responsibility toward tribal governments. The services include health care, education, housing, economic development assistance, and others.

In 2016 the US Department of the Interior announced an administrative procedure to allow for a unified Native Hawaiian government to enter into a formal government-to-government relationship with the United States. This would give Native Hawaiians a status similar to more than 567 Native American tribes that currently hold nation-to-nation status, which could allow federal considerations on issues ranging from land management to access to social services.

Today Indian gaming has also affected the way the general public perceives federal recognition of tribes. Under the Indian Gaming Regulatory Act of 1988, only federally recognized tribes in states that already allow a particular class of gambling can operate a gaming facility. Public opposition toward tribes seeking federal acknowledgment—whether or not the tribe intends to conduct gaming on its land—has been steadily growing since the mid-1990s and has even prevented some tribes from becoming federally recognized. The Eastern Pequots in Connecticut and the Schaghticoke Tribe in Rhode Island are recent examples of tribes that have had their federal acknowledgment efforts delayed or thwarted by strong public and political opposition.

—LIZ HILL

WHY DIDN'T INDIAN TRIBES BAND TOGETHER TO FIGHT OFF EUROPEANS?

The rapid and devastating spread of European diseases is the main reason that Indian tribes were not able to unify against the European invaders. Another primary factor was the autonomy that most communities enjoyed. Hundreds of Indigenous tribes were spread out across the continents. They spoke hundreds of different languages and governed their people in as many different ways. And, of course, not all the tribes were peaceful toward one another.

Imagine the Western Hemisphere—South, Central, and North America, including the Hawaiian Islands—as it might have been before the wave of European arrivals that began in the late 1400s. Some have estimated that the hemisphere's Indigenous population numbered more than 70 million before this time. Great civilizations flourished, such as the Inka in South America, the Maya and Mexica (Aztec) in Central America and Mexico, and the Mississippian culture of North America. These societies—their immense populations and their activities were well documented by the Europeans who first came across them—were sophisticated and bustling centers of commerce, culture, and religion. But they were thousands of miles apart, separated by formidable geographic barriers.

An important point to keep in mind is that Europeans didn't arrive in the Americas all at once. In fact, even before Columbus landed in 1492, some of the Western Hemisphere's Native peoples had already seen light-skinned people. The Vikings, for example, visited the far northeastern part of the continent in AD 1000, a little less than 500 years before Columbus. A number of tribes have centuries-old stories that mention white-skinned people.

The Shawnee leader Tecumseh (ca. 1768–1813).

Hulton Archive/Archive Photos/ Getty Images

Following Columbus's lead, Spanish explorers, including Hernando de Soto and Hernan Cortes, began more frequent travel between Europe and the Americas. With them came a variety of Old World diseases that spread with alarming rapidity to all corners of the Western Hemisphere in an extremely short time. Disease is now considered to be the major reason that Europeans—who came from much less populated countries (in 1492, Spain's population was only about 8 million) and who arrived with relatively few people aboard their ships—were able to overcome Native societies whose populations, particularly in South and Central America, were substantially larger. Swept by epidemics of bubonic plague, smallpox, measles, cholera, and influenza, Indigenous peoples, having no immunity, quickly fell ill and died in great numbers. In his book *Stolen Continents: The Americas through Indian Eyes since 1492* (1992), Ronald Wright writes, "The great death raged for more than a century. By 1600, after some twenty waves of pestilence had swept through the Americas, less than a tenth of the original population remained. Perhaps ninety million died, the equivalent, in today's terms, to the loss of a billion. It was the greatest mortality in history."

Disease is not the only reason that Europeans succeeded in taking over Native lands. Europeans brought with them metal weapons that had never been seen in the Americas, and they sometimes recruited tribes to fight with them against traditional enemies. The great Shawnee political and military leader, Tecumseh, championed the idea of Native political unity in 1810 and 1811, traveling from the Great Lakes to the Gulf of Mexico to promote concerted resistance to treaties that left Native Nations with ever-diminishing lands. Few tribal chiefs, however, were interested in giving up their ability to negotiate directly with European and American governments.

—LIZ HILL

WHAT WAS THE IROQUOIS CONFEDERACY AND HOW DID IT CONTRIBUTE TO DEMOCRACY?

In the 1600s the Iroquois Confederacy was a political and military alliance comprising the original five nations of the Haudenosaunee, or "People of the Longhouse": the Seneca, Mohawk, Cayuga, Onondaga, and Oneida. In 1722 the Tuscarora, driven out of North Carolina, increased the number of participating nations to six. One of the largest—and most politically and militarily powerful—groupings of Indigenous peoples in North America, the Haudenosaunee held territory that stretched some 1,000 miles south to Kentucky and north to Quebec, east to Pennsylvania and west to Illinois. The document that laid out the Haudenosaunee Confederacy's system of government, or its constitution, was called the Great Law of Peace.

According to oral tradition, the Great Law of Peace, or Kaianere:kowa, was introduced to the Haudenosaunee people by Deganawidah, the "Peacemaker," who is said to have been a man of non-Iroquoian descent, and Ayonwatha (Hiawatha), a Mohawk or Onondaga. The Great Law of Peace is an ancient document. In Haudenosaunee oral tradition, it appeared as early as AD 1142. According to Charles C. Mann, author of *1491: New Revelations of the Americas Before Columbus* (2005), "The Haudenosaunee would have the second-oldest continuously existing representative parliament on earth. Only Iceland's Althing, founded in AD 930, is older." Further, as Emory Dean Keoke and Kay Marie Porterfield point out in an article about the Great Law in *American Indian* magazine (Fall 2004), "Many scholars believe the Great Law was the longest-lived international constitution at that time.

The only possible exception to this was the unwritten English Constitution, which had its origins in the English Magna Carta. Certainly, in fifteenth-century Europe nothing existed to rival this American Indian constitution."

The Haudenosaunee Confederacy was a consensus-driven form of government, meaning that all decisions that came before the confederacy had to be unanimous. The confederacy was represented by fifty *sachems*, or chiefs, chosen from among each of the Haudenosaunee nations. Its sessions were convened by the Todadaho, who represented the confederacy in diplomatic relations with other governments and who was always a member of the Onondaga Nation. Women, who headed the clans, chose the sachems (who were all men). The confederacy had the power to negotiate treaties but not to declare war.

The Great Law of Peace was by all accounts a sophisticated, effective, and modern system of governing, one in which political power was held in balance by an elaborate system of checks and a view of individual freedom that was truly revolutionary, at least for American settlers.

The constitution of the Haudenosaunee Confederacy made an indelible impression on the United States' Founding Fathers, including Benjamin Franklin, who used it as one model for the Articles of Confederation, which later were incorporated into the US Constitution (ratified in 1789). In 1987 the US Senate formally acknowledged, in a special resolution, the influence of the Haudenosaunee Great Law of Peace on the US Constitution.

—LIZ HILL

Are Indians US Citizens?

American Indians hold two distinct forms of citizenship. They are citizens of the United States (if they are born in the United States or to a US citizen living outside the United States), and they are citizens of their tribal nations. As citizens of the United States, American Indians—like all other citizens—enjoy all the rights guaranteed in the US Constitution, including freedom of speech, religion, and the press.

United States citizenship for America's original inhabitants was a long time coming. It is one of history's great ironies that American Indians—the first peoples of North America—were not guaranteed US citizenship until 1924. Although two-thirds of Indian people (women who married US citizens, for example) had gained citizenship through piecemeal laws enacted during the previous fifty years, American Indians were the last group in the United States to enjoy citizenship as a birthright. Charles Curtis (Kaw/Osage, 1860–1936), the first American Indian US senator and later the vice president under Herbert Hoover, sponsored the Indian Citizenship Act while he was serving as the chairman of the Senate Committee on Indian Affairs. Congress supported the law as an extension of the government's assimilation policy. Some 12,000 American Indians had served in the US military during World War I, thus demonstrating, the thinking went, their ability to assimilate into white society.

Some traditional American Indian peoples do not embrace American citizenship, believing it interferes with tribal status as sovereign nations. Some tribes, such as the Haudenosaunee (Iroquois), have in the past issued their own passports. The 1924 act, however, grants US citizenship to American Indian peoples regardless of individual personal and political beliefs.

Citizenship for American Indian peoples did not automatically mean the right to vote in the individual states in which they resided. Like African Americans living in the southern states, American Indians faced oppression, racism, and discrimination, particularly when it came to voting rights. Discrimination was expressed most openly in the states with large Native populations, including Alaska, Arizona, Colorado, New Mexico, and Utah. American Indians could not vote in New Mexico until 1948; in Arizona, not until 1964. In South Dakota, Indian people were still fighting for the right to vote in county elections well into the mid-1970s.

Suzanne Evans, of the University of California, Berkeley, writes in the *Encyclopedia of North American Indians* (1996), "The right to vote is arguably the most significant characteristic of American citizenship. . . . But, despite its significance, the franchise has been denied to many groups throughout history, including blacks, women, and Indians. However, whereas blacks were formally enfranchised with the Fifteenth Amendment (1870) and women with the Nineteenth Amendment (1920), Indians cannot claim one defining historical moment when their right to vote was constitutionally secured."

—LIZ HILL AND NEMA MAGOVERN

Did Native Americans Own Slaves?

Slavery as an economic means to an end had been an alien concept to most Native peoples before contact with Europeans. Some version of slavery or servitude, however, had existed among Indigenous populations, particularly among the wealth-conscious tribes of the North Pacific Coast. In the *Encyclopedia of North American Indians*, Theda Perdue wrote, "On the Northwest Coast, where material wealth assumed greater significance, slaves did acquire a value unknown elsewhere and became a species of property to be bought, sold, and given away." Both the North Pacific Coast tribes and the Aleut people of Alaska and the Aleutian Islands had three primary social divisions: nobility or wealthy, high-status people; commoners; and slaves. Among the Plateau tribes of Idaho, eastern Oregon and Washington, and southern British Columbia, slaves also held the lowest social ranking.

After European contact, a number of tribes recognized the economic benefits of selling Native slaves to the Europeans and began engaging in this practice. The Indian slave trade among the Native peoples of the Southwest intensified after the arrival of the Spanish. The Comanche of the Great Plains raided Apache, Navajo, and Pueblo settlements for slaves to use as currency in business deals with Mexicans, New Mexicans, and Americans. The Catawba people in South Carolina also traded in slaves, as did a number of other Southeastern tribes, who discovered early in the 1700s that the British were keenly interested in obtaining slaves. Some of the more stratified societies of Caribbean, Central American, and South American peoples also included types of servitude.

Slaves were usually taken during raids of neighboring tribes, with women and children preferred. Female slaves often became wives. The Aleut would free the children of female slaves if the father was Aleut. Slaves among North Pacific Coast tribes, such as the Tlingit, were sometimes killed, freed, or given away to demonstrate that their owners were so wealthy, they could afford to part with them. Not all captives became slaves. Conditions varied a great deal, with slaves in some cultures gaining their liberty and even tribal honors. Iroquoian peoples, for instance, had procedures for adopting captives into Iroquoian society. These adopted captives often replaced men killed during a raid. Among the Seminole, slaves who were bought, kidnapped through raids, or escaped plantations and joined Native communities could reduce their marginality within those communities over time.

Some of the Five Civilized Tribes, which included the Cherokee, Chickasaw, Choctaw, Creek, and Seminole, held African American slaves during the years leading up to the American Civil War. (The Seminole, however, later harbored runaway slaves, even accepting them into their communities.) Other tribes known to have played prominent roles in America's enslaving past were the Apache, Pawnee, and Comanche. While some tribes bought African American slaves from white plantation owners and adopted the plantation system, slavery often functioned differently within Native society. Unlike slavery in the American South, which operated on a rigid race-based system, Native slavery operated on a spectrum. Ideas of belonging were fluid. Native slaves comprised black, white, Mexican, and other Native peoples. Their concept of freedom probably aligned with Native ideas of belonging, which often meant gaining admittance into a matrilineal clan.

Some tribes, like the Cherokee, however, adopted a system of slavery similar to that of the American South, buying and selling slaves not as people but as property and vehicles of free labor. This was largely due to the overwhelming pressures of Euro-American territorial expansion. The Cherokee were forced to shift their tribal economies to a plantation system as a means of maintaining control of their land and sovereignty prior to removal. In an effort to compete in a Southern agricultural market, where white plantation owners grew, harvested, and sold crops by exploiting the free labor of slaves, the Cherokee also moved to implement a race-based chattel slavery system.

Today issues of race and bloodlines among Native nations that owned African American slaves are much discussed and remain a source of intense controversy. Decisions to deny citizenship to slave descendants, known as Freedmen, have led the Cherokee, Choctaw,

Creek, Chickasaw, and Seminole into contentious lawsuits with their Freedmen descendants that are still playing out today. As sovereign nations, these tribes claim the right to determine their own criteria for citizenship and belonging. The descendants of Freedmen argue that "blood quantum" laws that require members to have at least one-quarter Native blood and receive sponsorship from an established citizen are overtly exclusionary and were enacted to discriminate against black members and deny their shared history.

—BETHANY MONTAGANO, ARWEN NUTTALL, AND LIZ HILL

DID WOMEN SERVE AS CHIEFS AND LEADERS OF NATIVE AMERICAN TRIBES?

Native women held considerable leadership authority before Europeans arrived. While gender roles were usually clearly divided in Native society, the contributions of both genders were equally prized and respected. Native women's leadership following Contact went largely unnoticed by European observers, whose cultural filter dismissed and devalued the contribution of women. As a result, women's roles are not well documented in colonial records. However, Native histories indicate that women played highly important political and social roles within most communities and provide many examples of women leaders. Women did not usually serve as the political heads of their tribes, although there are occasions when this happened.

More commonly, they were spiritual and clan leaders who held profound economic power within the community. This power often overrode that of their male counterparts. Several formidable leaders stand out in the historical record—no one more than Awashonks, who led the Saconet band of Wampanoag in Rhode Island in the mid-1600s. Unlike other contemporaneous Native women leaders, Awashonks reportedly did not inherit her role but earned it through the quality of her leadership. Called Sunsqua, or female chief, she was known for her talents in negotiation and diplomacy. She negotiated an alliance with the English in 1671, albeit under threat by the Plymouth leaders.

Cockacoeskie (ca. 1640–ca. 1686), also called Queen Ann, led the Pamunkey of Virginia for thirty years. She became the *weroance* (leader) in 1656 after the death of her husband, Totopotomoi. When Bacon's Rebellion erupted, the colonial governor sought military assistance from Cockacoeskie. In turn, she wanted protection against the settlers' raids on her people. The

Washington and Gist visit Queen Aliquippa, by John McNevin (1821–1894). Engraving by John Rogers (ca. 1808–ca. 1888).

Art and Picture Collection, The New York Public Library
Gado Images / Alamy Stock Photo

English offered up a weak effort to defend the Pamunkey, despite the tribe's many sacrifices for the colonial government. In 1677, Cockacoeskie and her son signed the Treaty of Middle Plantation in which she relinquished claims on ancestral land in return for protection and reserved land—in essence, this created the first reservation in America.

Haudenosaunee, or Iroquois Confederacy, women hold significant power. In particular, clan mothers nominate, install, and remove male leaders, and their counsel is taken as equal to a chief's. Given this strong matrilineal society, it is not surprising that a female Seneca leader rose to prominence during the tumultuous colonial period. "Queen" Aliquippa (d. 1754), as colonists called her, was a leader of the Mingo Seneca who lived near what is now Pittsburgh, Pennsylvania. She was a key ally of the British leading up to the French and Indian War. Aliquippa commanded great respect among colonial leaders (including a young Maj. George Washington), who honored her requests to pay tribute when in her territory.

More than a 100 years later on the other side of the continent,

Liliuokalani (born Lydia Lili'u Loloku Walania Kamaka'eha, 1838–1917) was the first queen and last monarch of Hawai'i. During her short reign, she attempted to draft a new constitution that would have restored the monarchy's power as well as voting rights for the disenfranchised. Feeling threatened by this assertion of sovereignty, American settlers and businessmen staged a coup d'état, backed by the US government, overthrowing the monarchy. Liliuokalani continued to advocate for an independent Hawai'i for the rest of her life.

In 1757, Cherokee leader Attakullakulla traveled to South Carolina to negotiate trade agreements with the colony's governor. Upon arriving, he was surprised that no white women were present, commenting, "Since the white man as well as the red was born of woman, did not the white man admit women to their council?" Confused, the governor took a few days to respond with: "The white men do place confidence in their women and share their councils with them when they know their hearts are good." Europeans were shocked to find that Cherokee women were considered the equals of men. A Ghigau, or Beloved Woman, held a voting seat in the council of chiefs and headed the council of women. She could also pardon or sentence offenders. Attakullakulla's niece Nanyehi (Nancy Ward, ca. 1738–ca. 1822) was the last and most famous Beloved Woman, renowned as a warrior in battle and also as a leader for peace. One of the most prominent female leaders in modern tribal history is Wilma Mankiller (Cherokee, 1945–2010), who was the first woman elected as principal chief of the Cherokee Nation, serving from 1985 to 1995.

Without a doubt, Native women have played an important role in tribal cultures/communities for centuries. Their knowledge and accomplishments have been passed on to the daughters and granddaughters who continue to walk in their footsteps.

—ALEXANDRA HARRIS

CAN INDIANS LEAVE THE RESERVATIONS? WHY DO RESERVATIONS STILL EXIST?

Indian people, as citizens of the United States, are entitled to live wherever they choose, just like other American citizens. In fact, in 2005 approximately two-thirds of Indian people in the United States lived away from reservation lands in rural areas, towns, and cities. In Canada about 57 percent of government-recognized Indians were living off reserves (the Canadian term for reservation), according to the census for 2006.

Reservations and reserves are made up of lands that were set aside by and for tribes when they gave up enormous portions of their original landholdings in treaties with federal governments. In the past, US reservations also were created through presidential executive orders and acts of the US Congress, or a combination of both.

Today much original Indian reservation land in the United States is inhabited by both Indians and non-Indians. Such "checkerboarding," or splintering of lands that comprise Indian reservations, is a result of unwise federal policies, in particular, the General Allotment Act (also known as the Dawes Act) of 1887. This law mandated the conversion of Indian lands that tribes had previously held in common into smaller parcels open to individual Indian ownership. More than 90 million acres were subsequently taken from US tribes as a result of the General Allotment Act. These lands fell into the hands of non-Indian landowners who could afford to purchase the parcels that Indian people lost through bankruptcies or the inability to pay newly levied taxes.

Many of the 326 US reservations and approximately 3100 Canadian reserves (in Canada, many First Nations communities have rights to more than one reserve within a province or territory) are incapable of sustaining agriculture and other economic

Sign outside tribal government buildings, Pawhuska, Oklahoma, June 2006.

pursuits. But over the years many Indian people have come to consider the reservations "home," despite having been initially forced to move there. Beginning in the early decades of the 1800s, for example, the government forced a number of East Coast tribes from their ancestral homelands to faraway, inhospitable lands west of the Mississippi.

In Mesoamerica and South America, very few of the approximately 50 million Indigenous people live on land set aside for them. Some village communities in the Mesoamerican highlands and Andes Mountains are oficially recognized as the collective owners of their lands, and some Latin American governments created reservations for lowland peoples in the early 1900s. But most of Latin America's Indigenous people live in the countryside or large cities.

Many reservations, reserves, and Indigenous villages continue to be socially and economically depressed, with very high levels of poverty and unemployment among residents, few economic opportunities, and high incidences of alcohol and drug abuse. But Indian people who are living elsewhere often return to them to visit their families and participate in a variety of cultural activities. Most elders were born on the reservations or in villages, and many still live there. Reservation lands, which may or may not have been part of ancestral homelands, continue to be imbued with cultural and religious significance for the people.

—LIZ HILL

WHY DO AMERICAN INDIANS RUN CASINOS?

Indian casinos are not owned by individuals, nor are they the same type of commercial gambling enterprises as those located in Las Vegas and Atlantic City. Instead, they are owned and operated by tribal governments. In the 1980s, tribal governments argued that their sovereignty guaranteed them the right to open gaming enterprises to the public. A compromise with the federal government eventually resulted in the Indian Gaming Regulatory Act (IGRA). Passed by Congress in 1988, IGRA guaranteed tribes the right to conduct gaming on their reservation lands as a means of developing their economies.

Another difference between commercial casino operations and Indian gaming casinos is that the profits of the latter—by law—must support the following: Indian community infrastructure; diverse, self-sufficient tribal economies; and charitable causes. Although some tribes pay their members a share of casino revenues (called "per capita payments," or "per caps"), most do not have enough left over after setting aside operating expenses and revenues earmarked for community needs.

Almost all states allow some form of gambling. In 2016, according to the American Gaming Association, 47 states and the District of Columbia allowed charitable gaming, and forty states and the District of Columbia had state lotteries. Indian gaming facilities are currently located in twenty-eight states. Perhaps the most important fact to remember is that Indian tribes are not commercial businesses or "special interest groups"; they are governments, each with its own structure, priorities, and jurisdiction. Because Indian gaming is a form of gambling that exists to provide revenue for Native tribes—much the same as state lotteries provide revenues for education and other state needs—

and because tribes are sovereign governments, government gaming is allowed on reservation lands, which are free of state jurisdiction.

The Indian Gaming Regulatory Act did not create Indian gaming; gaming had existed for a decade or more on reservations in the form of large-scale bingo games and, even earlier, in traditional games. In 1987 the Supreme Court upheld in *California v. Cabazon* the right of American Indian tribes as sovereign nations to conduct gaming on Indian lands free of state control when similar gaming is permitted by the state outside the reservation. At the same time, the IGRA aµrmed that tribes had the power to conduct gaming on Indian lands but also gave states the ability to negotiate—via tribe-state compacts—gaming regulations and the kinds of games played.

—LIZ HILL

WHAT HAPPENS TO THE REVENUE FROM INDIAN CASINOS?

In accordance with the Indian Gaming Regulatory Act (IGRA), which was enacted by the US Congress in 1988 to provide a new means of economic development for American Indian tribes, revenues from Indian casinos are used primarily to help rebuild Native communities. Many Native American communities in the United States remained in various stages of poverty due to neglect by the federal government, and Indian gaming was seen as a way to enable tribes to become more self-sustaining.

Not every tribe has a casino. According to a National Indian Gaming Commission fact sheet, out of 567 federally recognized tribes, only 238 tribes operate 474 gaming facilities in 28 states. Thus, 329 tribes (58 percent) have no gaming operations. Indeed, the rural and unpopulated geographic locations of many Native nations discourage gaming.

In 2015 a substantial portion of the estimated $29.9 billion national Indian casino revenue was used to operate, maintain, and regulate tribal gaming facilities. American Indian tribal governments used the rest of the revenues in their communities to continue building much-needed infrastructure such as police and fire stations, hospitals and health clinics, schools, daycare and Head Start facilities, eldercare centers, and sewer and water systems. Examples of facilities built with gaming revenues during the past few years include an elder citizen care center at the Mille Lacs Indian Reservation in north-central Minnesota; a hospital at the Pueblo of Isleta in New Mexico; a Head Start center for the Mandan, Hidatsa, and Arikara Nation in North Dakota; and a high school for the Mescalero Apache tribe in New Mexico—where tribal history and culture are important parts of the curriculum.

Tsali Manor, a Cherokee senior citizen's center financed by revenue from the local casino. Cherokee, North Carolina, 2003.

While other legal gaming institutions may do with their net profits as they please, tribal nations are governed by strict rules. Per IGRA (25 U.S.C. 2710), gaming net profits may be used only to:

1) Fund tribal government operations or programs,
2) Provide for the general welfare of their members,
3) Promote tribal economic development,
4) Donate to charitable organizations, and
5) Help fund operations of local government agencies.

Revenues from gaming casinos also give Native tribes the capital to invest in other businesses besides gaming. A number of tribes, including the Shakopee Mdewakanton Sioux (Dakota) Community in Minnesota, the Winnebago Tribe of Nebraska, and the Tulalip Tribes in Washington State, have invested in convention centers, movie theaters, gas stations, hotels, spas and health clubs, and golf courses, thus diversifying their economies. By doing so, communities hope that future tribal governments will be less reliant on gaming, which many

Indian people believe will not always be the only viable means of improving tribal economies.

Indian gaming facilities also provide revenue to federal, state, and local communities. Through the more than 628,000 jobs that tribal gaming generated in 2013, the federal government benefited by receiving $6.2 billion in tax revenue and $1.4 billion in revenue savings through reduced welfare and unemployment benefit payments. In 2013 Indian gaming also generated $2.4 billion in state revenue and $100 million more for local governments.

—LIZ HILL

Do THE RICH CASINO TRIBES HELP OUT THE POOR TRIBES?

Yes. The more successful casino tribes do assist less-fortunate gaming and nongaming tribes. Sometimes the less-successful tribes have gaming facilities of their own that don't reap the same kinds of revenues; sometimes they do not. Unfortunately, stories about how the wealthier tribes are helping those with less robust economies do not interest the mainstream news media, and many instances of tribe-to-tribe giving also go unnoticed.

For tribes, generosity is tradition. Some recent examples of tribe-to-tribe generosity include:

- In Arizona, Gaming Device Operating Rights have enabled tribes—including many that do not have casinos—to lease their gaming devices to other tribes in the state. As of 2015, of the state's 22 federally recognized tribes, 16 operate active gaming entities while five others lease their slot machine rights to tribes in larger markets. In this manner, tribes that do not have casinos can generate revenues to operate their tribal governments and programs.

- The Forest County Potawatomi Tribe in Wisconsin periodically provides assistance through their gaming revenues to the Red Cliff and Mole Lake bands of Ojibwe, also located in Wisconsin.

In 2017 the Shakopee Tribe awarded nearly $3 million to tribes and Native causes across the country:

- Cheyenne River Sioux Tribe (South Dakota)–The tribe received a $150,000 grant, the majority of which will help create opce space for a new radio station.

- Eastern Shoshone Tribe (Wyoming)–The tribe received a $180,000 grant for shuttle buses and driver training.

- Flandreau Santee Sioux Tribe (South Dakota)–A $435,000 grant will help the tribe purchase dental equipment for its tribal health clinic.

- Kickapoo Tribe in Kansas–A $150,000 grant will help the tribe purchase three police patrol cars.

- Leech Lake Band of Ojibwe (Minnesota)–The tribe received a $75,000 grant for a playground project.

- Ponca Tribe of Nebraska–A $500,000 grant will support the tribe's health and wellness center construction project.

- Rosebud Sioux Tribe (South Dakota)–The tribe received a $75,000 grant for its Rosebud Economic Development Corporation community garden and farmers' market.

- Shoalwater Bay Indian Tribe (Washington)–The tribe received a $75,000 grant to equip and furnish its community library and gift shop.

- Standing Rock Sioux Tribe (North Dakota)–A $40,000 grant will support the tribe's Nutrition for the Elderly program.

- Yanktonai Tribe (South Dakota)–The tribe received a $25,000 matching grant for a storage building to support its buffalo program (based on receiving an equal or greater donation[s]).

- Blackfeet Community College (Montana)–The tribal college received a $200,000 grant for a new health science education building.

- Native American Rights Fund–The nationally recognized nonprofit law firm, which provides legal assistance to Native American tribes, organizations, and individuals, received $200,000 for legal program support.

- Northwest Indian College Foundation–The tribal college, with seven locations in Washington and Idaho, received a $100,000 grant for its capital campaign.

- Thunder Valley Community Development Corp. (South Dakota)–The nonprofit organization received a $100,000 grant for the construction of an apartment building, and an additional $500,000 grant toward the construction for fiscal year 2018. The building is a part of the nonprofit's 34-acre development on the Pine Ridge Reservation.

- Tiwahe Foundation (Minnesota)–The American Indian-led community foundation received a $100,000 grant for its Seventh Generation Endowment Campaign. The Tiwahe Foundation works to renew and build capacity in Native communities.

"The Dakota people have a long-standing tradition of *wo'okiye*, or helpfulness, and one of the ways the SMSC [Shakopee Mdewakanton Sioux Community] honors that tradition is through philanthropy," said SMSC Chairman Charles R. Vig. "We are glad to support other tribes and Native organizations that are taking important steps to improve their communities and the lives of Native Americans across the country." The SMSC is the single-largest philanthropic benefactor for Indian Country nationally, and it has donated approximately $350 million to organizations and causes in the past 25 years.

Throughout history, Indian people have been known for sharing with others. That spirit of giving continues. According to a 2015 report released by the National Indian Gaming Association, which represents 184 of the country's 228 gaming tribes, gaming tribes are committed to providing charitable assistance to both Natives and non-Natives. Tribal governments made more than $100 million in charitable contributions to other tribes, nearby state and local governments, and nonprofit and private organizations. Through these contributions, Indian gaming revenues support thousands of jobs for American health care workers, firefighters, police officers, and many other local officials who provide essential services.

—LIZ HILL

Why is there still poverty on some reservations?

One in four Native Americans and Alaska Natives are living in poverty. In 2015 the US Census Bureau's American Community Survey reported that 26.6 percent of American Indians and Alaska Natives continue to live in poverty—annual incomes remaining below about $38,530. This compares with $55,775 for the nation as a whole.

While gaming has brought a measure of financial well-being to some tribes, it has not provided enough to overcome the effects of more than a century of neglect by the federal government. Gaming has worked well for tribes with reservations and casinos close to large urban centers. The casinos provide jobs and economic opportunity to tribal citizens as well as to many non-Natives. But for small, remote communities, economic gains have been modest, to say the least.

A wide range of social ills continue to plague reservation peoples. In addition to the age-old problems of disease, poor nutrition, and alcohol abuse, illegal drug and gang activity have devastated many Native communities. Suicide is too common, with young boys most at risk. Domestic abuse also is a problem on many reservations.

Years of neglect by, and dependence on, the federal government continue to shape the legacy that Indians on reservations have inherited. The long-standing effects of this history constitute the major reason that poverty and lack of education, among many other social and economic ills, continue to affect Indian people living on reservations. Everyday domestic comforts that average Americans take for granted—such as running water, sewer systems, housing, electricity, heat, food, transportation, and telephone service—are often in woefully short supply on reservations. In many places, individuals hold little hope for a better life. The most immediate effect of reservation poverty is the overall lack of economic opportunity for tribal citizens. Without jobs or financial stability on their reservations, many Indians move away.

The monies made available to tribes from the federal government have accomplished only the bare minimum. Today there is a profound shift away from the idea that US government support alone can solve tribal economic problems. The emphasis is on what the tribes themselves can do. A new sense of self-determination is influencing the way tribes operate their governments and businesses.

Since 1987 the Harvard Project on American Indian Economic Development at Harvard University has been studying social and economic development on Indian reservations and in Alaska Native villages. The project poses the question, "How, amidst well-documented and widespread poverty and social distress, are an increasing number of tribes breaking old patterns and putting together economies, social institutions, and political systems that work?"

Through more than 300 field research reports, the project has been able to observe the systems that work and those that do not work on reservations. In the words of the Harvard Project on American Indian Economic Development, here are the latest research findings:

- **Sovereignty Matters:** When Native Nations make their own decisions about what development approaches to take, they consistently outperform external decision makers on matters as diverse as governmental form, natural resource management, economic development, health care, and social service provision.

- **Institution Matters:** For development to take hold, assertions of sovereignty must be backed by capable institutions of governance. Nations do this as they adopt stable decision rules, establish fair and independent mechanisms for dispute resolution, and separate politics from day-to-day business and program management.

- **Culture Matters:** Successful economies stand on the shoulders of legitimate, culturally grounded institutions of self-government. Indigenous societies are diverse; each nation must equip itself with a governing structure, economic system, policies, and procedures that fit its own contemporary culture.

- **Leadership Matters:** Nation-building requires leaders who introduce new knowledge and experiences, challenge assumptions, and propose change. Such leaders, whether elected, community, or spiritual, convince people that things can be different and inspire them to take action.

—LIZ HILL

WHAT BENEFITS DO INDIANS RECEIVE FROM THE US GOVERNMENT?

Before the government of the United States was formed, Native American tribal peoples governed themselves, held lands in common for their members, and clearly related to one another as sovereign entities. Beginning in the earliest days of the English colonies, government-to-government treaties, court decisions, acts of the US Congress, and presidential actions recorded nearly 200 years of huge American Indian contributions to state and federal landholdings. In return, tribes were offered payments, ever-smaller reservation lands, and a number of government services. Over the decades, the services have varied widely in quantity and quality. Today federally recognized tribes have access to more than 600 government programs, including health care through the Indian Health Service (which has clinics and hospitals on a number of reservations), education grants and programs, and housing assistance.

Tribal members may be eligible for monetary payments from the federal government if, for example, the tribe has settled a land claim with the federal government and a payment is divided among individual tribal members. In some cases, the federal government leases out tribal lands for cattle grazing or other purposes. The Bureau of Indian Affairs then places the monies collected in federal trust accounts, either for individuals or the tribal government, depending upon who, specifically, owns the land. Tribal members also can exercise, often after a struggle against competing interests, the hunting and fishing rights accorded them by federal treaties.

Tribal members are eligible to apply for "Indian preference" that certain federal agencies, such as the Indian Health Service and the Bureau of Indian Affairs, have established for various

Cheyenne, Arapaho, and Sioux Nation leaders meeting with members of the US Indian Peace Commission, 1868. Fort Laramie, Wyoming. Under the provisions of the Treaty of Fort Laramie (1868), in exchange for ceded lands, the tribes were promised a payment issued as annuities to be paid out over thirty years in the form of food, clothing, and other goods and in the form of services to assist in their "civilization." The treaty also guaranteed the Lakota ownership of the Black Hills, and further land and hunting rights in South Dakota, Wyoming, and Montana. A separate agreement with fewer provisions for land and hunting rights was made with the Northern Arapahos and Northern Cheyennes. The US government broke the treaty less than ten years later.

Photo by Alexander Gardner.
National Anthropological Archives, Smithsonian Institution
NAA INV 00514500

federal government jobs. Artists who are members of federally recognized tribes are also allowed by law—the 1990 Indian Arts and Crafts Act—to identify themselves as Indian artists and to advertise their products as Indian made.

Native people also receive assistance from their tribal governments. Today, owing to the success of gaming and other enterprises, members of some tribes are eligible for new and enhanced programs and services. Some—but by no means all—federally recognized tribes that engage in gaming give each of their tribal members an individual payment. College scholarships for academically eligible members, new preschool programs, and senior citizen centers are just a few of the benefits that business development has brought to entire communities.

—LIZ HILL

Do Indians Have to Pay Taxes?

Yes. Indians have to pay federal income taxes, the same as all other American citizens. In the Supreme Court case *Squire v. Capoeman* of 1956, the court stated, "We agree with the Government that Indians are citizens and that in ordinary affairs of life, not governed by treaty or remedial legislation, they are subject to the payment of income taxes as are all other citizens."

Taxation issues regarding Indian tribes have continued to be reexamined in recent years, causing much contention among the federal government, states, and tribes. Because of the ongoing debates, the general public has often been misled into thinking that Indian individuals, rather than tribes, do not pay taxes.

The difference—and confusion—often lies in the status of Indian tribes, which are governments. As such, tribes are not subject to taxation by other state or federal governments, including those of the United States. To cite a misunderstanding from recent years: Indian gaming revenues are considered tribal government revenues and are not taxed, since they are used to provide essential government services.

Two cases in which individual Indians are not taxed by the federal government are notable. In the first instance, no taxes are levied on federal monies that have been used to compensate individual Indians for the taking of their private land, such as treaty land, for government use. In the second instance, the income from trust land, the legal title to which is held by the United States, is not taxed. With regard to state taxes, Indians living on reservations do not pay state income taxes on the income they earn while working on their reservations. Indians also do not pay state sales taxes for goods or services purchased on their reservations, but those who live off the reservation do pay both kinds of state taxes. Because tribes are governments, however, they have the right to tax their members—and non-Indians—living on their reservations.

—LIZ HILL

An advertisement for Indian land that has been made available to white settlers, 1879.

MPI/Archive Photos/Getty Images

Do Indians have to follow state hunting and fishing regulations?

Not necessarily. In the United States, Indian peoples have the right to hunt and fish their traditional lands—even if those lands are not within the current boundaries of a tribal reservation—to provide food and the other basic necessities of life for themselves and their families. Early in its history the US government signed treaties with many tribes that included the continuance of these rights in perpetuity.

Because Indian tribes hold the right to self-government, they also have the right to regulate the hunting and fishing activities of their citizens. It is because tribes are governments that state hunting and fishing laws do not apply to Indian people who hunt and fish on their traditional lands.

With the increase of non-Indian commercial and sport hunting and fishing, however, have come inevitable conflicts. Some of the clashes have led to lengthy litigation and even violence. According to Stephen L. Pevar in his book *The Rights of Indians and Tribes: The Basic ACLU Guide to Indian and Tribal Rights* (1992), "Few areas of Indian law have created more conflict than Indian hunting, fishing, and gathering rights."

He continues:

> The right to hunt and fish was expressly guaranteed to many tribes in their treaties with the United States. However, this right is presumed to exist even if the treaty does not mention it. As the Supreme Court explained in 1905, a treaty is not a grant of rights to the Indians, but a taking of rights from them. Consequently, if a treaty is silent on the subject of Indian hunting and fishing rights,

Movie star Marlon Brando supports a Native fish-in demonstration at the Nisqually and Puyallup rivers, south of Tacoma, Washington, March 2, 1964.

MOHAI, *Seattle Post-Intelligencer* Photograph Collection, 1986.5.4414.1

then these rights are not limited by the treaty and still exist in full force.

In the twentieth and twenty-first centuries, state laws that regulate hunting and fishing have often clashed with Indian hunting and fishing rights, especially when Indian people's traditional hunting and fishing grounds are off their reservation lands. In recent decades several notable cases have challenged Indian rights to subsistence hunting and fishing. One well-known example concerns several Washington State tribes.

In Washington the state fishing law dictated in 1963 that all Indians needed to fish with hooks and line rather than their traditional nets. The ruling completely disregarded the treaties that had been established with the tribes in the mid-1800s. In 1964 the conflict became violent in an incident in which the police brutalized Indian people who had gathered to fish at Frank's Landing on the Puyallup River, south of Tacoma. By 1973 the federal government, which represented fourteen of the tribes, sued the state of Washington. The court decision, which became known as the Boldt Decision, came down in favor of the tribes and upheld their original treaty rights. In 1979 the Supreme Court agreed, supporting Boldt's original ruling.

—LIZ HILL

DO MUSEUMS HAVE TO GIVE BACK EVERYTHING IN THEIR COLLECTIONS THAT WAS TAKEN FROM TRIBES WITHOUT PERMISSION?

Museums and American Indian tribes have had a difficult and complicated history. Many tribes face the agonizing reality that some of their ancestors' remains, as well as the sacred objects buried with them, were taken without permission and eventually made their way into museum collections. In addition to items taken from burial sites, countless other objects of cultural importance—some considered sacred and strictly ceremonial—were excavated, stolen, traded, and occasionally purchased outright. The 800,000-object collection at the Smithsonian's National Museum of the American Indian (NMAI), in fact, is the result of the obsession of German American banker George Gustav Heye (1874–1957), who sent collectors on expeditions to Indigenous communities in Canada, Peru, Patagonia, Chile, Alaska, and throughout the continental United States. In 1924 alone, he amassed more than 22,000 objects. Although Heye was greatly concerned about the diversity and authenticity of his collection, he cared far less about how objects were acquired.

Nearly a century after he bought the first item in his vast collection (a hide shirt), Heye's entire legacy was transferred to the newly established National Museum of the American Indian. The NMAI Act of 1989 (Public Law 101–185), which created the museum and its policies, included specific requirements for all Smithsonian museums regarding the repatriation, or return, of American Indian, Alaska Native, and Native Hawaiian human remains and objects in their collections. The law not only allowed individual descendants, American Indian tribes, Alaska Native

Georgianna and Joe Hotch (Tlingit) at a ceremony honoring the repatriation of a Bear Clan hat, NMAI's George Gustav Heye Center, New York City, 1999.

clans or villages, and Native Hawaiian organizations to rightfully claim their human remains and cultural items, but it also required each museum to work proactively with tribes to inventory, identify, and return these sacred cultural objects. Heralding a new era in museum-tribal relations, Congress a year later signed another bill into law—known as NAGPRA (Native American Graves Protection and Repatriation Act)—which empowered tribes to claim their human remains and cultural items from federal collections and non-Smithsonian museums. Museum, archaeological, American Indian, historical, and religious organizations across the country immediately stepped forward to support what they considered a long-overdue mandate on behalf of Native people and communities.

Proving a direct connection to a given item, however, requires a great deal of research and documentation; the process of repatriation, therefore, is long and complex for both museums and tribes. Museums are not under orders to return all American Indian objects in their collections, but they must inventory portions of their holdings and make those findings available to tribal representatives who request them. When a tribe can prove the ownership and cultural significance of an object, museums are required to repatriate it. Although the NMAI is active in its repatriation efforts, its collections will not be depleted, for most of its objects are not eligible for repatriation. Within the NMAI collection, approximately 25,000 of the museum's 800,000 objects fall

The Saxman, or Cape Fox, Tlingit community of Ketchikan, Alaska, have honored the story of Kaats the Bear Hunter—a traditional figure in the Bear Clan of the Saxman Tlingit people—by carving totem poles with his image and placing them outside their homes. In the early 1900s, one such Bear Clan totem pole was taken without permission. The 40-foot totem eventually made its way to George Gustav Heye's collection in New York City and became part of the National Museum of the American Indian's collection.

The Cape Fox community never forgot about its lost Bear Clan totem, however, and they approached the museum in the late 1990s to request the return of the pole. After extensive joint research by the NMAI staff and the community, the museum repatriated the pole in 2001. To express their gratitude, the Cape Fox Native Corporation presented a 20-foot cedar log to the NMAI. The museum then asked Tlingit carver Nathan Jackson and his family to use the log to create a new totem. Jackson again featured the traditional stories of Kaats. Using Tlingit carving techniques and colors, the Jackson family created in 2004 a new totem for the NMAI. As one of the museum's large "landmark objects," the totem pole serves as a gathering point for visitors.

To see the Kaats totem pole, go to page 15.

within the four categories of items—human remains, funerary objects, sacred objects, and objects of cultural patrimony—identified for repatriation by the NMAI Act and its 1996 amendment, which further defined the categories.

In most cases museum and tribal representatives work very closely throughout the process. For example, tribal delegations often visit the NMAI's Cultural Resources Center in Maryland, where they can view their tribe's material collections and begin discussions with the museum's Oµce of Repatriation. Since 1989 the NMAI has returned approximately 2,000 items to more than a 100 Native communities throughout the Western Hemisphere.

Once an object is repatriated, tribes can display it in their museums, if it is the type of item that can or should be kept in a public collection. Some items should not be viewed publicly at all, or handled by anyone other than religious leaders. Age and poor condition require special care of some items, so once they are returned to the community, fragile pieces are moved, used, or worn only during ceremonies or special occasions. When cultural and sacred items are returned by museums, it is a cause for celebration and, sometimes, solemn ceremony—honoring and welcoming the objects back to their rightful home.

—TANYA THRASHER

SCIENCE, TECHNOLOGY, AND SOCIETY

WHAT WERE SOME OF THE ACCOMPLISHMENTS OF NATIVE AMERICANS AT THE TIME EUROPEANS FIRST ARRIVED IN THE WESTERN HEMISPHERE?

The first European explorers in the Western Hemisphere, including Christopher Columbus, remarked on the ingenuity of the Indigenous population, claiming at times that its accomplishments surpassed those found in the Old World. But unable to find weapons, metal tools, or Christianity on the continent they had "discovered," Europeans for the most part characterized Native people as ignorant and heathenish.

Most history textbooks begin at 1492, ignoring the significant accomplishments of pre-Contact Native Americans. With specialized tradesmen and artisans as well as populous cities and economic stratification, European society may have seemed more advanced than the villages and even the cities of the Western Hemisphere. But filth and disease pervaded Renaissance Europe. Wars for land, wealth, and power destabilized European political and daily life, and religious intolerance led to injustice and brutality.

Native societies may have lacked metal tools and weapons, domesticated animals, or large-scale agriculture in the 1500s, but they were highly resourceful and adaptable to the varied environments of the Western Hemisphere. As for agriculture, many staple foods grown today, including corn, potatoes, tomatoes, squashes, peanuts, and chilies, were first cultivated by Native people and carried to Europe, Africa, and Asia by Europeans. Although Europeans created the process for making the sweet chocolate we eat today, the Maya and the Aztec were grinding

An Inka Road with sidewalls cuts through an agricultural valley. Colca Canyon, Peru, 2014. The Qhapaq Ñan was a 24,000-mile road system that connected all regions of the vast Inka Empire at the height of its power in the fifteenth century.

cacao beans to create a sugarless beverage long before the arrival of Columbus. It was some of these nutritious food exports from the Americas that provided a boost to Europe's population, which had never fully recuperated from the human devastation of the Black Death in the 1300s.

The domestication of animals in Southwest Asia ten thousand years ago introduced many diseases to the human population. In the crowded, unhygienic urban centers of Europe, diseases spread quickly. In contrast, the Western Hemisphere had few infectious diseases.

Communities in the American Southwest made soap and shampoo out of yucca. The Shoshone sterilized their surgical spaces hundreds of years before Western doctors recognized the spread of germs as a source of infection during surgery. More than fifty present-day prescription drugs have been developed by studying the ways in which plant extracts were used in traditional Native medicine. Most of the plants from which these medicines are derived are native to the Amazonian rain forest, an area where contemporary Indigenous peoples are facing the encroachment of pharmaceutical companies, pressures from local and foreign governments, and sometimes murder by loggers and miners.

Pre-Contact Native societies were also responsible for extensive road networks, such as those found in the Andes and southwestern North America as well as for architectural feats such as the Mississippian mounds and the Mesoamerican pyramids. The Olmec people of Mesoamerica invented rubber, an entrancing innovation to the *conquistadores*. One of the most important systems of government in the world today was developed by the Haudenosaunee (Iroquois). The Great Law of Peace, which may have appeared as early as AD 1142, described a democratic system in which the leader's political power is balanced by the rights of the individual.

While the moment of first contact between the Eastern and Western Hemispheres is usually told as the story of Columbus's "discovery" of the Americas, its far-reaching effects have made it probably the single most important event in history. In myriad ways, it changed the fabric of global life.

—ARWEN NUTTALL

DID INDIANS HAVE MATHEMATICS BEFORE CONTACT WITH EUROPEANS?

Yes. Native people used number systems long before contact with Europeans. American Indians developed decimal systems, as well as sequences based on the numbers five, ten, and twenty. Many Native languages also had words for the numbers one through ten. Inuit people of the subarctic regions, for example, counted to 100 using their hands and feet. Two hands equals ten; the addition of one foot equals fifteen; the other foot brings the total to twenty. Twenty represents one person; one person plus five fingers equals twenty-five; and so on. Five people equal 100, which also represents one bundle, such as a bundle of sticks or animal skins.

The Maya of Mesoamerica are said to have developed the most sophisticated mathematical principles and applications of all the Indigenous people of the Western Hemisphere. Numbers up to nineteen were written in combinations of bars, each of which had a value of five, and dots, each representing a value of one. "Head variant numerals," or portraits of the heads of Maya gods shown in profile, represented the number of each head's facial features or attributes. The Maya had three words for "twenty": *kal*, *may*, and *uinic*, the last of which was also the term for "human being." Multiples of twenty followed a regular sequence up to 380, after which came "one 400."

The Maya ceremonial calendar of 260 days is called the *tzolkin*, the Sequence of Days, the Sacred Almanac, or the Sacred Round. This calendar consists of a cycle of thirteen day numbers and a cycle of twenty day names. The day names are represented by glyphs. They also have a calendar of 365 days, which is referred to as the Vague Year because it does not preserve a precise alignment with the seasons over long periods. The Vague Year

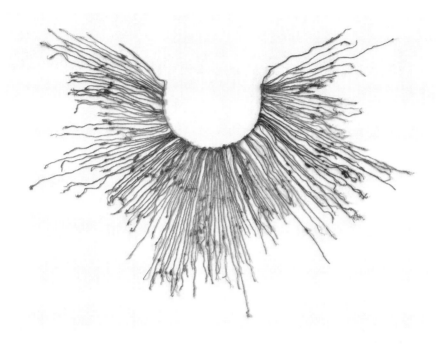

Inka *khipu*, a device used for recording statistics, AD 1400–1600. Nazca region, Peru.

17/8825

is made up of eighteen name months of twenty days each, with a residual period of five days. The Maya use both of these calendars to generate what is called the Calendar Round, which consists of 18,980 Calendar Round dates.

The Inka of the Andean regions kept statistics about crops, llamas, weapons, births, and deaths. These figures were recorded using *khipu*—knotted strings of different colors and lengths. The record keepers responsible for these tallies were called *khipucamayucs*, or rememberers. Each rememberer designed his own khipu, and the rememberers would get together to explain how their khipu were coded, so that the knotted strings could be interpreted by others. Khipu were not used for computation, but rather to record totals that had been obtained by using piles of grains, pebbles, or an abacus-like counting tray. The Inka used the decimal system; both the Inka and the Maya understood the abstract concept of zero.

In North America the Pomo of the West Coast used stick counting and tying knots in string. The number of days it took to complete a journey was recorded by tying knots on a string. One knot represented one day, so the strings were called day counts. The stick system could be applied to compile records of large quantities and could involve the use of two different-sized sticks. Most tribes used the principles of addition and multiplication, but only some used subtraction and division.

—MARY AHENAKEW

How did foods native to the Americas influence global cuisines?

Foods indigenous to the Americas changed what people cooked around the world and affected global economies in ways that are still felt today. The first contact between Native peoples and Christopher Columbus in 1492 began what is called the Columbian Exchange: the exchange of plants, animals, ideas, diseases, peoples, and goods between the Americas and the rest of the world. The introduction of foods from the Western Hemisphere such as cassava, maize (corn), potatoes, and sweet potatoes to Europe, Africa, and Asia resulted in a marked improvement in nutritional health throughout the Eastern Hemisphere and essentially brought an entirely new supply of calorically and nutritionally rich staples to the Old World. Additional crops, including tomatoes, cacao, and chili peppers, added both flavor and vitamins. Many of these new foods transformed local and national cuisines, changing the essential ingredients that define them. Can you imagine Italian food without tomatoes? Hungarian food without paprika? Or Thai, Sichuan, and Indian food without the heat of chili peppers? Five hundred years ago, these foods were known only to people in the Americas.

Indigenous American peoples influenced each other's cuisines through trade. Chocolate, for example, is arguably one of the world's favorite foods. Cacao trees from Central and South America (the seeds of which are processed into chocolate) made their way via trade to the Olmec in Mesoamerica, where they were domesticated more than two thousand years ago. Cacao thrived in Mexico and Central America, where it was a drink of status for the Aztecs, who also used the beans as currency. Evidence of the extensive cacao trade was found as far north as Chaco Canyon in New Mexico. Cacao remains a fundamental

Juanita Velasco (Ixil Maya) grinds cacao beans into chocolate during the 2011 Power of Chocolate Festival.

element of tradition—especially that of Día de los Muertos (Day of the Dead)—and diet throughout Mexico and Central America. Cacao was introduced to Europe after Columbus brought a pod back to Spain after his second voyage. Reserved primarily for use by aristocrats in the 1500s, cacao eventually spread from Spain to Italy and then France before the rest of the world embraced the "food of the gods." Today West African countries produce most of the world's cacao.

Other foods of the Americas arrived in Europe in the late fifteenth and early sixteenth centuries. After Europeans mistook them as poisonous, tomatoes enjoyed widespread cultivation throughout Spain, Italy, and France. Today Greece is the world's largest consumer of this originally South American fruit (surprisingly, Italy is sixth). Capsicums, or chili peppers, spread into Asia, influencing some of the world's hottest culinary legacies in India, Thailand, and China; Koreans incorporated chilies into their fermented staple, kimchi. While the Irish may be known for potatoes—and the tragic Potato Famine of 1845–49—the tubers originated in South America and were domesticated by pre-Inka cultures in the Andes at least 7,000 years ago. These cultures cultivated thousands of varieties of potatoes. After European contact, potatoes spread to Europe, where they were adopted by many countries as a staple food. In a study by researchers Nathan Nunn and Nancy Qian, it was found that the Old World countries that adopted the potato had a significant 12 percent increase in population growth over countries that did not adopt the vegetable. According to a 2010 study by the Food and Agriculture Organization of the United Nations, the top-consuming countries for various New World foods (maize, cassava, sweet potatoes, potatoes, tomatoes, and pineapples) are now almost entirely outside the Americas, namely in Europe, Africa, and Asia.

One food that originated in the Andes and has recently gained widespread popularity is quinoa. An Andean plant from the area surrounding Lake Titicaca in Peru and Bolivia, quinoa was domesticated between 5,000 and 7,000 years ago and remains an important food for the Quechua and Aymara peoples, descendants of the original cultivators. In the Quechua language, quinoa is called *chisiya*, meaning "mother grain." The seed is one of the only plants that contains a complete protein, providing all the essential amino acids. The United Nations declared 2013 as the "International Year of Quinoa" and this super-nutritious food has now been embraced the world over. While the growing popularity of quinoa has put pressure on small farmers in the Andes to produce enough to meet demand, it has also boosted their business. Today they face threats from larger farmers who can maximize production but who use monoculture farming that harms the environment. Quinoa's ability to thrive in harsh environments makes it a Native food with the potential to play a critical role in an agricultural future that must adapt to climate change.

—ALEXANDRA HARRIS

WHO REALLY BUILT THE MOUNDS?

Mounds, or man-made earthworks, hundreds of feet in length and height can be found throughout what is now the eastern, midwestern, and southern United States, from Minnesota to Florida and New England to Louisiana. Upon first encountering the mounds in the 1700s and 1800s, Europeans variously attributed the feat of building them to early Spanish explorers; an ancient, vanished civilization; the lost tribes of Israel; Vikings; and the survivors of the lost city of Atlantis. Noting similarities to stone edifices in Mesoamerica, late nineteenth-century scientists speculated that the Maya and the Aztec civilizations had extended farther north than previously supposed. Seeing no contemporaneous signs of a populous, specialized society that could have supported such an endeavor, explorers and archaeologists discounted any notion that American Indians had constructed the mounds.

In the twentieth century it became clear to archaeologists that the ancestors of the region's Indigenous peoples had indeed constructed the mounds without help from abroad. Between about AD 700 and 1700 the Natchez people of the lower Mississippi Valley built enormous and numerous flat-topped mounds, constructing houses and temples on the broad plateaus. The nation's leader, called the Great Sun, lived on the largest mound, orchestrating the orderly conduct of daily life. The mounds were also used as burial chambers. Elaborate ceremonies and cultural disciplines were formulated and followed, both in building the mounds and burying the dead.

The logistics required to accomplish these feats of construction are staggering. Monk's Mound, for example, covering sixteen acres in southwestern Illinois, is the largest pre-Columbian earth-

Aerial view of the Great Serpent Mound, ca. 1935. Adams County, Ohio.

Photo by Major Dache M. Reeves. P13211

work in North America. Larger at its base than the Great Pyramid at Giza, the mound still astonishes archaeologists with its sheer size.

In the nineteenth century, with most Indigenous nations forced to move west of the Mississippi, Europeans, intent on possessing the fertile lands, used or moved the mound soil to make way for farming. In the process, they destroyed many mounds. Some farmed on the broad surface of mounds, their plows uprooting human remains and burial goods. With such discoveries, looting proliferated, and many of the burial objects (including human bones) found their way into private and institutional collections.

The most renowned mound sites today are Cahokia, including Monk's Mound in Illinois, and Serpent Mound in the Ohio Valley. State and federal officials have passed laws to prevent looting, and in several states mounds are tourist attractions that draw thousands of visitors each year. Continued preservation of the mounds is an open question, owing to the cost of maintaining them. In addition, wind, snow, and rain have had a constant effect, causing erosion over time.

Indigenous nations with different languages, social conventions, and forms of leadership had a remarkably similar need to construct these monuments. Their systems and techniques remain the subjects of speculation. Questions about population, group discipline, work assignment, time of construction, methods for moving soil, workforce, and the ability to sustain interest and health over time remain unanswered. In the end, the mounds are an enduring testament to the skills, knowledge, social developments, religious and spiritual beliefs, discipline, and order of Native societies before Europeans arrived in North America.

—RICO NEWMAN

NATIVE KNOWLEDGE 360°
A NATIONAL EDUCATION INITIATIVE

The National Museum of the American Indian (NMAI) is joining with Native communities and educators nationally to help change the way American Indian histories, cultures, and contemporary lives are taught in K-12 classrooms. Known as NK360°, this experiential online project provides educational materials and teacher training and widens the lens through which to view new perspectives on the rich history and cultures of the Americas.

NK360° challenges common assumptions about Native peoples—their cultures, their roles in United States and world history, and their contributions to the arts, sciences, and literature. NK360° offers a comprehensive, accurate, and engaging connection to Native narratives of the past as well as to the vibrant peoples and cultures of today. Building on the ten themes of the National Council of Social Studies' national curriculum standards, the NK360° experience reveals key concepts, or Essential Understandings, that reflect untold stories and about American Indians that deepen and expand the teaching of history, geography, civics, economics, science, engineering, and other subject areas.

The NMAI acknowledges the support of the Montana and South Dakota Offices of Indian Education, as they first established Essential Understandings for their respective states and have partnered with NMAI to help guide this national framework. Visit the NK360° website at www.AmericanIndian.si.edu/nk360 to explore its latest offerings, classroom resources, and professional development activities.

FURTHER READING

Adovasio, J. M., with Jake Page. *The First Americans: In Pursuit of Archaeology's Greatest Mystery*. New York: Random House, 2002.

Anderson, Kat. *Tending the Wild: Native American Knowledge and the Management of California's Natural Resources*. Berkeley: University of California Press, 2005.

Archuleta, Margaret L., Brenda J. Child, and K. Tsianina Lomawaima, eds. *Away from Home: American Indian Boarding School Experiences, 1879–2000*. Phoenix: Heard Museum, 2000.

Banner, Stuart. *How the Indians Lost Their Land*. Cambridge, Mass.: Harvard University Press, 2005.

Belarde-Lewis, Miranda. *Meet Lydia: A Native Girl from Southeast Alaska*. Washington, D.C.: National Museum of the American Indian in association with Council Oak Books, 2004.

Berkhofer, Robert F., Jr. "White Conceptions of Indians." In *History of Indian-White Relations*, edited by Wilcomb E. Washburn. Vol. 4, *Handbook of North American Indians*, edited by William C. Sturtevant. Washington, D.C.: Smithsonian Institution, 1988.

Berlo, Janet Catherine. "Drawing (Upon) the Past: Negotiating Identities in Inuit Graphic Arts Production." In *Unpacking Culture: Art and Commodity in the Colonial and Postcolonial Worlds*, edited by Ruth B. Phillips and Christopher B. Steiner, pp. 178–196. Berkeley: University of California Press, 1999.

Blackburn, Thomas C., and Kat Anderson. *Before the Wilderness: Environmental Management by Native Californians*. Menlo Park, Calif.: Ballena Press, 1993.

Blanchard, Kendall. "Traditional Sports, North and South America." In *Encyclopedia of World Sport: From Ancient Times to the Present*, edited by David Levinson and Karen Christenson. Vol. 3. Santa Barbara: ABC-CLIO, 1996.

Bonar, Eulalie. *Woven by the Grandmothers: Nineteenth-Century Navajo Textiles from the National Museum of the American Indian*. Washington, D.C.: National Museum of the American Indian in association with Smithsonian Institution Press, 1996.

Brooks, James F. *Captives and Cousins: Slavery, Kinship, and Community in the Southwest Borderlands*. Chapel Hill, N.C.: University of North Carolina Press, 2002.

Browning, Tara. *Heartbeat of the People: Music and Dance of the Northern Pow-Wow*. Urbana: University of Illinois Press, 2004.

Bruchac, James, and Joseph Bruchac. *Native American Games and Stories*. Golden, Colo.: Fulcrum Publishing, 2000.

Champagne, Duane. *Contemporary Native American Cultural Issues*. Walnut Creek, Calif.: AltaMira Press, 1999.

Closs, Michael P. *Native American Mathematics*. Austin: University of Texas Press, 1989.

Cobb, Amanda J. "This Is What It Means to Say *Smoke Signals*: Native American Cultural Sovereignty." In *Hollywood's Indian: The Portrayal of the Native American in Film*, edited by Peter C. Rollins and John E. O'Connor. Lexington: University Press of Kentucky, 1998.

Code of Federal Regulations. Title 25, Indians. Chapter 1, Bureau of Indian Affairs, Department of the Interior. Part 83, Procedures for establishing that an American Indian group exists as a tribe. Subpart 7, Mandatory criteria for federal acknowledgment. Washington, D.C.: National Archives and Records Administration, Oµce of the Federal Registrar, and Government Printing Oµce, April 1, 2006.

Coe, Sophie D., and Michael D. Coe. *The True History of Chocolate*, 2nd ed. London: Thames & Hudson, 2007.

Cook, Noble David. *Born to Die: Disease and New World Conquest, 1492–1650*. New York: Cambridge University Press, 1998.

Davis, Jeffrey E. *Hand Talk: Sign Language among American Indian Nations*. Cambridge: Cambridge University Press, 2010.

Davis, Mary B., ed. *Native America in the Twentieth Century: An Encyclopedia*. New York: Garland Publishing, 1996.

Dejong, David H. *Promises of the Past: A History of Indian Education in the United States*. Golden, Colo.: North American Press, 1993.

Deloria, Vine, Jr., ed. *American Indian Policy in the Twentieth Century*. Norman: University of Oklahoma Press, 1985.

———. *Custer Died for Your Sins: An Indian Manifesto*. Norman: University of Oklahoma Press, 1970.

———. *God Is Red: A Native View of Religion*, 3rd ed. Golden, Colo.: Fulcrum Publishing, 2003.

———. *Red Earth, White Lies: Native Americans and the Myth of Scientific Fact*. New York: Scribner, 1995.

Deloria, Vine, Jr., and David E. Wilkins. *Tribes, Treaties, and Constitutional Tribulations*. Austin: University of Texas Press, 1999.

DeMallie, Raymond J., ed. *Plains*. Vol. 13, pts. 1 and 2, *Handbook of North American Indians*, edited by William C. Sturtevant. Washington, D.C.: Smithsonian Institution, 2001.

Densmore, Frances. *Chippewa Customs*. 1929. Reprint, St. Paul: Minnesota Historical Society Press, 1979.

Derounian-Stodola, Kathryn Zabelle, ed. *Women's Indian Captivity Narratives*. New York: Penguin Books, 1998.

Diamond, Jared. *Guns, Germs, and Steel: The Fates of Human Societies*. New York: W. W. Norton, 1999.

Divina, Fernando, and Marlene Divina. *Foods of the Americas*. Washington, D.C.: National Museum of the American Indian in association with Ten Speed Press, 2004.

Drinnon, Richard. *Facing West: The Metaphysics of Indian Hating and Empire Building*. Norman: University of Oklahoma Press, 1997.

Driskill, Qwo-Li, Chris Finley, Brian Joseph Gilley, and Scott Lauria Morgensen. *Queer*

Indigenous Studies: Critical Interventions in Theory, Politics, and Literature. Tucson: University of Arizona Press, 2011.

Dubin, Lois Sherr. *A History of Beads: 30,000 B.C. to the Present.* New York: H. N. Abrams, 1987.

Einhorn, Lois J. *The Native American Oral Tradition: Voices of the Spirit and Soul.* Westport, Conn.: Praeger Publishers, 2000.

Erdoes, Richard. *The Rain Dance People: The Pueblo Indians, Their Past and Present.* New York: Knopf, 1976.

Fleming, Walter C. *The Complete Idiot's Guide to Native American History.* New York: Alpha, 2003.

Food and Agriculture Organization of the United Nations. "2013 International Year of Quinoa." Accessed November 15, 2017. http://www.fao.org/quinoa-2013/en/

Frey, Rodney. *The World of the Crow Indians.* Norman: University of Oklahoma Press, 1989.

Gallay, Alan. *The Indian Slave Trade: The Rise of the English Empire in the American South, 1670–1717.* New Haven, Conn.: Yale University Press, 2002.

Ganteaume, Cécile. *Officially Indian: Symbols That Define the United States.* Washington, D.C.: National Museum of the American Indian, 2017.

Garroutte, Eva Marie. *Real Indians: Identity and the Survival of Native America.* Berkeley: University of California Press, 2003.

Goddard, Ives. "Introduction." In *Languages,* edited by Ives Goddard. Vol. 17, *Handbook of North American Indians,* edited by William C. Sturtevant. Washington, D.C.: Smithsonian Institution, 1997.

Gourse, Leslie. *Native American Courtship and Marriage Traditions.* New York: Hippocrene Books, 1995.

Green, Rayna D. "The Indian in Popular American Culture." In *History of Indian-White Relations,* edited by Wilcomb E. Washburn. Vol. 4, *Handbook of North American Indians,* edited by William C. Sturtevant. Washington, D.C.: Smithsonian Institution, 1988.

Hämäläinen, Pekka. *Comanche Empire.* New Haven, Conn.: Yale University Press, 2009.

Harjo, Suzan Shown. *Nation to Nation: Treaties Between the United States and American Indian Nations.* Washington, D.C.: National Museum of the American Indian, 2014.

———. "Note to Congress: Stop Shielding 'Indian' Mascots and Start Defending Indian People." *Indian Country Today,* June 9, 2006. https://indiancountrymedianetwork.com/news/note-to-congress-stop-shielding-indian-mascots-and-start-defending-indian-people/

Harkin, Michael E., and David Rich Lewis, eds. *Native Americans and the Environment: Perspectives on the Ecological Indian.* Lincoln: University of Nebraska Press, 2007.

Harvard Project on American Indian Economic Development. *Honoring Nations 2003: Celebrating Excellence in Tribal Government.* Cambridge, Mass.: Harvard Project on American Indian Economic Development, Harvard University, 2004.

Heth, Charlotte, ed. *Native American Dance: Ceremonies and Social Traditions.* Washington, D.C.: National Museum of the American Indian in association with Fulcrum Publishing, 1992.

Hill, Tom, and Richard W. Hill, Sr., eds. *Creation's Journey: Native American Identity and Belief*. Washington, D.C.: National Museum of the American Indian in association with Smithsonian Institution Press, 1994.

Hirschfelder, Arlene, and Paulette Molin. *The Encyclopedia of Native American Religions: An Introduction*. New York: Facts on File, 1992.

Hodge, Frederick Webb. *Handbook of American Indians North of Mexico*. 2 vols. New York: Pageant Books, 1959.

Horse Capture, George P. *Powwow*. Cody, Wyo.: Buffalo Bill Historical Center, 1989.

Horse Capture, George P., and Emil Her Many Horses, eds. *A Song for the Horse Nation: Horses in Native American Cultures*. Washington, D.C.: National Museum of the American Indian in association with Fulcrum Publishing, 2006.

Hoxie, Frederick E., ed. *Encyclopedia of North American Indians: Native American History, Culture, and Life from Paleo-Indians to the Present*. Boston: Houghton Miðin, 1996.

Hunt, H. F. "Slavery among the Indians of Northwest America." *The Washington Historical Quarterly* 9 (Oct. 1918): 277–83.

Jargstorf, Sibylle. *Baubles, Buttons, and Beads: The Heritage of Bohemia*. Atglen, Pa.: Schiffer, 1993.

Jensen, V. *Totem Pole Carving: Bringing a Log to Life*. Vancouver: Douglas & McIntyre, 2004.

Johansen, Bruce E., and Donald A. Grinde, Jr. *The Encyclopedia of Native American Biography: Six Hundred Life Stories of Important People, from Powhatan to Wilma Mankiller*. New York: Da Capo Press, 1998.

Johnson, Tim, ed. *Spirit Capture: Photographs from the National Museum of the American Indian*. Washington, D.C.: National Museum of the American Indian and Smithsonian Institution Press, 1998.

Johnston, Basil. *The Manitous: The Spiritual World of the Ojibway*. New York: Harper-Collins, 1995.

Josephy, Alvin M., Jr. *Five Hundred Nations: An Illustrated History of North American Indians*. New York: Gramercy Books, 1994.

———. *The Indian Heritage of America*. New York: Houghton Miðin. 1968. Reprint, 1991.

Kavasch, Barrie. *Native Harvests: Recipes and Botanicals of the American Indian*. New York: Vintage Books, 1979.

Keoke, Emory Dean, and Kay Marie Porterfield, eds. *Encyclopedia of American Indian Contributions to the World*. New York: Facts on File, 2002.

Kidwell, Clara Sue. "Food and Cuisine." In *Encyclopedia of North American Indians: Native American History, Culture, and Life from Paleo-Indians to the Present*, edited by Frederick E. Hoxie. Boston: Houghton Miðin, 1996.

Kilpatrick, Jacquelyn. *Celluloid Indians: Native Americans and Film*. Lincoln: University of Nebraska Press, 1999.

Krech, Shepard, III. *The Ecological Indian: Myth and History*. New York: W. W. Norton, 1999.

Lang, Sabine. *Men as Women, Women as Men: Changing Gender in Native American Cultures.* Austin: University of Texas, 1998.

Lincoln, Kenneth. *Indi'n Humor: Bicultural Play in Native America.* New York: Oxford University Press, 1993.

Liu, Robert K. *Collectible Beads: A Universal Aesthetic.* Vista, Calif.: Ornament, Inc., 1995.

Loadman, John. *Tears of the Tree: The Story of Rubber—A Modern Marvel.* New York: Oxford University Press, 2005.

Lyman, Christopher M. *The Vanishing Race and Other Illusions: Photographs of Indians by Edward S. Curtis.* Washington D.C.: Smithsonian Institution Press, 1982.

Machamer, Gene. *The Illustrated Native American Profiles.* Mechanicsburg, Pa.: Carlisle Press, 1996.

Mann, Charles C. *1491: New Revelations of the Americas before Columbus.* New York: Knopf, 2005.

Markstrom, Carol A. *Empowerment of North American Indian Girls: Ritual Expressions at Puberty.* Lincoln: University of Nebraska Press, 2008.

Marshall, Ann. *Rain: Native Expressions from the American Southwest.* Albuquerque: University of New Mexico Press, 2000.

McLuhan, T. C. *Dream Tracks: The Railroad and the American Indian, 1890–1930.* New York: Harry N. Abrams, 1985.

McMaster, Gerald, and Clifford E. Trafzer, eds. *Native Universe: Voices of Indian America.* Washington, D.C.: National Museum of the American Indian in association with National Geographic Books, 2004.

Medicine, Beatrice. "Gender." In *Native America in the Twentieth Century: An Encyclopedia,* edited by Mary B. Davis. New York: Garland Publishing, 1996.

Meyer, Carter Jones, and Diana Royer, eds. *Selling the Indian: Commercializing and Appropriating American Indian Cultures.* Tucson: University of Arizona Press, 2001.

Mihesuah, Devon A. *American Indians: Stereotypes and Realities.* Atlanta: Clarity Press, 1997.

———. *Cultivating the Rosebuds: The Education of Women at the Cherokee Female Seminary, 1851–1909.* Urbana: University of Illinois Press, 1993.

Miles, Tiya. *Ties That Bind: The Story of an Afro-Cherokee Family in Slavery and Freedom.* Berkeley: University of California Press, 2005.

Mithlo, Nancy. "No Word for Art in Our Language? Old Questions, New Paradigms." *Wicazo Sa Review* 27, no. 1 (Spring 2012): 111–26.

Moerman, Daniel E. *Native American Ethnobotany.* Portland, Oreg.: Timber Press, 1998.

Moorehead, W. K., and J. E. Kelly. *Cahokia Mounds.* Tuscaloosa: University of Alabama Press, 2000.

Mulroy, Kevin. *Freedom on the Border: The Seminole Maroons in Florida, the Indian Territory, Coahuila, and Texas.* Lubbock: Texas Tech University Press, 1993.

———. *The Seminole Freedmen: A History (Race and Culture in the American West Series).* Norman: University of Oklahoma Press, 2007.

Nabokov, Peter, and Robert Easton. *Native American Architecture.* New York: Oxford University Press, 1989.

——. "Indians, Slaves, and Mass Murder: The Hidden History." *The New York Review of Books,* November 24, 2016. http://www.nybooks.com/articles/2016/11/24/indians-slaves-and-mass-murder-the-hidden-history/

——. *Native American Testimony.* New York: Penguin, 1999.

——. *Where the Lightning Strikes: The Lives of American Indian Sacred Places.* New York: Viking, 2006.

National Museum of the American Indian. *Listening to Our Ancestors: Native Life along the North Pacific Coast.* Washington, D.C.: National Museum of the American Indian in association with National Geographic Books, 2005.

Niethammer, Carolyn. *Daughters of the Earth: The Lives and Legends of American Indian Women.* New York: Simon & Schuster, 1977.

Nunn, Nathan, and Nancy Qian. "The Columbian Exchange: A History of Disease, Food, and Ideas." *Journal of Economic Perspectives* 24, no. 2 (2010): 163–88.

Oaklander, Mandy. "Quinoa: Should You Eat It?" *TIME,* October 15, 2015. Accessed November 15, 2017. http://time.com/4052489/quinoa-health-benefits-nutrition/

Ohén:ton Kariwahtékwen/Thanksgiving Address: Greetings to the Natural World. Corrales, N.M.: Six Nations Indian Museum and Tracking Project, 1993.

Page, Jake. *In the Hands of the Great Spirit: The 20,000-Year History of American Indians.* New York: Free Press, 2003.

Paterek, Josephine. *The Encyclopedia of American Indian Costume.* New York: W. W. Norton, 1994.

Perdue, Theda. "Slavery." In *Encyclopedia of North American Indians: Native American History, Culture, and Life from Paleo-Indians to the Present,* edited by Frederick E. Hoxie. Boston: Houghton Miðin, 1996.

Pevar, Stephen L. *The Rights of Indians and Tribes: The Basic ACLU Guide to Indian and Tribal Rights.* Carbondale: Southern Illinois University Press, 1992.

Phillips, Ruth B. *Trading Identities: The Souvenir in Native North American Art from the Northeast, 1700–1900.* Seattle: University of Washington Press, 1998.

Rollins, Peter C., and John E. O'Connor, eds. *Hollywood's Indian: The Portrayal of the Native American in Film.* Lexington: University Press of Kentucky, 1998.

Roscoe, Will. *The Zuni Man-Woman.* Albuquerque: University of New Mexico Press, 1991.

Rose, Cynthia, and Duane Champagne. *Native North American Almanac.* Farmington Hills, Mich.: Thomson Gale/U.X.L, 1994.

Rountree, Helen. *Pocahontas's People: The Powhatan Indians of Virginia through Four Centuries.* Norman: University of Oklahoma Press, 1990.

Sale, Kirkpatrick. *The Conquest of Paradise: Christopher Columbus and the Columbian Legacy.* New York: Alfred A. Knopf, 1991.

Sayre, Gordon M., ed. *American Captivity Narratives.* Boston: Houghton Miðin, 2000.

Scarborough, Vernon L., and David R. Wilcox, eds. *The Mesoamerican Ballgame.* Tucson: University of Arizona Press, 1991.

Sciama, Lidia D., and Joanne B. Eicher, eds. *Beads and Bead Makers: Gender, Material Culture, and Meaning.* Oxford: Berg, 1998.

Secakuku, Susan. *Meet Mindy: A Native Girl from the Southwest.* Washington, D.C.: National Museum of the American Indian in association with Beyond Words Publishing, 2003.

Silver, Shirley, and Wick R. Miller. *American Indian Language: Cultural and Social Contexts.* Tucson: University of Arizona Press, 1997.

Smith, Huston, and Reuben Snake. *One Nation Under God: The Triumph of the Native American Church.* Santa Fe: Clear Light Publishers, 1995.

Smith, Laura E. *Horace Poolaw: Photographer of American Indian Modernity.* Lincoln: University of Nebraska Press, 2016.

Snyder, Christina. *Slavery in Indian Country: The Changing Face of Captivity in Early America.* Cambridge, Mass.: Harvard University Press, 2010.

Standing Bear, Luther. *Land of the Spotted Eagle.* Lincoln: University of Nebraska Press, 1978.

Stannard, David E. *American Holocaust.* New York: Oxford University Press, 1992.

Stewart, Hilary. *Totem Poles.* Seattle: University of Washington Press, 1990.

Stewart, Omer C. *Peyote Religion: A History.* Norman: University of Oklahoma Press, 1987.

Suttles, Wayne, ed. *Northwest Coast.* Vol. 7, *Handbook of North American Indians,* edited by William C. Sturtevant. Washington D.C.: Smithsonian Institution, 1990.

Sutton, Mark Q. *An Introduction to Native North America.* Hoboken, N.J.: Pearson Education, Inc., 2004.

Swanton, John R. *Chickasaw Society and Religion.* Lincoln: University of Nebraska Press, 2006.

Szasz, Margaret Connell. *Education and the American Indian: The Road to Self-Determination since 1928.* Albuquerque: University of New Mexico Press, 1999.

Tayac, Gabrielle. *Indivisible: Native and African Lives in the Americas.* Washington, D.C.: Smithsonian Institution, 2009.

Taylor, Allan R. "Nonspeech Communication Systems." In *Languages,* edited by Ives Goddard. Vol. 17, *Handbook of North American Indians,* edited by William C. Sturtevant. Washington, D.C.: Smithsonian Institution, 1996.

Tedlock, Dennis. *Popul Vuh: The Mayan Book of the Dawn of Life and the Glories of Gods and Kings.* New York: Touchstone Books, 1996.

Thornton, Russell. *American Indian Holocaust and Survival: A Population History since 1492.* Norman: University of Oklahoma Press, 1987.

Tiller, Veronica E. Velarde., ed. *Tiller's Guide to Indian Country: Economic Profiles of Indian Reservations.* Albuquerque: Bow Arrow Publishing, 2005.

Trafzer, Clifford E. *As Long as the Grass Shall Grow and Rivers Flow: A History of Native Americans.* Fort Worth: Harcourt College Publishers, 2000.

Trafzer, Clifford E., Jean A. Keller, and Lorene Sisquoc. *Boarding School Blues: Revisiting American Indian Educational Experiences.* Lincoln: University of Nebraska Press, 2006.

U.S. Department of Health and Human Services. *Trends in Indian Health, 1998–1999.* Rockville, Md.: Indian Health Services, 1999.

Utter, Jack. *American Indians: Answers to Today's Questions.* 2nd ed. Norman: University of Oklahoma Press, 2001.

Vennum, Thomas. *Lacrosse Legends of the First Americans.* Baltimore: Johns Hopkins University Press, 2007.

Viola, Herman J. *After Columbus: The Smithsonian Chronicle of the North American Indians.* Washington, D.C.: Smithsonian Books in association with Orion Books, 1990.

Walker, Willard B. "Native Writing Systems." In *Languages,* edited by Ives Goddard. Vol. 17, *Handbook of North American Indians,* edited by William C. Sturtevant. Washington, D.C.: Smithsonian Institution, 1997.

Washburn, Wilcomb E. "Introduction." In *History of Indian-White Relations,* edited by Wilcomb E. Washburn. Vol. 4, *Handbook of North American Indians,* edited by William C. Sturtevant. Washington, D.C.: Smithsonian Institution, 1988.

Weatherford, Jack McIver. *Indian Givers: How the Indians of the Americas Transformed the World.* New York: Ballantine, 1988.

Welburn, Ron. *Roanoke and Wampum: Topics in Native American Heritage and Literature.* New York: Peter Lang Publishing, 2001.

Wilkinson, Charles F. *Blood Struggle: The Rise of Modern Indian Nations.* New York: W. W. Norton, 2005.

Wright, Barton. *Classic Hopi and Zuni Kachina Figures.* Santa Fe: Museum of New Mexico Press, 2006.

———. *Hopi Kachinas: The Complete Guide to Collecting Kachina Dolls.* 1st rev. ed. Flagstaff: Northland Publishing, 2000.

Wright, Ronald. *Stolen Continents: The Americas through Indian Eyes since 1492.* Boston: Houghton Miðin, 1992.

INDEX

Page numbers in *italics* refer to illustrations.

Ababinli/Abainki (Chickasaw supreme being), 45
"aboriginal," as term, 132, 135
adobe, 93, 129
adoption of non-Natives, 76, 84–86, 138
African American slaves, 57, 191–92
African Americans, 148, 189
afterlife, 50–51
agriculture: before arrival of Europeans, *89*, 93–95, *94*, 220–21; ball game in Mesoamerica associated with agricultural fertility, 32, 33; combination-planting, 91, 105–6; environment, Native American relationship with, 91–92; Europeans settlers, assistance provided to, 2, 73; foodstuffs, 105–6, *107*, 125–26, 220–21, 226–28, *227* (*See also specific types*); plantation systems, Native Americans, adopting, 191; rain dances and, 39–40; on reservations, 196; spirituality and, 45; squash cultivation and migration patterns, 63; women's role in, 168, *169*, 170
Ahenakew, Mary (Cherokee/Piscataway-Conoy), 9, 36, 47, 88, 108, 124, 133, 144, 148, 174, 225
Akimel O'odham, 9
Alaska Natives, 98–99, *111*, *127*, 135, 144, 170, 181, 207
alcoholism, 125, 127–28, 206
Aleut peoples, 98, 132, 190
Alexie, Sherman (Spokane/Coeur d'Alene), 59, 100
Algonquian languages, 26, 35, 122, 142
Aliquippa (Mingo Seneca), *194*
Allen, Elsie (Pomo), 19
alphabets. *See* writing systems
Althing, Iceland, 186
American Gaming Association, 198
"American Indian," as term, 132–33

American Indian magazine, 186–87
American Indian Religious Freedom Act (1994), 47
American Indian sign language, 102
American Psychological Association, 145
ancestry, Indian, proving, 138–39
ancestry and origins of Native Americans, 62–64
Andean Indians, 8, 63, 105, 108, 197, 222, 228
Anderson, M. Kat, 96–97
animals: all parts, full use of, 110–12; clothing made from, *1*, *46*, 108; nature, Native American relationship to, 90–92, 95, 96–97; as relatives, 111–12. *See also* fish and fishing; hunting; *specific animals*
Anishinaabe. *See* Chippewa
Apache, 8, *85*, 152, 153, 154, 175, 177, 190, 191, 200
Arapaho, 117, *210*
Argall, Samuel, 79
Arikara, 80–81, 200
Arizona Board on Geographic and Historic Names, 142
art and artmaking, 17–22, *18*, *21*, 211
assimilation policies, 67–69, 71, 188
Assiniboine, 80
Atsugewi, 154
Attakullakulla (Cherokee), 195
Autry, Gene, 52
Awashonks (Saconet band of Wampanoag), 193
Axtell, James, 84, 87
Aymara, 8, 228
Aymara language, 67
Ayonwatha (Hiawatha; Mohawk or Onondaga), 186
Aztec (Mexica), 23, 30, 35, 70, 176, 220–21, 229

Bacon's Rebellion, 193

Bald Eagle Protection Act (1942/1962), 115

ball games, 30–33, *31*

baskets and basket making, 18–19

Baziliologia: A Booke of Kings (1618), *141*

beads and beading, 119–21, *120*

beans, 91, 105–6, 136

beauty pageant, Indian, 141

Beloved Woman or Ghigau, 195

benefits, payments, and services provided by federal governments, 138–39, 182, 207, 209–11, *210*, 212

berdache, 157

Bering Strait theory, 62–63, 113–14

Berry Creek Rancheria, 134

Betancourt, Stephanie (Seneca), 106, 130, 147

binge drinking, 127

bisexual, lesbian, gay, transgender, and queer individuals, 155–57, *156*

bison. *See specific entries at* buffalo

Black Death/bubonic plague, 184, 221

Blackfeet, 69, 80, 110, 117, 204

"blood quantum," 138, 150–51, 192

bloodroot, 10, *11*

boarding schools for Indian children, 67–68, 150, 164, 165–66, *166*, *167*

boat baskets, 124

Bois Forte Reservation, 41

Boldt Decision, 215

bounties for Indian scalps, 87–88, 148

Bradby, Marvin (Eastern Chickahominy), *150*

Brady, Rebecca (Cheyenne/Sac and Fox), Cheyenne three-hide dress and accessories (ca. 1995), *1, 46*

Brando, Marlon, *215*

bubonic plague/Black Death, 184, 221

Buffalo Bill Wild West show (1890), *159*

buffalo jumps, 111

buffalo/bison, 93, 106, 111, 112, 114, 129, 204

Bureau of American Ethnology, *Chippewa Child Life and Its Cultural Background* (1951), 41

Bureau of Indian Affairs, US, 181, 209

burials: mounds used as, 229; museum repatriation of grave goods and human remains, 216; NAGPRA (Native American Graves Protection and Repatriation Act; 1990), 63, 217; Native American burial practices, 50–51, *51*; treatment of ancient human remains, 63

Burke, Annie (Pomo), 19

Cahokia mounds, 230

calendars and calendar systems, 223–24

California Indians, 7, 18, 40, 80, 91, 93, 96, 124, *130*, 134, 154

California v. Cabazon (US Supreme Court, 1987), 199

Cameahwait (Shoshone), 82

Canada: boarding schools for Indian children in, 164, 166; contemporary population of Native Americans, 180; recognition of Native American identity in, 139; reserves (reservations) in, 196; terms for Native Americans in, 132, 135, 144

Canadian Aboriginal Festival Powwow, 26

cannibalism, 34

Cape Fox or Saxman Tlingit, 218

captives: Europeans as, 84–86, *85*; Indian women and children as, 88, 190–91; as slaves, 190–91

cardiovascular disease, 125

Caribbean Indians, 30, 32, 34, 35–36, 80, 190

Carson, Johnny, 54

Cartier, Jacques, 87

casinos and gaming/gambling, 198–205; *California v. Cabazon* (US Supreme Court, 1987) on, 199; charitable and philanthropic assistance provided by, 203–5; IGRA (Indian Gaming Regulatory Act of 1988), 182, 198, 199, 200, 201; individual payments to tribal members (per capita payments or per caps), 198, 211; leasing of gaming devices, 203; nongaming tribes assisted by profits from, 203–5; nontaxability of Indian gaming revenues, 212; number of tribes and facilities, 200; owned and operated by tribal governments, 198–99; poverty continuing despite, 206; resistance to recognition of some Native tribes and, 182; revenue and profits, use of, 198, 200–205, *201* cassava, 226, 228

Catawba people, 190

cattle grazing, tribal lands leased for, 209

Cayuga, 28, 137, 186. *See also* Haudenosaunee

Celilo Fall, Columbia River, Oregon, *91*

Census, US, and census taking, 180

Central America. *See* Latin America

ceremonies. *See* religion and spirituality

Charbonneau, Jean Baptiste (son of Sacagawea), 82, *83*

charitable assistance, 203–5

Cherokee/Cherokee Nation of Oklahoma, xv–xvi, 10, 69, 138, 170, 191–92, 195, 201

Cherokee language, 23–24, 67

Cherokee Phoenix (newspaper), 71

Cherokee syllabary, 23–24, *71*

Cheyenne, *46*, 117, *210*

Cheyenne River Sioux, 203

Chickasaw, 45, 191–92

chicken scratch music *(waila)*, 9

chili peppers/peppers, 105, 106, *107*, 226, 228

Chinese coins, Tlingit body armor using, 121

Chippewa (Ojibwe; Anishinaabe): doll in toy cradleboard with dream catcher (early 20th century), *42*; language, 136, 144; tribe, 35, 41–42, 80, 137, 152, 203, 204

Chiricahua Apache, *85*

chocolate, 105, 106, 220–21, 226–27, *227*

Choctaw, 10, 191–92

Choctaw code talkers in WWII, 174

cholera, 184

Chontales, 10

Christianity, *24*, 45, 51, 141, 155, 177

Chumash, 80

cigar-store Indians, 55–57, *56*

cirrhosis, 125

citizenship, 188–89, 196, 212

Civil War, 3, 191

Clark, William, 82

Cleveland, Grover, 156–57

clothing, *1*, 10, *46*, 108, *109*, 110, *111*, 119–21, *120*

Cobb, Amanda J., 59

cochineal, 10

Cockacoeskie (Queen Ann; Pamunkey),

193–94

code talkers, Native American, in WWII, 172–74, *173*

Coeur d'Alene reservation, 59

colors, 10–11

Columbia River dams, Oregon, *91*

Columbian Exchange, 226

Columbus, Christopher, 31, 54, 55, 72, 95, 132, 183–84, 222, 226, 227

Colville Reservation, Confederated Tribes of, 63, 92

Comanche, 117, 134, 190, 191

Comanche code talkers in WWII, 174

combination-planting, *91*, 105–6

coming-of-age ceremonies, *131*, 152–54, *153*

constitutions: English, 187; Great Law of Peace of Haudenosaunee Confederacy, 186–87, 222; US, 47, 181, 187, 188, 189

Cook, James, 175

Cooper, James Fenimore: *Last of the Mohicans* (1826), 142; *The Redskins* (1846), 148

copal, 33

Copper Inuit dialect, 99

Coriz, Joseph (Santo Domingo Pueblo), Storyteller Bracelet (ca. 1990), *21*

corn (maize), 12, 45, 63, 73, *91*, *94*, 105–6, *107*, 136, 170, 220, 226, 228

corn pollen, as symbol of fertility, *153*

cornmeal, placed with human remains, 50

Cortés, Hernán, 73, 184

Coté, Julianna (Osage), *68*

cotton textiles, 108

counterfeited Native art, 20–21

counting coup, 37, *38*

Courts of Indian Offenses, 47

The Cowboy and the Indians (film; 1949), 54

cradleboards, 41, *42*, 122–24, *123*

creation stories, 32–33, 45, 62, 64, 168–70

Cree, 35, 80, 174

Cree language, 24, 67

Cree syllabics, 24

Creek (Muscogee Nation), 136, 191–92

cross-gender individuals in Native American society, 155–57, *156*

Crow, 80, 81, 117, *123*, 174

Crow Fair, 118

cultural appropriation, 20, 48

Curtis, Charles (Kaw/Osage), 188

Curtis, Edward, 159

Dakota peoples, 136, 201, 205
Dalles hydroelectric dam, Columbia River, Oregon, 91
dances and dancing: ceremonies, non-Native attendance at, 43–44; chicken scratch music and, 9; Jump Dance, 40; powwows and, 27–28, 44, 115–16; rain dances, 39–40; Sun Dances, 45, 47
Daughters of Britannia, 140
Davis, Jeffrey E., 102, 104
Dawes Act (General Allotment Act; 1887), 150, 196
Dawes Roll, 138
de Bry, Theodore, *The Tovvne of Secota* (engraving; 16th century), 89, 94
death, burial, and afterlife, 50–51, 51. *See also* burials
Deganawidah (non-Iroquoian Indian), 186
Deloria, Vine, Jr. (Standing Rock Sioux), 64, 92
DeMallie, Raymond, 103–4
denigration. *See* stereotyping, misrepresentation, and denigration
Densmore, Frances, *Chippewa Customs* (1929), 41
Día de los Muertos, 51, 227
diabetes, 92, 125–26
dictionaries, 23
Diné. *See specific entries at* Navajo
diphtheria, 65
disease. *See* health and medicine
DNA, 63
Dobyns, Henry F., 65
domestic violence, 206
domesticated animals and infectious disease, 221
dream catchers, 41–42, 42
drug addiction, 128, 205
drums, 6, 7
Dry Creek Rancheria Band of Pomo Indians, 134
Dutch colonies. *See* European arrival in Western Hemisphere
dyes and paints, 10–11, 119

eagle feathers, 115–16, 116
Eastern Pequots, 182
Eastern Shoshone, 204
Eastern Shoshone pipe (ca. 1850), 36
Eastern Woodland Indians, 7, 28, 62, 177

economic depression. *See* poverty and social disadvantage
Ecuyler, Simeon, 80
education: before arrival of formal schools, 161, 162–63, 163; boarding schools for Indian children, government-run, 67–68, 150, 164, 165–66, 166, 167; casino revenue supporting, 200, 204; "civilization" and de-Indianization through, 164, 165–66, 167; coming-of-age ceremonies, 131, 152–54, 153; contemporary schooling, 164; kachina (katsina) dolls, role of, 12–13, 13; language loss and, 67–68, 165; mission schools, 164; NK360° program, xiii–xiv, 232; on reservations, 164, 165; tribal governments financing, 211
Eliot, John, 45
employment: casinos, jobs provided by, 202, 205, 206; "Indian preference" for federal government jobs, 209–11; low levels of, 197
Encyclopedia of North American Indians (1996), 87, 189, 190
English colonies. *See* European arrival in Western Hemisphere
English Constitution, 187
enrollment and membership in a tribe, 138–39, 150–51
environment, Native American relationship to, 90–92, 95, 96–97
Erdrich, Jennifer (Turtle Mountain Chippewa ancestry), 126, 128
Eskimo, as offensive term, 144
Essential Understandings, xiii, 232
European adaptation of Native foodstuffs, 220–21, 226–28
European arrival in Western Hemisphere: accomplishments of Native Americans at time of, 220–22; agriculture in Americas prior to, 89, 93–95, 94, 220–21; characterization of Native Americans, 220; diseases spread by, 65–66, 73, 80–81, 95, 150, 183–85; horses in Americas and, 117; Jamestown Colony, 2, 72–73, 75–77; land ownership, Native American versus European views about, 78, 96–97; Manhattan, "sale" of, 78–79, 79, 97; manifest destiny, concept of, 95, 150; multiple names for same tribe or nation and, 136; Native American

assistance for European settlers, 2–3, 72–74; nature and the environment and, 92, 95; "New World" and Americans as untouched wilderness, concepts of, 66, 93–95; overhunting after, 95, 112, 114; Plymouth Colony, 2, 73, 176; population of Native Americans affected by, 65–66, 184; population of Native Americans at time of, 65, 183; royalty, attributed to Native American leaders, 140; Thanksgiving, celebration of, 2–4, *3*, 72, 176; tobacco, European cultivation of and trade in, 35–36, 55, 73; trade between Europeans and Native Americans, 78, 82, 87, 120–21, 170; unified Native resistance, lack of, 183–85

Europeans, generally. *See* non-Natives

Evans, James, 24

Evans, Suzanne, 189

extinction: of Pleistocene mammals, 112, 113–14; of "real" Indians, 149–51

Eyre, Chris (Cheyenne/Arapaho), 59

fakes and frauds: Native art, 20–21; pseudo-shamans, 48

family groups and living arrangements, 177

farming. *See* agriculture

feathers, wearing, 115–16, *116*

federal government, US *See* US government

Fifteenth Amendment, 189

films. *See* movies and TV shows

"First Nations/First Peoples," as term, 132, 135

fish and fishing: fertilizer, fish used as, 73; land rights for, 96, 97, 209, 214–15, *215*; religious/spiritual ceremonies associated with, 5; resource and land management for, 95; salmon, *91*, 91–92, 106; state regulations, 214–15, *215*; tomcod caught in dip net, *111*

Five Civilized Tribes, 191. *See also* Cherokee; Chickasaw; Choctaw; Creek; Seminole

Flandreau Santee Sioux Tribe, 204

Florida State Seminoles, 147

flutes, 7

Food and Agriculture Organization of United Nations, 228

foodstuffs, 105–6, *107*, 125–26, 220–21, 226–28, *227*. *See also specific types*

Fort Laramie, Treaty of (1868), *210*

Frank's Landing, Puyallup River, Washington State, *215*

frauds. *See* fakes and frauds

Freedmen descendants of Native Americans' African American slaves, 191–92

French and Indian War, 80, 194

fry bread, 106

funerals. *See* burials

game hunting. *See* hunting

games and sports: at Haudenosaunee (Iroquois) funerals, 50; lacrosse, 28–29, *29*; Mesoamerican ball games, 30–33, *31*; Native American names for sports teams, 145–47, *146*, 148; rubber balls, use of, 30–31, *31*, 32; stickball, 28, 29

gaming/gambling. *See* casinos and gaming/gambling

Ganteaume, Cécile, 140

Gardner, Alexander, *210*

Gathering of Nations Powwow, Albuquerque, 26, 141

gay, lesbian, bisexual, transgender, and queer individuals, 155–57, *156*

gender equality and autonomy, 168–71, 195

gender issues: division of gender roles and duties in Native American culture, 168–71, *169*; in education, 162–63, 165; katsinam, male and female characteristics of, 12; lacrosse, women not originally allowed to play, 29; matrilineal and matrilocal social structures, 162, 194; Mesoamerican ball games, boys and men playing, 30; painting, male versus female, 11; politics, women's involvement in, 168–71, 187, 193–95, *194*; pregnant women, ceremonies for, 152; puberty ceremonies, *153*, 153–54; sexuality and gender, Native American view of, 155–57, *156*; *squaw*, as offensive term, 142–43

gender variance in Native American society, 155–57, *156*

General Allotment Act (Dawes Act; 1887), 150, 196

generosity, as Native American tradition, 37, 72, 203

genetic explanations: for alcoholism, 127–28; for diabetes, 125–26; for migrations of Native Americans, 63

geomythology, 64

Geronimo (Apache), 85

Ghigau or Beloved Woman, 195

Giles, Justin Bruce (Muscogee [Creek] Nation of Oklahoma), 29

glass beads, 119–21, 120

global adaptation of Native foodstuffs, 226–28

glyphs, 23, 70

golden eagles, 115

Goodyear, Charles, 31

government and politics: benefits, payments, and services provided by, 138–39, 182, 207, 209–11, 210, 212; Haudenosaunee Confederacy, political structure of, 186–87; tribes as, 44, 138, 182, 188, 198–99, 212, 214 (See also tribal governments); women's involvement in, 168–71, 187, 193–95, 194. See also constitutions; US government

Grand Entry, at powwows, 28

graves. See burials

Great Basin tribes, 154

Great Lakes tribes, 28, 41, 137, 185

Great Law of Peace of Haudenosaunee Confederacy, 186–87, 222

Great Plains tribes. See Plains Indians

Great Serpent Mound, 230

Greenland and Greenlanders, 144

Guacanagarí (Taíno), 72

Guaraní language, 67

Hariot, Thomas, A briefe and true report of the new found land of Virginia (16th century), 89, 94

Harjo, Suzan Shown (Cheyenne/Hodulgee Muscogee), 146–47, 148

Harris, Alexandra (Cherokee ancestry), 19, 25, 29, 74, 95, 97, 104, 112, 124, 141, 151, 154, 157, 171, 195, 228

Harvard Project on American Indian Economic Development, 207–8

Haudenosaunee (Iroquois), 186–87; cannibalism opposed by, 34; captives, treatment of, 85–86; cradleboards, 124; embroidery and beadwork, 119; Great Law of Peace, 186–87, 222; interment

practices, 50; Iroquois Thanksgiving Address (Ohen:ton Kariwahtekwen: Greetings to the Natural World), 39; lacrosse played by, 28–29, 29; long houses of, 130; marital practices, 178; maternal uncles, role of, 162; Native photography and, 160; passports issued by, 188; political structure of, 186–87; totem poles, 15; tribes comprising confederacy, 28, 137, 186; women as political leaders and Clan Mothers, 170, 187, 194

Hawaiian Natives, 69, 98, 101, 175, 182

headdresses, 116

The Healing Pole (2002), 15

health and medicine: diet of Native Americans and, 106, 125–26; disparities of health between American Indians and general population of US, 125–28; domesticated animals and infectious disease, 221; environmental change exacerbating medical conditions, 92; Europeans, diseases spread by arrival of, 65–66, 73, 80–81, 95, 150, 183–85; plant extracts used in Native medicine, 222; shamans or medicine men, 28, 48–49, 163; sterilization of surgical spaces, 222. See also specific illnesses and medical conditions

Hero Twins, 32–33

Herodotus, 87

Herrera y Tordesillas, Antonio de, 31

Heye, George Gustav, 216, 218

Hiawatha (Ayonwatha; Mohawk or Onondaga), 186

Hidatsa, 80–81, 82, 200

hide clothing, 1, 46, 108

hide painting, 10, 70

Hilger, M. Inez, 41

Hill, Liz (Red Lake Band of Ojibwe), 4, 13, 31, 34, 42, 69, 81, 99, 101, 139, 157, 176, 182, 185, 187, 189, 192, 197, 199, 202, 205, 208, 211, 213, 215

Hodge, Frederick, Handbook of American Indians North of Mexico (1959), 87

hogans, 129

Hohokam, 119–20

hoop baskets, 124

Hoover, Herbert, 188

Hopi, 12–13, 40, 174

Hopi Snake and Antelope ceremony (Hopi Snake Dance), 49, 158
horse masks, 118
horses, Native American acquisition and use of, 117–18, 118
hospitality, as Native American tradition, 72, 175
Hotch, Georgiana and Joe (Tlingit), 217
Houle, Terrance (Blood), Urban Indian Series (2007), xiv
House of Tears Carvers, 15
housing, 129–30, 130
Huichol, 46
human sacrifice, 32–33
Hun Hunahpu (Maya god), 32
hunting: all parts of animals, full use of, 110–12; buffalo/bison, 93, 106, 111, 112, 114; European overhunting, 95, 112, 114; to extinction, 112, 113–14; for foodstuffs, 105, 106; land rights for, 96, 97, 209, 210, 214–15; men's role in, 168, 170; migration theories related to, 63; musical instruments used in, 8; religious/spiritual ceremonies associated with, 5, 43, 45, 111; in Secoton village engraving, 94; sign language, use of, 103; state regulations, 214–15; subsistence hunting, 110; whales and whaling, 114
Hupa, 40
Hupa language, 122
Huron people, 80, 119

IACA (Indian Arts and Crafts Act; 1935/1990/2000/2010), 20, 21–22, 211
ice age, 114
identity, Native American. See racial identity as Native American; recognition of Native American identity
igloos, 129, 130
IGRA (Indian Gaming Regulatory Act of 1988), 182, 198, 199, 200, 201
Indian Arts and Crafts Act (IACA; 1935/1990/2000/2010), 20, 21–22, 211
Indian Arts and Crafts Board, 22
"Indian," as term, 132–33, 135
Indian Citizenship Act, 188
Indian Commerce Clause, US Constitution, 181
Indian Country Today (newspaper), 147
Indian Gaming Regulatory Act of 1988

(IGRA), 182, 198, 199, 200, 201
Indian Health Service, 209; Trends in Indian Health, 1998–1999, 127
"Indian preference," 209–11
Indian Princess motif, 140–41
"Indigenous American/indígenas," as term, 132, 133, 135, 139
influenza, 184
Inka, 25, 221, 224
International Lacrosse Federation, 29
Inuit, 98, 99, 129–30, 132, 144, 223
Inuktitut syllabics, 24
Iñupiaq (pl. Iñupiat), 98, 144
Iñupiaq language, 98
Irish Potato Famine, 228
Iroquois. See Haudenosaunee
Isleta Pueblo, 200

Jackson, Jack (Navajo), 142
Jackson, Nathan (Tlingit), 218
James, George Wharton, 158
James I (king of England), 73, 75, 141
Jamestown Colony, 2, 72–73, 75–77
Jefferson, Thomas, 82
Jesuits, 28, 157, 164, 177
Johnston, Philip, 172
Josephy, Alvin, Jr., The Indian Heritage of America (1968), 34
Judd, Steven Paul (Kiowa), The Summer They Visited (2014), ii–iii, xiv
Jump Dance, 40

Kaats totem pole, 15, 218
kachina (katsina) dolls (katsinam), 12–13, 13
Kalaallit, 144
Karuk, 91–92
Kaw, 27
"Keep America Beautiful" (TV ad), 90
Kennedy, John F., xv
Kennewick Man, 63
Keoke, Emory Dean, 186–87
khipu, 224
Kickapoo, 204
King, Charles Bird, oil painting of Sequoyah with Cherokee syllabary (1828), 61, 71
King Philip's War (1675–1676), 176
kinnikinnick, 35
Kiowa, 117

INDEX

247

Kiowa drawing of mounted warrior counting coup on Mexican or white man (1875–1877), 38
Kiowa language, 122
Kittamaqua (Piscataway), 177
kivas, 158
Kixunai, 40
Kokopelli, 13
Koshari, 13

lacrosse, 28–29, 29
Laguna Pueblo, 160
Lakota, 50, 90, 120, 136, 210. See also Sioux
Lakota Sun Dance, 45
Lamar, Cynthia Chavez (San Felipe Pueblo/Hopi/Tewa/Navajo), xiii–xiv
land: management practices, 91; Native American relationship to, 90–92, 95, 96–97; ownership of, Native American versus European views about, 78, 96–97; rights to use, 96, 97, 209, 210, 214–15, 215; taken by federal government, payments for, 209, 210, 212, 213; taken from Indians and made available to white settlers, advertisement for, 213
languages: code talkers, Native American, in WWII, 172–74, 173; educational policies, loss of language due to, 67–68, 165; losing and regaining, 67–69, 68, 165; polysynthetic languages, 98; sign language, 102–4, 103; smoke signals, 100–101; snow, number of words for, 98–99; spelling variations for Native American words, 23–25; writing systems for, 23–25, 70, 70–71, 97. See also terminology; *specific languages*
Latin America: contemporary population of Native Americans, 180; definition of Mesoamerica, 32; Día de los Muertos, 51, 227; pyramids, Mesoamerican, 222; recognition of Native American identity in, 139; reservations in, 197; slaves and slavery in, 190; terms for Native Americans in, 132, 133, 135, 139
Lenni Lenape, 15, 78–79, 168–70
lesbian, gay, bisexual, transgender, and queer individuals, 155–57, 156
Lewis, Meriwether, 82

Lewis and Clark Expedition, 82–83
LGBTQ individuals, 155–57, 156
Liliuokalani (Native Hawaiian), 195
Lincoln, Abraham, 3
Linnaeus, Carolus, *Systema Naturae* (1735), 148
Little Bighorn, Battle of, 104
liver disease, 125
Lomahaftewa, Clifford (Hopi), *Rain: Native Expressions from the Southwest* (2000), 40
The Lone Ranger (radio, from 1933, and TV show, 1949–1957), 52–54, 53
long houses, 130
Lono (Native Hawaiian god), 175
Lumbee, 181
Lumbee Act (1956), 181
Lummi, 15
Lummis, Fletcher, 85

Magna Carta, 187
Magovern, Nema (Osage), 11, 37, 99, 137, 189
Makah, 81
Malinalli (Malintzin/Doña Marina/La Malinche; Mexican Native American), 72, 73–74
Mandan, 80–81, 82, 200
Manhattan, "sale" of, 78–79, 79, 97
manifest destiny, 95, 150
Mankiller, Wilma (Cherokee Nation of Oklahoma), xv–xvi, 195
Mann, Charles C., *1491: New Revelations of the Americas before Columbus* (2005), 114, 186
Markstrom, Carol A., 153
Marmon, Lee (Laguna Pueblo), 160
marriage practices, 177–78, 190–91
mascots for sports teams, Native American, 145–47
Massachusett language, 97, 142
Massasoit (Wampanoag), 176
mathematics and number systems, 223–25, 224
matrilineal and matrilocal social structures, 162, 194
Maya, 30, 31, 32, 34, 35, 70, 114, 176, 220–21, 223, 229
Maya bas-relief depicting ball player (AD 600–750), 31

Maya calendar systems, 223–24

Maybee, Dallin (Northern Arapaho/ Seneca), *Conductors of Our Own Destiny* (2013), *xii*, xiv

Mayflower, 73

McCullough, John, 84

McKinn, Santiago, *85*

McNevin, John, *Washington and Gist visit Queen Aliquippa* (engraving, early 19th c.), *179, 194*

measles, 65, 184

Medicine, Beatrice (Lakota), *Native America in the Twentieth Century* (1996), 155

medicine generally. *See* health and medicine

medicine men or shamans, 48–49

membership and enrollment in a tribe, 138–39, 150–51

menstruation, onset of, 153–54

Mesa Grande Reservation, *169*

Mescalero Apache, 152, 200

Meskwaki, 174

Mesoamerica. *See* Latin America

mestizos (people with Spanish and Indian ancestry), 139

Métis (Canadian peoples of Indigenous and French descent), 132

Mexica. *See* Aztec

Mexico. *See* Latin America

Middle Plantation, Treaty of, 194

migration of Native Americans to America, 62–64, 113–14

Mi'kmaq, 10, 177

Mille Lacs Indian Reservation, 200

Miller, Bill, 9

Mingo Seneca, 194

Minuit, Peter, 78–79, *79*

misrepresentation. *See* stereotyping, misrepresentation, and denigration

Miss Indian World, 141

mission schools, 164

Mistanaskowew (Badger Calling; Cree), 24

Mohawk, 28, 137, 186. *See also* Haudenosaunee

Mohawk language, 142

Mohegan, 10

Molina, Alonso de, *Vocabulary in Castilian and Mexican Language* (1555–1571), 23

molybdenum mining, 92

Monk's Mound, 229–30

Monongye, Jesse (Navajo/Hopi), Bracelet (ca. 1983), *21*

Montagano, Bethany, 22, 118, 121, 192

Mooney, James, 65

Moore, Clayton, 52, *53*

Morningstar Institute, 146–47

moss sacks, 123

mounds and mound builders, 222, 229–31, *230*

movies and TV shows: contemporary movies told from Native perspective, accuracy of, 58–60; *The Cowboy and the Indians* (1949), 54; "Keep America Beautiful" (TV ad), 90; Native American Film and Video Festival, 58; *Powwow Highway* (1989), 58; *Skins* (2002), 59; *Smoke Signals* (1998), 58–59, *59*, 100; smoke signals in, 100; stereotyping, misrepresentation, and denigration in, 52, 54, 60; Tonto and *The Lone Ranger* (1933/1949–1957), 52–54, *53*

Mudhead, 13

multiple names for same tribe or nation, 136–37

Muscogee Nation (Creek), 136, 191–92

museum repatriation of Native American materials, 216–18, *217*

music and musical instruments, 5–9, *6, 8*

Myaamia language, 122

NAGPRA (Native American Graves Protection and Repatriation Act; 1990), 63, 217

Nahuatl, 23

Naismith, James, 30

Nakota peoples, 136

Nampeyo (Hopi/Tewa), 18

Nantucket people, 97

Nanyehi (Nancy Ward; Cherokee), 195

Narragansett language, 122

Narragansett peoples, 80, 122

Natchez people, 229

"nation" versus "tribe," 134–35

National Archives and Records Administration, 139

National Collegiate Athletic Association (NCAA), 147

National Congress of American Indians, 145

National Council of Social Studies, 232
National Eagle Repository, 115
National Education Association, 145
National Indian Gaming Association, 205
National Indian Gaming Commission, 200
National Museum of the American Indian (NMAI): Cultural Resources Center, 218; mission of, xiii–xiv, xv; Native American Film and Video Festival, 58; NK360° program, xiii–xiv, 232; NMAI Act (1989/1996), 216–17, 218; Oµce of Repatriation, 218; origins of collection, 216; repatriation of items from, 216–18, 217
National Powwow, 6, 27
"Native American," as term, 132–33
Native American Church, 45–46, 46
Native American Film and Video Festival, 58
Native American Graves Protection and Repatriation Act (NAGPRA; 1990), 63, 217
Native American identity. See racial identity as Native American; recognition of Native American identity
Native American Rights Fund, 204
"Native," as term, 132–33
Native Knowledge 360° (NK360°), xiii–xiv, 232
nature, Native American relationship to, 90–92, 95, 96–97
Navajo (Diné), 11, 17, 40, 50, 129, 134, 136–37, 152, 154, 163, 166, 177
Navajo code talkers in WWII, 172–73, 173
Navajo language, 67, 172–73
Navajo Reservation, 172
Nazca poncho, camelid and plant fiber (AD 1000), 109
NCAA (National Collegiate Athletic Association), 147
"New World," concept of, 66, 93–95
New York cigar-store Indian (ca. 1895), 56
Newman, Rico (Piscataway/Conoy), 16, 54, 64, 178, 231
Nez Perce, 63, 117
9/11, 15
Nineteenth Amendment, 189
NK360° (Native Knowledge 360°), xiii–xiv, 232
NMAI. See National Museum of the American Indian

non-Natives: adoption of, 76, 84–86, 138; attendance at Native ceremonies by, 43–44, 48–49; captured by Native Americans, 84–86, 85; casinos providing jobs for, 205, 206; charitable assistance to, 205; movies telling stories from Native perspective by, 58; photographs and photography, 158–59, 159; scalping and scalp bounties, 87–88; schooling in spiritual ways and medicinal knowledge for, 48–49. See also European arrival in Western Hemisphere; tourists and tourism
Northeastern tribes, 8, 10, 28, 70, 97, 105, 178
Northern Arapaho, 210
Northern Cheyenne, 210
northern Plains Indians, 110, 117, 177
Northwest Coast Indians, 62, 81, 117, 121, 170, 190
Northwest Indian College Foundation, 204
Northwest Passage, 82
number systems and mathematics, 223–25, 224
Nunn, Nathan, 228
Nuttall, Arwen (Cherokee ancestry), 33, 49, 51, 69, 71, 86, 164, 192, 222

Obama, Barack, 63
Ohen:ton Kariwahtekwen: Greetings to the Natural World (Iroquois Thanksgiving Address), 39
Ojibwe. See Chippewa
Olmec, 30, 222
Olmos, Andres de, 23
Omaha people, 27, 170
Oneida, 28, 137, 186. See also Haudenosaunee
Onondaga, 28, 137, 186, 187. See also Haudenosaunee
oral tradition, 68, 70–71
origins of Native Americans, 62–64
orphans, raising, 178
Osage, 27, 197
"other," Native Americans positioned as, 84, 160
Owen, Angie Reano (Santo Domingo Pueblo), Bracelet (ca. 1988), 21

Pacific Northwest Indians, 62, 81, 117, 121,

170, 190

Page, Jake, *In the Hands of the Great Spirit: the 20,000-Year History of American Indians* (2003), 34

paints and dyes, 10–11, 119

Paipai, *130*

Pamunkey, 193–94

Papago. *See* Tohono O'odham

papoose, as term, 122

Pavil, Ella (Uliggaq; Yup'ik), 111

Pawnee, 27, 191

peanuts, 105, 220

Peek, Walter W., 142

Peepeekisis Indian Band, 135

Pena, Anita (Kumeyaay), *169*

peppers/chili peppers, 105, 106, *107*, 226, 228

Perdue, Theda, 190

petroglyphs, 70

Pevar, Stephen L., *The Rights of Indians and Tribes: The Basic ACLU Guide to Indian and Tribal Rights* (1992), 214–15

peyote, 46

philanthropic assistance, 203–5

Philip II (king of Spain), 31

photographs and photography, 158–60, *159*

pictographs, 10, 23, 70

Piestewa, Lori (Hopi), 142–43

Pilgrims, 2, *3*

pineapple, 105, 228

pipes, pipe ceremonials, and tobacco, 35–36, *36*, 47

Piscataway, 15

Piscataway Confederacy, 177

Plains Indian sign language, 102

Plains Indians: beads and bead work, 121; buffalo, dependence on, 110, 111, 129; cigar-store Indians resembling, 57; counting coup, 37; cradleboards, 124; diseases contracted from European settlers, 80; foodstuffs of, 106; horses, acquisition and use of, 117–18; interment practices, 51; musical instruments, 7; northern Plains Indians, 110, 117, 177; paints and dyes, 10; portable tipis used by, 93; powwows, 26, 27; sign language used by, 102, 103; slaves and slavery, 190; smoke signals used by, 100; war bonnets of, 116; writing systems, 70

Plateau tribes, 177, 190

Pleistocene extinctions, 113–14

Plymouth Colony, 2, 73, 176

Pocahontas (Amonute/Matoaka/Rebecca; Pamunkey), 72–73, 75–77, *76*, *77*, 140–41, *141*

politics. *See* government and politics

polygamy, 177–78

polysynthetic languages, 98

Pomo, 18–19, 124, 134, 225

Ponca, 27, 204

Poolaw, Horace (Kiowa), 159–60

Popol Vuh, 32

population of Native Americans in Western Hemisphere: contemporary population, 180; effects of European arrival, 65–66, 184; at time of European arrival, 65, 183

Porterfield, Kay Marie, 186–87

Potato Famine, 228

potatoes, 10, 35, 105, 106, 220, 226, 228

Potawatomi, 203

potlaches, 14–15

pottery, 18

poverty and social disadvantage: alcoholism, drug addiction, and suicide, 125, 127–28, 205; casino tribes, use of profits from, 203–5; continuing high levels of, 206–8; diet of Native Americans, 106, 125–26; Harvard Project on American Indian Economic Development, 207–8; on reservations, 196–97, 206–8. *See also* employment

Power of Chocolate Festival (2011), *227*

Powhatan (Pamunkey leader), 72, 75, 76, 140

Powhatan confederation, 15, 140

Powwow Highway (film; 1989), 58

powwows, *6*, 26–27, *27*, 43–44, 115–16, 150, 159

pregnant women, ceremonies for, 152

Pretty Beads (Crow), *118*

puberty ceremonies, *153*

Pueblo communities, 12, 50, 108, 111–12, 117, 129, 134, 160, 162, 178, 190, 200

Pueblo Revolt of 1860, 117

pumpkin, *94*, 105, 106

pyramids, Mesoamerican, 222

Qhapaq Ñan, *219*, *221*

Qian, Nancy, 228
Quechua, 8, 31, 228
Quechuan language family, 67
Queen Aliquippa (Mingo Seneca), 194
Queen Ann (Cockacoeskie; Pamunkey), 193–94
queer, bisexual, lesbian, gay, and transgender individuals, 155–57, 156
quinoa, 228
Quonset huts, 130

racial identity as Native American: historical classification of, 148; official recognition of, 132, 138–39
racism: Indian experience of, 189; scientific, 150
rain dances, 39–40
Rainbow Coalition, 145
Raleigh, Sir Walter, 35
rancherias, 134–35
rasps and rattles (as musical instruments), 8
Rau, William H., Chief Iron Tail—Sinte Maza (ca. 1901), 116
"real" Indians, belief in extinction of, 149–51
recognition of Native American identity: Freedmen descendants of Native Americans' African American slaves, 191–92; tribal membership and enrollment, 132, 138–39; tribes recognized by federal government, 134, 138, 150–51, 181–82; unrecognized tribes, 150, 181
Red Horse (Lakota), 104
redskin, as offensive term, 146–47, 148
religion and spirituality, 45–47; agricultural practices as part of, 39–40; attendance at ceremonies by non-Natives, 43–44, 48–49; Christianity, 24, 45, 51, 141, 155, 177; creation stories, 32–33, 45, 62, 64, 168–70; death, burial, and afterlife, 50–51, 51 (See also burials); drums, 7; eagle feathers, 115–16, 116; education in, 163; games and sports related to, 28, 32–33; gender in, 168–70; gods, Europeans initially venerated as, 175; hunting and fishing, ceremonies associated with, 5, 43, 45, 111; katsinam, 12–13; museum repatriation of sacred/ceremonial objects, 216, 218; non-Native attendance at ceremonies, 43–44,

48–49; photographs and photography, 158–59, 160; pipes, pipe ceremonials, and tobacco, 35–36, 36, 47; pregnancy and puberty ceremonies, 152–54, 153; religious freedom for Native Americans, 47; sacred music and songs, 5–6; shamans or medicine men, 28, 48–49, 163; thanksgiving, 4; totem poles, role of, 16; traditional dwelling spaces used as places of, 130
reservations, 196–97; Alaska Native village corporations as alternative to, 181; census taking on, 180; checkerboarding or splintering of lands comprising, 196; Courts of Indian Offenses on, 47; education on, 164, 165; environmental concerns, 92; gender roles and, 170; Native American view of, 197; Native diet on, 106, 138; photography and confinement of western tribes on, 158; poverty and social disadvantage on, 196–97, 206–8; rancherias as type of, 134–35; state taxes, freedom from, 212–13; Treaty of Middle Plantation creating first reservation, 194; as tribal lands under tribal government, 44. See also casinos and gaming/gambling; specific reservations
Revere, Paul, 140
Rickard, Jolene (Tuscarora), 160
road networks, 219, 221, 222
Rogers, John, Washington and Gist visit Queen Aliquippa (engraving, early 19th c.), 179, 194
Rolfe, John, 36, 72–73, 75, 141
Rolfe, Thomas (son of Pocahontas), 75
romanticization of Native peoples, 55–57
Romero, Mateo, 147
Roscoe, Will, The Zuni Man-Woman (1991), 157
Rosebud Sioux, 204
royalty, Native American, 140–41
rubber and rubber balls, 30–31, 31, 32, 222
Ryan, Georgetta Stonefish (Delaware), 64, 79, 143, 166, 180

Sacagawea (Shoshone), 82–83, 83
Sahagún, Bernardino de, 23
Sale, Kirkpatrick, 95
salmon, 91, 91–92, 106

San Juan Pueblo, 50, 134
Sanders, Thomas E., 142
Saxman or Cape Fox Tlingit, 218
scalping, 87–88, 148
Schaghticoke, 182
Schemitzun, Connecticut, 26
Schoolcraft, Henry Rowe, *Oneóta, or, Characteristics of the Red Race of America* (1845), 148
Schupman, Edwin (Muscogee), 6, 9, 40, 44, 92, 137
scientific racism, 150
scientific theories about migration of Native Americans to America, 62–64, 113–14
Secakuku, Scott (Hopi), *13*
Secoton village (North Carolina?), 89, *94*
Seda, Tepexi de la, painted tribute record of (18th c. copy of 16th c. original), *107*
Sekakuku, Susan, *Meet Mindy: A Native Girl from the Southwest* (2003), 13
Seminole, 191–92
Seneca, 28, 137, 186, 194. *See also* Haudenosaunee
September 11, 2001, 15
Sequoyah (Cherokee), 23, *61*, *71*
Seri, 8
services, benefits, and payments provided by federal governments, 138–39, 182, 207, 209–11, *210*, *212*
sexual abuse of boarding school children, 166
sexuality and gender, Native American view of, 155–57, *156*
Shakopee, 203
Shakopee Mdewakanton Sioux Community (SMSC; Dakota), 201, 205
shamans or medicine men, 28, 48–49, 163
Shawnee, 84
Shoalwater Bay Indian Tribe, 204
Shoshone, 80, 82, 83, 222; Eastern Shoshone, 204; Eastern Shoshone pipe (ca. 1850), *36*; pipe bag (ca. 1870), *36*; Western Shoshone, 124
Sicangu Lakota, *120*
sign language, 102–4, *103*
Silverheels, Jay (Harry Smith; Mohawk), 52–54, *53*
singing and songs, 5–6

Sioux, *116*, 117, 136, 174, 203, 204, *210*.
    See also Lakota
Sioux hymnals and bible, *24*
Six Nations Confederacy. *See* Haudenosaunee
Six Nations Indian Reserve, 52, 54
Six Nations Powwow, 150
Skagway Village, 135
Skins (movie; 2002), 59
slaves and slavery, 190–92
smallpox, 65, 80–81, 184
Smith, John, 75–77
Smith, Laura E., 19
Smithsonian NMAI. *See* National Museum of the American Indian
smoke signals, 100–101
Smoke Signals (film; 1998), 58–59, *59*, 100
smoking. *See* tobacco
SMSC (Shakopee Mdewakanton Sioux Community; Dakota), 201, 205
snow, number of words for, 98–99
social disadvantage. *See* poverty and social disadvantage
songs and singing, 5–6
Sons of Liberty, 140
Soto, Hernando de, 87, 184
South America. *See* Latin America
Southeastern tribes, 28, 29, 62, 190
Southwestern tribes: adobe dwelling houses of, 93, 129; art and artmaking, 18; clothing of, 108; corn pollen as symbol of fertility for, *153*; deer as ancestors of, 111–12; kachina dolls, 12, 13; marital practices, 178; musical instruments, 7; paints and dyes, 11; rain dances, 39; shamans, 49; slave trade, involvement in, 190; smoke signals used by, 100; spear points used by, 62; tourists and photography in, 158; yucca, soap and shampoo made from, 222
Spanish conquest. *See* European arrival in Western Hemisphere
spellings for Native American words, 23–25
spirituality. *See* religion and spirituality
Squanto (Tisquantum; Northeastern Indian), 72, 73
squashes, 63, 91, 105, *107*, 220
squaw, as offensive term, 142–43
Squaw Lake, Minnesota, renamed as Nokomis Lake Pond, 143

Squaw Peak, Arizona, renamed as Piestewa Peak, 142
Squire v. Capoeman (US Supreme Court, 1956), 212
Stadaconans, 87
Standing Bear, Luther, *Land of the Spotted Eagle* (1978), 90
Standing Rock Sioux, 204
Stannard, David E., 95
Starr, Arigon (Kickapoo/Creek), *8*
states: casinos and gaming/gambling in, 198, 199; hunting and fishing regulations, 214–15; with largest American Indian populations, 180; taxes, Native payment of, 212–13; tribal recognition by, 181; voting and racial discrimination in, 189
stereotyping, misrepresentation, and denigration: art and artmaking, 17–19; cannibalism, 34; cigar-store Indians, 55; Eskimo, as offensive term, 144; European settlers, characterization of Native Americans by, 220; human sacrifice, 32–33; Indian Princess motif, 140–41; movies and TV shows, 52, 54, 60; names for some Indian tribal groups, 136–37; NMAI's mission regarding, xiii, xvi; *papoose*, as term, 122; peacefulness/warlike traits, groups stereotyped for, 175–76; persistence of, xv; photographs and photography, 158–59, *159*; racism, Indian experience of, 189; rain dances, 40; "real" Indians, belief in extinction of, 149–51; *redskin*, as offensive term, 146–47, 148; scalping, 87; scientific racism, 150; smoke signals, 100; sports teams, Native American names for, 145–47, *146*, 148; *squaw*, as offensive term, 142–43; terms for Native Americans, 132–33, *133*; treatment of Europeans captured by Native Americans, 84
stickball, 28, 29
subsistence hunting, 110
substance abuse, 125, 127–28, 206
suicide rates, 128, 206
Sun Dances, 45, 47
sunflowers, *94*, 105
Supreme Court, US *See* US Supreme Court
Swan Lake First Nation, 135

sweatlodges, 47, 48
sweet potatoes, 105, 226
Swentzell, Roxanne (Santa Clara Pueblo), *Don't Shoot* (1990), *18*
syllabaries and syllabics, 23–24, *71*

Taíno, 35, 55, 72, 80, 175
taxes, Indian payment of, 212–13
Tecumseh (Shawnee), *184*, 185
television. *See* movies and TV shows
Teller, Henry M., 47
Tendoi (Shoshone), *103*
terminology: early popularization of Native American words in English, 122; Eskimo, as offensive term, 144; gender-variant individuals, terms for, 156, 157; multiple names for same tribe or nation, 136–37; Native Americans, terms for, 132–33, *133*, 135; *papoose*, as term, 122; *redskin*, as offensive term, 146–47, 148; sports teams, Native American names for, 145–47, *146*, 148; *squaw*, as offensive term, 142–43; "tribe" versus "nation," 134–35. *See also* languages
territorial claims, 96–97
Tewaaraton Award, 28
Thanksgiving, 2–4, *3*, 39, 72, 176
Theresa of Bavaria, *159*
Thornton, Russell, *American Indian Holocaust and Survival* (1987), 65–66
Thrasher, Tanya (Cherokee Nation of Oklahoma), 27, 77, 116, 135
Three Sisters (corn, beans, and squash), 105–6
Thunder Valley Community Development Corp., 204–5
tipi, spelling of, 24–25
tipis, 10, 11, 93, 129–30
Tisquantum (Squanto; Northeastern Indian), 72, 73
Tiwaho Foundation, 205
tlachtli, 30
Tlingit, *217*, 218
Tlingit body armor, 120–21
tobacco: cigar-store Indians, 55–57, *56*; dried plant materials mixed with, 35; European cultivation of and trade in, 35–36, 55, 73; Native cultivation and use of, 35–36, 55; pipes and pipe ceremonials, 35–36, *36*, 47

Togiak, Traditional Village of, 135
Tohono O'odham, 9, 126, 136
tomatoes, 105, 106, 220, 226, 227–28
tomcod caught in dip net, *111*
Tonto (from *The Lone Ranger*), 52–54, *53*
totem poles, 14–16, *15*, 218
Totopotomoi (Pamunkey), 193
tourists and tourism: Native art and, 17–19, 20–21; photographs and photography, 158–59, *159*
trade and trade networks: cacao beans, 226–27; between Europeans and Native Americans, 78, 82, 87, 120–21, 170; between Native Americans, *91*, 95, 103, 117, 119–20, 226–27; tobacco, European cultivation of and trade in, 35–36, 55, 73
transgender individuals in Native American society, 155–57, *156*
treaties and treaty negotiations, 70, 103, 181, 185, 194, 209, *210*, 214–15
Treaty Clause, US Constitution, 181
tribal governments: benefits and services provided by, 211; casinos owned and operated by, 198–99; citizenship in, 188; federal taxation, not subject to, 212; hunting and fishing regulations, 214; reservations as tribal lands under, 44; taxation by, 213
tribal membership and enrollment, 138–39, 150–51
"tribe" versus "nation," 134–35
tribes, unrecognized, 150, 181
tribute records, *107*
Tsali Manor (Cherokee senior citizens center), North Carolina, *201*
Tshimshian, 170–71
tuberculosis, 125
Tulalip, 201
Tuscarora, 28, 137, 186. *See also* Haudenosaunee
TV. *See* movies and TV shows
two-spirit individuals, 157
typhus, 65

Uliggaq (Ella Pavil; Yup'ik), 111
Umatilla Reservation, Confederated Tribes of, 63
umbilical cords, 124, 152
unemployment, high levels of, 197
United Nations, 228

United States: contemporary population of Native Americans, 180; Indian Princess used to symbolize, 140; states with largest American Indian populations, 180. *See also specific entries at* U.S.
University of Oklahoma, 145
University of Southern Utah Utes, 147
unrecognized tribes, 150, 181
untouched wilderness, concept of Americas as, 66, 93–95
Ursuline nuns, 119
US Army Corps of Engineers, 63
US Army Signal Corps, 174
US Bureau of Indian Affairs, 181, 209
US Census and census taking, 180
US citizenship, 188–89, 196, 212
US Constitution, 47, 181, 187, 188, 189
US Department of the Interior, 181, 182
US government: assimilation policies, 67–69, 71, 188; benefits, payments, and services provided by, 138, 182, 207, 209–11, *210*, 212; boarding schools for Indian children, 67–68, 150, 164, 165–66, *166*, *167*; disease deliberately spread by, 80–81; land taken by, payments for, 209, *210*, 212, *213*; National Eagle Repository, 115; taxes, Indian payment of, 212–13; treaties and treaty negotiations, 70, 103, 181, 185, 209, *210*, 214–15; "tribe" preferred to "nation" by, 134; tribes recognized by, 134, 138, 150–51, 181–82
US Indian Peace Commission, *210*
US Marines, 172–73, *173*
US. Supreme Court: Boldt Decision upheld by (1979), 215; *California v. Cabazon* (1987), 199; *Squire v. Capoeman* (1956), 212
usufruct, 96

Vague Year, Maya calendar, 223–24
van de Passe, Simon, *76*, *141*
"vanishing Indian" motif, 149–51, 158
Vaughn, Alden T., 148
Velasco, Juanita (Ixil Maya), *227*
Vig, Charles R., 205
Vikings in Americas, 183
villages, Alaska Native communities known as, 135

255

Viola, Herman J., *After Columbus: The Smithsonian Chronicle of the North American Indians* (1990), 81
Virginia Colony, 35–36, 79
vision quests, 154, 163
Vogel, Clayton, 172
voting discrimination, 189
Vucub Hunahpu (Maya god), 32

waila (chicken scratch music), 9
Wakan Tanka, 90
Walters, Harry (Navajo), 17
Wampanoag, 2–3, 122, 176, 193
wampum, 70
Wanapum Band of Priest Rapids, 63
war: ceremonial war dances, 26–27; counting coup, 37, *38*; European metal weapons, 185; between Europeans and Native Americans, 175–76; games and sports as substitute for, 28, 32; horses, Native American acquisition and use of, 117; Native American groups stereotyped as peaceful or warlike, 175; sign language used in, 103; unified Native resistance to Europeans, lack of, 183–85. *See also specific wars and battles*
war bonnets, *116*
Ward, Nancy (Nanyehi; Cherokee), 195
Ware, Shawn (Kiowa), 102
Washakie (Eastern Shoshone), *36*
Washington, DC Redskins, 146–47, 148
Washington, George, *194*
water, in Native American culture, 40
West, Sir Thomas, third Lord de la Warr, 79

Western Shoshone, 124
We'wha (Zuni), *156*, 156–57
whales and whaling, 114
Whip Men, 27
whistles (as musical instruments), 8–9
White, Andrew, 177
wigwams, 129
Williams, Roger, *A Key Into the Language of America* (1643), 122
Winnebago tribe, 201
Winslow, Edward, 73
winter counts, 70
women. *See* gender issues
World War I, 188
World War II, 52, 172–74, *173*
Wright, Ronald, *Stolen Continents: The Americas through Indian Eyes since 1492* (1992), 184
writing systems, 23–25, 70, 70–71, 97

Xibalba (lords of Maya underworld), 32–33

Yakama Nation, Confederated Tribes and Bands of, 63
Yanktonai, 204
Youngblood, Mary, 9
yucca: soap and shampoo, 222; textiles, 108
Yup'ik, 98, 132, 144
Yup'ik language, 67, 98

Zah, Peterson (Diné), 136
Zia Pueblo, 50, 134
Zuni, 12, 50, 156–57
Zuni language, 156, 176